YIAYIA AND PAPOU

Christine Skoutelas

A MORNING GROUCH PUBLICATION

Chapbook Press

Schuler Books
2660 28th Street SE
Grand Rapids, MI 49512
(616) 942-7330
www.schulerbooks.com

ISBN 13: 9781943359943

Library of Congress Control Number: 2018933192

Copyright © 2018, Christine Skoutelas

All rights reserved.

No part of this book may be reproduced in any form without express permission of the copyright holder.

Printed in the United States by Chapbook Press.

For my husband, Lambros, and our daughters, Penelope and Daphne. Also for my sister-in-law Voula and her children, Simon and Leo; and for my sister-in-law Athena and her children, Aleko and Nina.

PROLOGUE

When you marry someone, you don't just marry them. You marry their family. This is important. Make sure you like your spouse's family. Even if their family lives far away or if their parents are on their deathbeds, know that no matter what, they will always be a part of your spouse's life and by proximity that means they will be a part of yours as well.

No one can escape the dueling privilege and pain-in-the assery that is Family. They're in your head, they're in your heart, and they usually share a considerable chunk of your genetic makeup. They're there in your traditions. They're there in your family recipes. They're there in your world view. They're there in your greatest accomplishments and in your darkest fears.

You cannot escape where you came from. Sorry if that worries you, but it's the doggone truth. Cross my heart.

A large chunk of who you are is shaped by your parents, your grandparents, your great-grandparents, your great-great grandparents, and so on. You don't just become you from the experiences you've had in your life; you are you because of the experiences of your ancestors as well. You are shaped and molded by the countless others who came before you. And so is your spouse. Keep this in mind when you're searching for The One.

When I first met my husband, he was introduced to me as Bobby. I had no idea then that Bobby was a nickname his mother had given him and that his real name was Lambros—a hint at his hidden heritage.

Soon though, I became obsessed with learning more about this handsome Greek boy. I learned that he inherited his dark eyes, thick brows, passion for cooking, and incessant phone calling "just to check in" from his mother, Glykeria. I learned that his quick wit, sharpness of mind, and outrageously short temper came from his father, Tom.

His strong work ethic and inability to talk about his emotions he inherited equally from both sides.

I fell in love with him immediately, and as I got to know his parents I fell in love with them too. From the beginning, they made me feel at home.

Our wedding was a celebration of our love and of the merging of our families. When we got engaged I was teaching high school science and finishing up my master's degree. Lambros was working as a project manager and completing his MBA. Thank goodness for my sister-in-law Athena, who planned and booked just about everything for us. We were so swamped with our jobs and our schooling that we let the organ player pick the music we walked down the aisle to, we let the DJ pick out our wedding song, we let the florist pick out the flowers.

On the day of our wedding, we did not care that the flower girl threw ferns cut from the bridesmaid bouquets instead of the rose petals we had forgotten. It was no big deal that the air conditioning in the reception hall didn't work and everyone was dripping with sweat. It did not matter that we stood there with nothing to cut our cake with until somebody handed us a butter knife from a nearby table. All we cared about was that we were married. We were joined, and so were our families.

There was only one bit of frippery I kept thinking about, even though I never actually followed through and carried it out. I envisioned a matching pair of 20 x 24 photographs—our parents' wedding portraits—standing in thick, gold, antique gesso frames on a long rectangular table leading into the reception area. Beside each large frame, I imagined a smaller frame containing a short description that would give our guests the background stories behind the images.

My parents' photo: a couple of teenagers in the mid-seventies, my dad, with black hair, long and shaggy, accentuated by coke-bottle glasses and a thick mustache, his arm around my mother with her feathered, shoulder-length brown hair and silky empire-waist dress that only slightly concealed her rounded, swollen belly.

His parents' photo: A grainy black and white, Tom atop a short gray mule, Glykeria, in lacy white, sitting on a tall dark one, riding through the rural Greek mountainside.

Both photographs are hilariously unconventional. This is the kind of warped human being I am—the only ornamentation I truly desired on my wedding day was one that made me shake my head and snicker.

The thing is, though, the photographs depicted more than just a couple of lovesick teenagers, hastily married two days before my birth; and two hillbilly Greeks, goat herders from a remote mountainous village who met only a couple of days before their arranged marriage. The photographs also displayed successful marriages despite all odds. Both sets of parents are still together, several decades later, and are two of the happiest couples we know.

I never got around to buying a guest book or arranging the table with the photograph display. But even though it wasn't there for everyone else, it was there in my mind, endearing and inspiring. The image of my parents will forever be ingrained in my brain. I'd heard their story, or at least pieces of it, countless times.

But it is the image of my in-laws, and the story behind their arranged marriage, that continued to resonate in my mind, bouncing off my skull and shouting at me to capture the story behind the photo. This story grabbed me with its exotic intrigue. I promised myself I'd uncover and record their wedding story eventually.

It wasn't until four years later that I actually did it. It happened spontaneously, when the four of us were on a day trip to the Soo Locks. Lambros and I sat in the front in his black Volkswagen Jetta, and my in-laws were in the back. I had my laptop with me, and within the first hour or so of our trip I remembered that I had always wanted to put the details of their matrimonial adventure down on paper.

We had the time, so I asked if they would tell me how the two of them ended up together. They agreed and orated from the back seat while I listened from the passenger seat and eagerly typed as Lambros drove.

It turned out that they were exceptional storytellers, and it was clear that they enjoyed sharing their tale, as they piggybacked off one another, feverishly adding details and anecdotes. They told me the entire wedding story and then began divulging information about the tiny impoverished village they grew up in as I continued my frenetic typing.

We visited the Locks and headed to lunch. At this point the switch in my brain had clicked over to manic production mode, and I had become greedily obsessed with getting more information. So I lugged my laptop into the family restaurant, demanding a table near an outlet so I could charge the battery and get a few more words down while we chatted over our meal.

When we left the Locks, we drove to the casino, planning to gamble a bit and then stay the night. But all the hotels were booked, so Tom suggested we drive to Traverse City to stay at a casino there. This is how my husband and his father both operate—they jump into a vehicle early in the morning without clear-cut plans and end up driving across the state.

Normally the lack of a regimented schedule causes me to break out in hives while my heart palpitates from anxiety, but in this case additional hours in the car equated to more captured tidbits, so I was more than okay with the sudden change of plans.

By now the stories were flowing and could not be contained. Tom and Glykeria talked and I typed the whole way to Traverse City. We didn't have any luck finding a room there or anywhere else in the vicinity. At this point, it was close to midnight. We gave up and drove back home.

My laptop battery died on this stretch of the trip, so for the last couple of hours I was scribbling furiously under the tiny interior light on a stack of crumpled up oil-change receipts. I was a little shocked the next day when I typed up the notes from the scribbled papers—adding them to the stories I had collected during the trip—and discovered I had forty single-spaced pages of text.

To myself, I thought, *I already have forty pages. I have no choice but to make this into a book.* And in a moment of naive euphoria I may even have thought, *I mean, it's practically a book already!*

But, no. It wasn't a book already. It was forty pages of Greek-lish stand-alone sentences and fragments, each sentence colorfully underlined by spellcheck. I had a jumbled literary puzzle to be sorted and pieced together one painstakingly tedious word at a time.

On more than one occasion during the book-writing process I asked myself, *What the hell was I thinking?* But it was too late to turn back. By the time I truly realized just how hard this task would be, I had scavenged seventy pages of stories and it was a year and a half later. I had started to tell a few people about the project, so I couldn't stop. I'm a little too proud and a lot too stubborn for that.

More importantly, by then I had my first daughter, Penelope. We had our second child, Daphne, in our hearts before she was in our hands, and suddenly the stories took on even more meaning. They weren't just my in-law's stories. They were now also my children's. So I kept asking questions, and Tom and Glykeria kept supplying answers.

So, here we are, many years later, and the write-up I had envisioned of the wedding couple on their donkeys is complete. I'm still not wholly able to articulate why it's so critical that they have this information. I just know that it is.

While I might not be smart enough to fully understand why these stories are so important, I'm certainly not stupid enough to let them become forgotten. The text won't fit in the art gesso frame I had originally envisioned, but I can finally share the story.

I have documented events and conversations from my elderly in-laws. All information is true, as far as they can remember. As you will find, they did argue about the day of the week they met, and as it turns out they were both wrong - so, instead of a biography or a memoir, let's just call this is a book of memories, shall we? I have changed the names and identifying characteristics of some people and places, just in case what they remember isn't as true as they think it is.

We are not solely ourselves. We are, in part, our parents, our grandparents, and everyone else who came before us. We do not begin as a blank slate, but rather as a mishmash of genetic code and world views given to us by our ancestors.

AN INTRODUCTION

AN INTRODUCTION TO GREEK COOKING
A quick lunch

The first time Lambros took me to his parents' house they were not there, but I met his *yiayia*, his dad's mom. She wore an ankle-length, dark navy dress—her usual attire as I would come to find out—and her long gray hair was twisted into a tight bun that rested on the nape of her neck. Her hands were thick and wide, strong from a lifetime of manual labor. The skin covering them was stretched out and creased and would hold the shape of an object long after she pressed her hands down upon it; the elastin was long gone. They were also very soft. Maybe due to the muscle underneath, or maybe because she had been in the States long enough for the callouses to wear away.

She walked slowly but steadily as she led me to the backyard and introduced me to her garden. She spoke to me in Greek, which I couldn't understand, but that didn't deter her from chatting away. And her not understanding English didn't stop me from chatting right back.

She loved me from the get go, she smiled at me and held my hand and looked at my husband and winked as she rubbed my back. We visited for a couple of hours and then prepared to head back home.

"*Meinete kai na fate,*" she insisted. Stay for lunch. Lambros tried to say no, but in a way that wasn't all that convincing, and his weak protest did no good. I was confused about why he would say no. We were college students, and what college kid doesn't want a free meal? He relented, as it was clear he would, and she nodded and took my hand and led me to her garden again, where she started picking the fresh onions, parsley, and spinach from the bed.

She washed and chopped the greens and then mixed some dough and rolled it into thin sheets with a narrow wooden dowel. She was making homemade filo dough. For her, a "quick lunch" was making *spanakopita* from scratch. It was a solid six hours later before we were out of there. But damn, that spinach pie was good!

I've learned that for a Greek matriarch, feeding her family is the ultimate expression of love. Feeding her family *often*. The amount of food you offer someone directly correlates to the amount you like them or want to impress them.

For my in-laws, this stems from living as goat herders in a village. They were in a near constant state of hunger that could easily border on malnourishment. They dealt with illness without doctors, and exposure to the elements without shelter. They feasted because there could be famine. From this perspective, "food is love" never made more sense.

Even though my in-laws now have only themselves to cook for, my mother-in-law still uses her standard recipes, filling the same gigantic bowls and pans she has used for years. Since we live close to them, we are often the beneficiaries of this overzealous cooking. We get frequent calls to come over for homemade grape leaves or spinach pie. Sometimes instead of calling, my mother-in-law just sends me a picture of whatever it is that just came out of the oven. It's a visual memo that means come now and eat. It's like her Bat-Signal.

When I get those kinds of texts, I picture a circular beam of light illuminating the night sky, but instead of the bat at the center, there's Yiayia holding a pan of *pita*. I rush toward the beacon every time. Sometimes I feel guilty going over there and eating so much of her food, but my husband alleviates my guilt by saying things like, "It works out well. My dad hates leftovers, and my mom cooks for thirty."

AN INTRODUCTION TO GREEK COOKING
A simple recipe

I generally hate to cook, but my mother-in-law's recipes are worth taking the time to learn (and sometimes even make). They are worth dirtying up a million dishes or having to chop for hours. The meals are made from scratch and filled with copious amounts of garlic, oregano, butter, and love. They are nothing like the food that I grew up eating or what I find in any recipe book. They are heavenly.

If I want to ask her about a recipe, it's a gamble to try to get her answer over the phone. She can't remember. Or she can't articulate it. Or she assumes I know anything about cooking.

When she cooks she relies on muscle memory. It's like her brain might not really know what she's doing but her hands and her eyes do. They remember, even if her mouth doesn't. What she tells me very rarely aligns with what she shows me.

I shouldn't be surprised by this. This is a woman who consistently calls potholes "pot holders" after all. If I want to know how to make a dish, I have to watch her make it.

When I do watch her make something, and I jot down the directions as I observe, there is still much room for error. You see, she doesn't measure. She doesn't necessarily make things the same way every time. Much depends on the ingredients she has on hand. And—partly due to her naturally flippant speech and partly due to English not being her native language—she sometimes (often . . . always . . .) omits important information. Or says one thing and then the exact opposite in the next breath.

I am 100 percent positive that at one point she told me you could bake baklava and freeze it, but you had to do this before adding the syrup. Once the baklava was thawed, she said, you could make the syrup and add it. When I finally got around to making some baklava, I hoped maybe I could make extra to freeze for later. I asked her about this, but she said she had no clue and had never done that. Then she told me I could bake the baklava, add the syrup, *and then* freeze it. I know this is completely different information than I heard before, and it can't be trusted.

I thought maybe we were having communication difficulties about this because she had given me the information over the phone. So I waited until I saw her in person, and I asked her, "If I'm going to make baklava and freeze it, do I add the syrup before or after I put it in the freezer?"

Her response? "Yes."

I asked my husband's sisters. His cousins. NO ONE KNOWS. Except his aunt, who told me to freeze the baklava but to make sure the whole thing is frozen prior to baking it. So there you go.

The other day, a solid decade or so after I first learned how to make my mother-in-law's baklava, I was making a batch at home. I thought I was finally close to perfecting it. Glykeria, came over and stirred the syrup while it simmered on the stove. Her back was to me, her eyes were focused on the sticky liquid, and she asked, "Do you have any lemon juice?"

Lemon juice?! I have never heard her say anything about adding lemon juice to the syrup!

"Are you serious?"

It's stuff like this that just kills me. How does she never once mention lemon juice over the past decade?

"Do you have any of the liquid kind?"

"No. No, I don't," I said, shaking my head. *Eesh.*

I won't be surprised if one of these days someone pops up and tells me I've been getting punked all this time. Some kind of innovative reality TV cooking show, perhaps.

Ultimately, unless I watch them do it, I'll never learn how to cook like they do. And, let's be honest, even when I watch them, a) they make it differently each time and b) mine still tastes like *mine* and theirs still tastes like *theirs*.

I'll take it, though. The *mine* version is better than anything I would ever come up with on my own.

Periodically, I meet with my mother-in-law and watch her make a recipe I love so I can add it to my culinary repertoire. All of her recipes, just like all of her stories, cannot be lost when she's gone.

Here are a few classic scenarios that occur every time I am furiously scribbling one of her recipes down.

ONE:
"How much flour do I add?"

"A handful."

I look at her little elfish hands. I look at my gigantic man hands. *blink blink*

TWO:
"How many walnuts do you put in for one batch?"

"About four handfuls."

THREE:
"How much salt should I add?"

"Just a little," (said with a tone that implies I should understand what she means).

"A pinch?"

"Yeah, a pinch. Not too much." She pours out how much she needs into her hands, and then transfers it into a measuring spoon so I can record the amount.

I nod my head in acknowledgment. A teaspoon. I totally understand what a teaspoon is.

"But you need enough. Not too little either." She takes the salt shaker and pours an ungodly amount, unmeasured, into the mixing bowl.

FOUR:
"See?" She dips a spoon into the pot and lifts it up, letting the liquid pour back out. She's trying to get me to recognize the correct viscosity of the syrup.

I see pouring liquid. I don't see what I'm supposed to see.

"Um. How many minutes until it's done?"

"Until it is thick enough."

I will my eyes to be smarter. I stare harder. I might as well have a blindfold on. Some people are color blind. I'm cooking blind.

FIVE:
"So, I need three scoops?"

"Three scoops. Full ones."

"Got it." I put three scoops in and smile. *I did it!*

She looks at it with a critical eye and says, "Maybe a little extra."

BONUS! YIAYIA'S SPINACH PIE RECIPE
Spanakopita

<u>You will need:</u>

A Yiayia-sized mixing bowl: She can curl up and fit in it. Yes, she's only 4' 10", but still. You don't have one this size, trust me.

A Yiayia-sized pan: Yiayia uses a dented pan made from an unknown metal that has been passed down from the women in her family since the late 1800s. Good luck finding one like that. You could use a sheet cake pan. Or 2 9 x13 pans. I can't tell you what size because it depends on how thick you make your spinach pie.

Salt: Way more than you would ever guess. But definitely not too much.

Dill: Copious amounts. Full disclosure: Yiayia doesn't put this in hers. Except for the times that she does.

Feta: A huge hunk. But not so much that you ruin it by making it taste like there is too much feta.

Cottage cheese: A 1-lb container. This is the only thing you will know for sure.

Cornmeal: A large handful (1 cup or so).

Green onions: 3 bunches. Unless you forget to buy it. Or don't have it in your garden. In which case, zero bunches.

Yellow onions: If you want.

You will do:

1. Chop the greens and onions until your hands are sore and you have developed a newfound respect for the strength Yiayia possesses. Be nicer to her because you now realize she could crush your windpipe with her bare hands, based on this hand-strength metric.

2. Add the cornmeal and squeeze to soak up some of the water.

3. Combine the rest of the ingredients.

4. Butter the bottom of your pan(s) and place 8-10 layers of filo in it/them.

5. Alternate layers of spinach mixture, then 3 layers of filo, then layers of spinach mixture, etc., until the spinach mixture is used up.

6. Top with another 8-10 layers of filo. Brush butter on the top layers (and by brush I mean SOAK). Then add more. Pro tip: Add a bit of olive oil on top of all that butter.

7. Bake at 350 degrees until top is golden brown (1 – 1 ½ hours)

A CONVERSATION ABOUT SPINACH PIE

A friend of mine read this *spanakopita* recipe when I posted it on my blog and told me she was upset that I didn't put a "real" recipe up there.

This IS the real recipe! *It really is.*

My husband said to me one time after biting into his mom's spinach pie, "I really like your spinach pie. But my mom's tastes different. I'm not saying yours isn't good. It is. But it's different than hers."

"I know. I know," I nod in agreement.

Mine will never taste like hers, as much as I would like it to. My brother-in-law, Tom, once told me that a family recipe is like a story that is passed down from generation to generation. My spinach pie just has a different story to tell.

Maybe another day I'll share my story, but this book is about theirs. And holy hell, what a story they have!

THE STORIES

XORIO (hoar-ee-oh)
A mountain village

My husband and his family refer to themselves as "mountain people" because of where his parents grew up. I hear this reference when I ask my husband if he wants to kayak with me when we're on a camping trip, for example. He'll say, "No. I don't go in water."

His sisters have similar preferences: "We're mountain people, not water people," they tell me. While I don't think this is a valid defense for missing out on a pontoon ride around the lake at the cottage, geographically there's truth behind their excuses.

"You both grew up in in the same village, right?" I ask my father-in-law. I knew they were both raised in a very remote space, high on a mountain in central Greece.

"Yeeaaah," Tom says slowly as he wobbles his hand back and forth. *Kind of.* "Different neighborhoods." We're in his living room and he's sitting in his recliner. He's got both of my toddlers on his lap and is balancing his laptop on his knees so they can watch cartoons. He'll do anything to get them to cuddle with him. He puts his hand down and adjusts the laptop so it won't fall.

The Skoutelas siblings grew up in a small village comprised of roughly fifteen to twenty square miles of steep, rocky land. Glykeria and her Economou siblings were raised nearby. Her family still owns and keep up their old family home as a vacation spot. Tom and his siblings own their house as well, though it has not been kept up and is slowly falling apart. The population level of the area peaked when my in-laws were young, at around five hundred residents, and very few people remain there today. It is *so* high up in the mountains, *so* far from civilization.

During the years that they lived there, the late 1940s to the late 1960s, each neighborhood was made up of a handful of homes. Most of the neighborhoods had a *caffeneio*—a meeting place where the men could sit and relax while sipping coffee or a measure of *tsiporo,* a liquor similar in taste and appearance to ouzo but with a zest more on par with paint thinner.

Many of the *caffeneios* housed a general store as well. Some of the neighborhoods had their own schools, while others didn't. They all had their own church. Other than that, there was almost nothing except the ubiquitous dirt and rocks, goats and sheep, and the steep edges of cliffs at every turn.

Just about everything their families had came from the earth or their animals. Handmade wasn't cute, it wasn't a hobby, it wasn't a novelty. It was the story of their lives. Store bought was pretty much a fairytale.

If items weren't made from scratch, they were usually traded for at the general store.

"What did you typically trade for?" I ask Tom. I want to understand their bartering system.

He takes a sip of black coffee from his insulated metal mug. It's the only mug he ever drinks out of. I can hear Glykeria in the kitchen, hand-washing the dishes. She got her first dishwasher a few years ago when they moved into their new house, but she rarely uses it.

Tom swallows and sets the mug back down on the oak end table, making sure it's out of reach of tiny hands.

"Take two eggs, or a little butter, get a dram of dye or a handful of raisins or salted chickpeas," he says. "Every once in a while I'd go down, every couple of weeks, to buy a liter of fuel for the light. Eh, they usually took whatever we had."

Quite often when he talks, he raises his pitch at the end of the sentence, even though he's not asking a question. It's like he's asking himself if what he's saying can actually be true. Items that the families grew or procured from their animals were traded for coffee, ouzo, canned foods, quarts of oil for their kerosene lamps, fabric dyes, thread, needles, books, or pencils.

"Sometimes the kids would charge things and my dad would pay later," Tom adds. "They trusted my dad. He always paid when he got back." He nods proudly.

He continues to talk and I continue to type.

The different neighborhoods were only a few miles apart, but walking anywhere up and down the ungroomed mountainous terrain would take hours or even days, depending on the weather. The steep hills were jagged and rocky with rough gravel, and trees poked out sporadically from the coarse crevices.

"Here, you can walk four miles in one hour," he says, waving his finger around, tracing the loop in his head of strolls he and his wife sometimes take from the house. "There, it would probably take you three hours."

But walking was the only option. There were no bikes. There were no cars. There were only strong feet, strong calves, and strong quads. Refueling meant sitting down and eating a piece of bread and some cheese.

"If you wanted to walk to the nearest town from the *xorio*, sometimes it would take five days," Glykeria adds as she walks in and sits down with us in the family room. The closest town was about forty miles to the south.

Daphne starts to fuss.

"What, baby?" Tom asks her. He hates it when the babies cry. "What's the matter? You want to go *volta*?" He is asking her, in his Greek English, if she wants to go for a walk. "Let's go *volta volta*." He moves the laptop onto the coffee table, and Penelope moves over to the couch to watch it from there. Tom and Daphne trek around the living room and kitchen, returning back to the family room before heading out for another loop.

The mountain is harsh but it is also beautiful. Anticlines and synclines provide a most pleasant pattern. At its peak grows the delicious mountain tea, chai. It is the village version of Sudafed; the only remedy for head colds. The plant is dried whole, boiled, strained, and drunk with honey. It is earthy and smooth and lacks even a hint of bitterness.

We recently had Lambros's cousin ship us the biggest box he could find on his recent trip to Greece. "The biggest box. It doesn't matter how much it costs, we'll pay you back. The BIGGEST box!" we emphasized. We need it; we're both prone to sinus infections in the winter.

As the elevation drops, the mountain hosts bay trees, and a further descent toward the valley reveals pines and needles, cedars, oaks, and maples. Wide-leaf trees and hollys dripping with red berries can be found by the river. Shrubs and grains exist in patchy areas, wherever they can grow. Green grass is virtually non-existent.

Glykeria's childhood home sits two or three miles below the Skoutelas house, on the same side of the mountain. A river cuts through a valley about a half mile below her place. The river now is about a quarter mile across at its widest point, but my in-laws remember it being much wider years ago. The river is full of rocks and ridges, which creates waterfalls and rapids.

Tom and Glykeria remember the river being difficult to cross in the summer and impossibly dangerous to pass in the winter. "That river is ancient," Tom tells me, standing, still holding Daphne in his arms. "Probably Homer mentioned it in some of his poems." She is no longer crying, but he continues to pat her gently on the back with his thick, calloused fingers.

The peak of the mountain is covered in snow, and as the ice melts it seeps into the rock and travels downward. Cool, fresh water, naturally filtered from running through the stone and gravel, pours from openings on the sides of the mountain. Many of these springs have been fitted with spouts screwed into the rock to allow the flow to be directed into a bottle or straight into a mouth.

I think about how we drank out of a couple of these springs while visiting on our honeymoon. Even though in the back of my mind I worried about parasitic infection, I trusted the filtration the mountain provided and reminded myself that my in-laws had drunk this water throughout their entire youths. Even if it was full of microbes I couldn't see, I didn't become ill and it tasted cool and fresh.

I remember that driving up the winding roads that lead to the village tests even the strongest of stomachs as the car swings back and forth, back and forth. Even with the guard rails, it looks like you are going to go over the edge at every turn. And there are *so many* turns.

From what I understand, those guard rails are very new, put up only in the last few years. There are still some stretches of road without any.

Glykeria finishes the dishes and comes into the living room. She sets a plate of *tiropitakia*, fresh from the oven, on the end table before she sits with us on the couch. She and Tom fuel my fears of the mountain edge. The cliffs were just as dangerous to walkers as they are to drivers.

"We lost a lot of people in winter. Lost them going over the mountain. One time we lost six or seven at once. A big gust of wind and—poof!" she moves her hand in front of her, tracing the shape of a rainbow.

"One time a guy fell over and hooked on a branch," Tom says. The motion he makes with his hand tells me that the man may have actually been impaled. "He stayed there frozen for a while," he adds dryly.

"Did you actually see a guy hooked on a branch?" I'm not sure if I want him to say yes or no. I'm sometimes intrigued by disgusting things. I eye my children and hope we aren't traumatizing them. Penelope's eyes are still glued to the cartoons on the screen. Daphne is petting her papou's sandpaper beard. *They're just fine,* I reassure myself.

"I don't remember it myself, but the older people used to talk about it. I knew their families, and I knew their names, but I didn't know them. It was the older generations," Tom says.

He tells me more about what he remembers hearing. "Big group of people in the '50s. Whole bunch. They figure they'd be safer, but they got caught, twenty of them, all from the surrounding villages. Not sure if it was an avalanche or the wind."

"They have a nice memorial now," he adds.

When they tell me these stories I picture the little memorials that stand on the sides of the roads on the mountain. Small wooden boxes sticking up from wooden posts, covered with colorful icons, sometimes with a glass door and a candle inside that loved ones can light in remembrance on name days, holidays, or anniversaries of deaths, keeping memories eternal. There were a lot of these, particularly near the curved edges of the cliffs. Tragically beautiful reminders that someone had died near that spot.

I ask him if the memorial he mentioned is like the ones I saw, with a candle and an icon.

"Those are oil lamps, not candles," Tom says as he pulls the coffee cup away from his lips to correct me.

I nod. *That makes sense.* Oil lamps wouldn't get blown out as easily as candles would.

"This memorial was much bigger," he continues. "Big plaque made of stone where it happened, a nice big memorial with everybody's name on it and ages and the date it happened. Professionally built, in other words. . . . You didn't want to travel yourself at that time of year. That's a bad mountain."

The closest town that had decent roads at the time was located about a hundred miles west of the *xorio*. From their homes in the village, Glykeria and Tom could sometimes see headlights from a distance or hear *vroom! vroom!* from across the mountain. They were intrigued by these other places where cars zoomed by on a regular basis. The closest vehicles to the village required a ten-mile hike across the valley and the river—and there was only a single pickup truck in the area at a time—which came solely to transport villagers who were traveling to more populated areas.

At this same time, around 1955, the children living where my parents grew up were being taught to look both ways when they crossed their suburban Detroit streets so they didn't get hit by a Ford Fairlane Crown Victoria or a Packard Four Hundred.

My in-laws, meanwhile, were being taught to pay attention so they wouldn't get butted by a goat and fall off a cliff. Neither Tom nor Glykeria stood close enough to touch an automobile until they were in their teens.

In the 1960s, when my in-laws were pre-teens, a hand-powered cable car was installed so people could cross the river more safely. A metal frame, about four by eight feet, was lined with wood. A bench seat could hold two or three people at a time. The car was mechanically powered by hand using pedals connected to a chain at the top. The contraption operated in exactly the same fashion as pedals powering a bike.

According to Tom, the first half of the journey was an uphill struggle but the second half was a downhill glide.

The cable car is still there, but it hasn't been used since a bridge was built nearby for automobiles. Tom doesn't anticipate anyone removing the cable car. "They'll probably just leave it there until it falls off," he says.

BONUS! YIAYIA'S CHEESE TRIANGLES RECIPE
Tiropitakia

You will need:

Filo: 1 package, thawed overnight.

Cottage cheese: 1 lb. The convenient thing about cottage cheese in recipes is you always know how much, because you buy it in 1-lb containers at the store.

Eggs: 2 or 3.

Feta: If you buy feta in 10-lb tubs like we do, you can measure your feta by filling your empty cottage cheese container with your brined cheese and call it good.

Butter: Copious amounts. Melted.

You will do:

1. Combine cottage cheese, feta, and eggs.

2. Fold 1 piece of filo (lengthwise) and brush with butter.

3. Drop a dollop of cottage cheese mixture on the end of the filo.

4. Fold filo over cottage cheese mixture like a flag, making sure to brush butter over dry filo along the way. The butter is what makes the cheese triangles turn golden and flaky in the oven.

5. Bake at 350 degrees until golden brown.**

**If desired, you can freeze prior to baking. Lay triangles flat in a bag and separate layers with a sheet of wax paper. You can place frozen *tiropitakia* directly in the oven when you're ready to eat.

These babies make perfect party appetizers.

THE VILLAGE
A trench for water

"Do you care if I come over later and get some more stories from you guys?" I ask.

"That's fine, Christine, but ahhhh . . . ." Glykeria hesitates.

Is she okay? Maybe she doesn't feel up to company.

"But, I didn't make anything to eat," she finishes.

"I'm not coming over for you to feed me. You don't have to feed me!" I almost yell at her because I'm so relieved nothing is actually wrong. "I'm coming over with my computer to ask you some questions."

"Ooookay . . .," she says in her high-pitched tone. She sounds unsure. "We'll be here."

When I walk in, she pulls out several serving platters from the fridge and sets them on the counter. What she meant was she hadn't cooked anything *that day*. But, as usual, she has a bounty of leftovers in her fridge.

I make myself a plate and sit down at their small kitchen table. I tell her she doesn't have to feed me, but it's not like I'm going to refuse if it's in front of me. I pull my computer out and open it up. Today's topic is water.

Nobody in the *xorio* had indoor plumbing. This I knew.

"So, did you guys just get buckets of water from the river, or what?" I ask Tom as I take a bite of day-old homemade *loukanika*. Sausages.

Tom is sitting on his recliner and my question makes him look up from the novel he's currently reading on his Kindle. He's recently buzzed his gray hair quite short and is wearing a navy blue sweatshirt and jeans that are streaked with white from painting the walls at his rentals. I notice that he didn't trim his beard when he cut his hair. He must be growing it out.

Tom explains how water was distributed from the source at the peak of the mountain to every home. "We didn't have pipes or anything, just dug little trenches for water." Installing this system meant digging a route in the ground, by hand, for the water to flow through. The villagers started digging near the melting snow at the peak of the mountain and continued digging a path to each household in the *xorio*.

The way he says this, so nonchalantly, makes my mouth drop open. I shut it so he can't see my partially chewed food, and I take a sip of water, eyeing the glass a little differently than I did a few seconds ago.

Just dug them.

I complain about having to plunge a toilet or snake out the shower drain when my hair clogs it up. Oh, who am I kidding? I complain about having to help my husband when *he* snakes it out. I can't imagine having to actually dig out and maintain the paths that the water travels through in the first place.

To my water-privileged self, it seems ludicrous. I think I'll hear his "just dug them" line echoing through my brain forever. I very rarely "just" do anything without complaint. When I'm feeling sorry for myself because I have to do something difficult, I often hear Tom tell me that in my head. That, or one of his other classic lines, "What else you going to do?" *Suck it up, buttercup.* My father-in-law has no idea how much he shouts at me inside my own brain.

He does most of the work at his rental houses on his own: he does plumbing, roofing, drywall, electrical, even painting, which I know he hates. Doing all of that is impressive, but creating a mountain-top plumbing system from scratch—without a single plumbing tool—is on a whole other level. It makes a little more sense now why he refuses to pay anyone to do menial labor for him.

Digging the mountainside trenches wasn't a one-time deal, either.

"Each year, the springtime, we go down there clean them out, you know, get them ready," Tom tells me. The trenches required continual refurbishing or reconstruction.

"Huh." I shake my head, still trying to process it all. "How wide were these trenches?"

"Oh, I don't know, Christine," he growls. I'm not usually on the receiving end of his temper, but sometimes I get a peek at his underlying gruffness. "It wasn't like we had much of a choice, some parts were rock. You couldn't get a shovel through."

I just stare at him. He needs to give me more information than that. I can't picture this trench, not even a little bit. Even when I go camping, I go places where there are bathrooms with pipes and plumbing. I have no background knowledge to pull from here. Nothing to help me fill in the gaps in his descriptions. This isn't the first time I have encountered this difficulty. Documenting these stories is sometimes like pulling teeth. Each detail is rooted deeply, its extraction complicated by barriers in memory, language, and frame of reference.

Sometimes it seems like it might have been easier to dig the damn trench than it is to get information out of him about what the trench was like.

Tom ignores my staring and reads from his novel as he takes a sip of his coffee, so I am forced to use my words and hassle him further in an attempt to get an answer I am happy with. Something I can visualize.

Glykeria comes over with the plate of sausages and scoops a few more onto my plate. "Feta?" she asks me.

"Sure." *Why not?* "I can get it," I tell her.

"Sit down, Christine, I get it for you," she says before holding the dish out toward Tom and asking him if he wants anything to eat.

"No, no," he says as he waves her away. "Later."

"He never eats anymore, Christine," she whispers to me, shaking her head as she heads back into the kitchen. "Drive me crazy."

I give her a sympathetic look as I eye the plate of sausages she carries back to her black and white speckled granite counter. *More for me.* She heaves the ten-pound tub of feta out of the fridge and forks a hunk out of the brine and into a bowl.

As I start in on my second serving of *loukanika*, with feta this time, I learn that the areas that were primarily stone were harder to dig through, so at those points the trench would be narrower, and it would be wider in the areas of softer earth that were easier to dig through. On average, the trenches were about four to six inches wide. Where the rock was too hard to cut through at all, troughs were constructed from pine boards so the water could be channeled over them.

The households in the *xorio* were surrounded by a canyon on one side and a huge ditch on the other, which resulted in them being stacked up on top of one another in a relatively straight line down the mountain. Wherever the farmers needed water for their crops, they could create a dam with some dirt or a large stone, blocking the flow coming through the trenches so the water would overflow and pour onto their grounds, soaking into the earth and irrigating their crops.

"Dammed them up wherever you needed it. Didn't completely stop it, so some still flowed down to the rest of the people below," Tom explains.

Either the discussions about water or the salty sausages I just ate make me thirsty. I pour myself a glass of water from the tap, move over to the couch, and keep typing as Tom talks from his recliner.

Once the farmers were done using the water, they would deconstruct the temporary dams and let the water flow freely to the next person below. Each family only owned between half an acre and one acre of land, yet there wasn't enough water coming from the source for all of them to water their fields every day.

During the late 1940s until the early 1960s, my family in Detroit was exposed to all kinds of innovation and technological wizardry—juke boxes, televisions, dishwashers, audio cassettes, and boxed cake mix—while my in-laws were digging trenches through the dirt for their water. My mother-in-law was still there up until 1971, still irrigating the fields with the same dug-out trenches when my parents were flipping through the first editions of *The Smithsonian* magazine and listening to The Beatles' new release of *Yellow Submarine*.

Members of the village sat down and constructed a plan to help ensure no one would be left without water. They calculated how much water each household would need for irrigation based on the size of each plot. From this, they created a schedule for how much water-usage time each household would receive.

"They said, 'You get three days, and you get three days, and you get two days,'" Tom explains, his coffee sloshing back and forth as he points to his imagined neighbors with his mug. "They made a schedule so every week or ten days, you get a few days in a row to water. When it's your time, you dam it up." He nods his head as he recalls, "Oh, and they go by the hours, and sometimes you end up getting up at 2 o'clock in the morning because that's what time your time starts. But, that's the best way they could do. I mean, you know." He takes another swig of his Maxwell House.

I think about how as a child I'd run through sprinklers and on slip-n-slides. I would splash in kiddie pools and drink out of the garden hose and sometimes leave that hose running, creating a soggy marsh in the lawn. I think about how as an adult I often take two showers a day. How I leave the water on when I brush my teeth or wash the dishes. *No Tom, I totally do not know.*

Beneath their village, other villages needed water too. "We wanted some water to run down for the rest of the people and some days if the people below didn't get enough water, we couldn't use for another day or two," Tom says. The Skoutelas family was allotted thirty-six hours of water usage each week, and if they didn't finish watering their fields during the allotted time, "Too bad, it was the next person's turn."

It sounded to me like regulating water usage could be difficult. "What if someone just went into the next person's time?"

"Oh yeah, then they had a lot of argument with that. 'Oh, it's my turn, your turn,'" Tom says.

Glykeria comes over and tops off Tom's coffee, and then sets a full mug for me on the end table to my right.

"When did the village start this system?" I ask, as I give her a thankful nod.

"Started it in the '50s, right after things settled down after the civil war. Started '49, '50 or whenever things started settling down."

While water for the crops was mostly accessed via the trench system, it wasn't fit for drinking. Water for regular household use was retrieved by walking down to the river or a natural spring several hundred feet from the house and filling up a wooden bucket they could draw from throughout the day.

During the heavy rains in the fall, people would set out buckets and collect rainwater. But the spring water was preferred since it had been filtered through the mountainous rock.

A small cistern was built near the Skoutelas house that was used for irrigation and household use. Tom laughs as he howls, "There were little green frogs in there! And we just drank that water!" He tips his head back and chuckles. "Oh, man!"

During the drier summer months, there wasn't much water available. When they placed the empty wooden barrels beneath the springs, the water would flow so slowly it would take hours to fill up.

In the 1980s, the *xorio* began to boast pipes made from PVC, which replaced the trenches and carried water from the mountain peak down to each house, the pipes lying atop the paths that were once dug out. Tom remembers visiting Glykeria's parents' house in 1981 and creating a makeshift shower by connecting a hose to the PVC piping and hanging it from the branches of a mulberry tree. I suppose you could call that outdoor plumbing.

"It got SO HOT, you had to wait until an hour after the sun went down to take a shower," Tom says, explaining that the sun would heat up the water traveling through the plastic pipes as it ran down the mountainside, so they'd have to take showers very early in the morning or late at night to prevent scalding.

In the 1990s most of the houses got regular indoor plumbing. The real kind. The kind that utilizes a water heater. The kind that I can picture, that doesn't need to be explained to me.

THE VILLAGE
A load of laundry

When Glykeria was debating whether or not to go visit her family in Greece one year, she told me, "I feel bad to leave Tom alone. No one to cook."

I didn't tell her this, but the last time she went out of town without him he said to me, "My wife is gone for a week, I lose five pounds. I feel great!"

As if she heard me speak this out loud she added, "He doesn't know how to do the laundry."

"I'm pretty sure he can figure out how to use the washing machine," I said to her.

"Well, yeah, but he doesn't like to do it."

That, I believed. Compared to the village though, throwing clothes into the washing machine is pretty damn easy. In the *xorio*, all the laundry was done by hand.

Glykeria is sitting on her navy leather recliner, and I'm across from her on the couch, with my feet on the edge of her coffee table. She leans forward on her chair and starts explaining how laundry was done: "You warm the water in the big pot." She sets down her cup of coffee and raises her arms in front of her, forming a gigantic "o" with her arms.

Tom interrupts her from his recliner, "Ahhh the other secret!" He's yelling so loudly someone who didn't know any better might think he was angry with me, but I know that's just how Greeks talk sometimes. Plus, he grinning. "You boil the water, but you put ashes in there!" He knows I'll be impressed with this bit.

"Okay, I was going to say it, but I wasn't there yet!" Glykeria admonishes him, clearly annoyed.

Tom continues talking, quite loudly, as Glykeria continues her explanation. I try to focus on what she's saying, staring at her mouth and lip-reading her message, which is being drowned out under Tom's booming voice.

"Let the ashes go down the bottom, and then you take the water and wash [the clothes]," she explains. "That's the best. Soft water. The water is so soft afterwards you don't need soap." She explains how they used to scrub the clothing or linens together in the water treated with wood ash.

Tom is still chattering, and since Glykeria has stopped I turn my attention back to him. "We used to make those tubs. Smooth oval tubs carved from wood. That's what we used for washing clothes. Rub the clothes together. Rub, rub, rub, rub, and then put it into cold water."

He puts his palms together, his wide fingers on one hand scrubbing the fingers on the other. I see the tendons in his forearms tighten and his muscles flex. He's still strong enough to do it, I'd bet. The tub he's describing is basically just a shallow, oblong bowl made of wood that was brought to the river or the spring. They would light a fire and heat up a kettle full of hot water and add the wood ash.

"Wash in hot, rinse in cold. Or you mix it. Some clothes you can't wash in hot water, like the wool," Tom says.

I find out that the wood ash wasn't used solely for laundry. "That is the ones we used to wash our hair too," Glykeria admits, as she combs her small fingers through her short, dark brown bob. She continues talking, and I learn that wood ash was used for almost everything. "For baking too," she adds. "Just add a couple teaspoons. When making *kourambiedes* we used that."

"Why did you put it in the *kourambiedes*?" I ask.

"That was like instead the baking powder. So it could fluff it up."

I nod as if I remember exactly what type of Greek pastry *kourambiedes* are. Were they the cookies covered with so much powdered sugar that you had to exhale every time you took a bite so you didn't choke? Were they the custard-filled pastries rolled in filo dough and drizzled with syrup?

I nod as though I can picture the pastry in my head, this pastry that I know I've been exposed to for the last couple of decades. I nod as if I know that making *kourambiedes* requires baking powder. I nod as if I could have recalled on a standardized test that the job of baking powder is to "fluff things up."

I'm the one with multiple college degrees, yet during the entire duration of documenting my in-laws' stories, I nod and pretend I am not as ignorant as I feel. As I am.

Apparently the ashes fluffed up the *kourambiedes* quite well. "Oh, that was awesome, Christine," she says, briefly lifting up both of her hands, her small palms pointing my way.

"Did you ever try using ashes here instead of using baking powder?" I wonder aloud.

"No," she says quickly, firmly. A definite no. "It's chemicals. It's poison here. No, I never tried it here, no." She doesn't have an abundance of fresh oak trees on hand, and she worries about using treated wood. Plus, she can now readily buy baking powder.

Glykeria returns to explaining how she did the washing: "Blankets and big stuff, you never wash them with ashes water. Put them to the river, wet them, beat them with a wooden thing. Bom! Boom! Bom! Boom!" she yells as she swings her arm repeatedly in a motion that looks like a very powerful underhand tennis stroke. "Wash them up. The wood we used to flap them we call it *kopanos.*"

"So, you'd put a plank of wood in the water, drape the blanket over it, and then beat it?" I ask.

"Yeah. Or put it on a rock or something," she says casually as she walks into the kitchen, pulls a cantaloupe out of the fridge and starts slicing it on her wooden cutting board. She slants the board and scrapes the knife across it, tipping the orange cubes into a ceramic bowl, which she offers to me when she walks back in. "Munch?" she asks me. I pop a piece in my mouth. She hands Tom a fork and his own bowl of melon.

Tom tries explaining what they beat the laundry with: "A big baseball bat, flat on one side, triangle on top."

Uh huh.

I slept through pretty much every history class I took in high school, so I missed out on the 1800s farmhouse unit and have no idea what this flat-baseball-bat-with-a-triangle-on-top thing is. Someone who actually passed their ninth grade history final exam would probably have had an easier time writing up my in-laws' stories. One incentive to pay attention in school, kids. You never know when you're going to need that knowledge.

Tom snorts and, with his eyebrows raised, looks at me and adds, "Fancy ones weren't straight across." He draws a horizontal line in the air with his fork, and after a foot or so continues drawing his imaginary line at a forty-five degree angle upwards. "The handle was angled up a bit." He shakes his head, understanding how ridiculous it sounds to call a stick you beat laundry with in the river "fancy," no matter how swanky it might have seemed to them at the time.

I smirk as I grab another piece of fruit and ask them, "Did you guys have fancy ones?"

Glykeria says, "No, I don't remember having a fancy one."

"I think we did, I think we did," Tom says. "That's what I remember."

Glykeria and I look at each other and raise our eyebrows and cluck our tongues and mentally take a sip of tea with our pinky fingers held out and make "Well, wasn't HE fancy" expressions at each other as we giggle.

The two of us, we giggle a lot. We both enjoy being silly for silliness's sake, and we find each other to be hilarious, something that our husbands don't always understand. But we don't care about that when we're cracking ourselves up. The two of us are proud of our strong husbands and know how lucky we are to have them, but we also support each other in a Greek-wife solidarity kind of way when they're acting like stubborn little mules. Whenever we can, we giggle.

I try Googling an image of what a fancy laundry-beating stick looks like. I show a couple of pictures to my in-laws but none of them look quite right to them.

Tom is not surprised. "Everyone in the *xorio* made his own tool. No two tools alike," he says. "You go chop down to make whatever you like. A rolling pin or whatever. Everyone made his own." He explains that some people were particularly good at making one type of tool or another, so they would make them for everyone. "Some people made them but even then they never make them same."

Glykeria goes on to explain that sometimes instead of beating the blankets by hand in the river, they took them to the water mill for a proper walloping. "You can wash at the water mill, you know the one that does . . ." She finishes her sentence by making a spinning gesture with her hands, and looks at me to make sure I understand what a mill is.

She tells me how they used to take their blankets to the area outside the gristmill where the waterwheel was, and launder them by leaving them there to get pummeled by the churning water for a few days.

"At the mill, where the water's going around to, at the bottom they have a little round circle and it go around like wave water. And you have to go there and put them and leave them two or three days and it would move them around and hit them." She tells me that taking them there not only made them cleaner, but also made them feel more comfortable. "Beating them makes them softer than cotton. That's where we take the *flotakis*." Blankets. "Right there, makes them soft and smooth."

    Tom looks at me and says, "Now, they have the mill just for tourists. You look at it and go, 'Remember that? Oh yeah!'" He's gripping his fork like he once gripped the *kopanos*, and I watch a piece of cantaloupe bob around as he gesticulates. "There's no grain to mill. Nobody farms that much anymore."

THE VILLAGE
A bucket for a bath and a bush for a toilet

Glykeria talks in a hushed tone about their "bathroom." They didn't even have an outhouse, they just had a special bush designated for this. "You went behind it to hide a little bit, and if people happened to see you, too bad," she says.

I told Penelope about this the other day. We were at an outdoor Greek festival, and she had to use the porta-potty. Like all of us think when we enter one, she said out loud, "Ew. Yucky. I don't like it in here. It's *disgusking.*" She might not be old enough to pronounce the word correctly, but she certainly understands the meaning.

"No one likes these. We just use them because we have to," I responded.

"Why do we have to?"

"Otherwise we wouldn't have anywhere to go potty and we'd have to go potty outside," I said before adding, "Hey, did you know that your yiayia didn't have a potty when she grew up? She had to go outside. Under a bush."

Penelope squinted her eyes and looked at me, trying to figure out if I was telling the truth or if I was making up a story, like I sometimes do about silly dragons that eat up all the clementines in the fridge or talking socks that can't breathe when they are trapped in sweaty shoes.

"I'm serious. Ask her. We're lucky we have a porta-potty, even though it's disgusting."

I'm not sure she believed me.

"But we didn't care about it," says Tom, looking at me with no trace of a smile on his face. "We didn't know!" he yells, meaning that was all they knew.

"Even in the bigger towns, not just us way out in the woods. But you know what we did for toilet paper?" he asks before immediately answering himself: "Newspaper. Chop them in squares and hang them in the stall so people could wipe up. Newspaper or any other paper that was available."

He takes a sip of his coffee. "Toilet paper," he scoffs. "Nobody had that!" he insists, shaking his head.

"Sometimes didn't have paper either and had to get big leaves. Leaves. Grass. Whatever you found," Glykeria says as she raises her eyebrows.

There was no bathing in the houses, with the exception of small babies and toddlers, who were washed up in little wooden barrels. Once they reached school age, they washed their hair, feet, armpits, and other essential body parts in the barn or down at the river.

"Why did you bathe in the barn?"

"That's where you go to wash because we don't have no room to go in the house. There's nobody in the barn."

"So just to have privacy? What did you do, take a bucket of water?"

"Yep. Go wash your hair, your feet, and whatever you think. Freshen up a bit."

At school, the teachers would periodically check their students' hands and the bottoms of their feet, and if they weren't deemed clean enough they would send them to wash up. Tom says he never experienced a proper bath or shower until he left the *xorio*.

"Summertime didn't have a problem," Tom laughs. "Jump in the pond and wash up. We were swimming. Were clean in the summertime." Tom smiles as he shakes his head.

"Ahhhh, Christine. It was not easy," Glykeria sighs.

"What did you use for soap?"

"Soap? Didn't have the soap," Glykeria bluntly states. Tom nods in confirmation.

A lot of times when we have these discussions, we're all sitting together in the living room and I'm listening intently, but my eyes are glued to my keyboard to double check that I am typing what I intend to. When I look up it's either the rare instance that they are talking slowly enough for me to be able to type accurately without looking or, as in this case, when I am so shocked I just have to make eye contact.

Sometimes they return my gaze with a *Yeah, I know Christine!* expression and sometimes they return it with a *What? That's just how it was.*

"What? No soap?" I lock eyes with her.

What? That's just how it was, her gaze replies to me.

"Some people made soap," Tom says. "Got lye or potash. But then they needed grease. We didn't have any grease." He means they didn't have grease they were willing to sacrifice for the sake of sanitation. "Grease we ate."

I shake my head as I picture all of the grease I toss after making bacon and sausages on lazy weekend mornings.

Glykeria amends her original answer: "Later on we got Tide, like we have here, the powdered Tide."

"Where did you get Tide?"

Glykeria tells me they went to closest town, several hours walk away.

"And when we had it, we washed our hair with the Tide." She shakes her head, knowing how crazy this might seem. But Tide was certainly better than nothing, "We didn't have no other soaps!"

"When did you guys start using Tide?" I ask.

"Ohhhh, '60s?" Glykeria estimates, looking at Tom for confirmation. He doesn't respond. He's reading a book on his Kindle. He's always reading on his Kindle.

I turn to my husband later that night and asked him, "Did you know your parents washed their hair with Tide?"

He shrugs. He doesn't have a lot to say when I ask him questions about his parents. He'll talk all day about his Jeep, or about politics, or soccer, or real estate. He knows about and talks about a lot of things. But get him on the subject of family, something I know is most important to him, and he clams up.

"You did?" I ask.

He just shrugs again before saying, "They had to wash it with something."

I guess the laundry detergent was a step up from the wood ash.

THE VILLAGE
A handmade house

My mother-in-law sends me a picture text. She never texts words. I'm not sure if it's because she doesn't want to, doesn't know how, or just doesn't want to deal with trying to figure out how to spell whatever it is she would write. But every now and again she'll send a photo of an outfit she's thinking of buying the girls, something she's knit for them, or something she's cooking. This time it's *gigantes*. Baked fava beans. They're one of my favorite dishes—tomatoey and creamy and comfort-foody satisfying.

Yummm.

I pack up my computer and head over immediately. My stomach rumbles.

"Ah hah!" she yells when she hears me walk in. "You got my picture?" she laughs.

"You're the best mother-in-law."

She laughs again and pulls a casserole dish from the oven, where the beans have been kept warm.

I stuff my face with *gigantes* topped with feta, and once my stomach feels slightly uncomfortable from all the beans I just consumed, I take out my computer and get to business. I ask them to tell me about their houses growing up.

The Skoutelas house was made of stone and cedar planks and built into a hill on the side of the mountain. A basement, accessible only from the outside, was used to house the goats. After the civil war, a trap door was installed, a simple square cutout on the floor with a couple of planks of wood and a wooden handle atop. It was located in the middle of one of the two rooms on the main floor, not-so-discreetly hidden under a handmade undyed wool rug that showcased the natural gray of the goat's hair.

"We were afraid of the communists," Tom explains. "Another exit just in case you saw something." The trap door also served a practical purpose: a "passageway from the house to the basement where the animals were, instead of going outside and all around the house."

The livable space was connected to an outdoor balcony shaded by holly trees and, since the house was built on the steep slope of the mountain, the balcony was overhanging a small patch of grass. Vines full of grapes were close enough for members of the family to reach out and pluck.

Glykeria's house was built in 1916. She describes it as containing "two rooms and that's about it." Her house overlooked the valley and the White River. I'm curious how their houses were built, since there were certainly no construction companies building up there. I learn that the walls and roofs of the houses in the area were hand-built from thin sandstone rocks, stacked and cemented together with plaster. A mixture Tom and Glykeria refer to as "mud" coated the exterior, to tightly seal the spaces between the rocks.

"We used to get a, like you paint your house, we used to get mud and . . ." she lowers her voice to a whisper, ". . . cow poop . . ." She continues, slightly quieter than before, ". . . and mix it up to make mud, and paint it down to make it nice and smooth."

Her explanation reveals that this "mud" was a mixture of clay, cow dung, hay, and water. Once dried, the cow dung had no odor, Glykeria tells me, triggering a flashback to a study abroad experience I had in college. I visited the Masai Mara in Kenya, and the Masai insulated their huts using a similar substance. She's right. There was, surprisingly, no odor from the dung.

I find myself daydreaming about the quintessential U.S. home during the 1950s that had bathrooms covered with teeny-tiny baby blue or light pink tiles, kitchens that housed padded chairs and tables edged with metal that sat atop black and white checkered flooring, and living rooms garnished with geometric shapes and patterns.

I compare this vision in my mind to my in-laws who had no indoor plumbing and cow shit floors.

Hay was added to the mixture to give reinforcement against erosion when the mud was used on the exterior. Glykeria explains that inside the house the same dung mixture was used on the floors, but the hay was omitted to provide a smoother surface, "so you could sweep it up and make it more formal like."

"Was it shiny?" I ask.

"Yes. Not *really* bright shiny, but yes, shiny. That's why we did that, to make it nice and clean."

"How often did you have to redo the floors?"

"Three, four times a year," she estimates.

"What did your mom paint the floors with?" I ask. My mother-in-law looks at me like she isn't sure what I mean, so I add, "With a tool? With her hands?"

"Her hands. A broom. Or a little piece of wood and scrape it like a scraper. But we didn't have a scraper so we'd use wood. Or hand or broom. Whatever we had."

I get up and take my dish to the sink. I look around at the spotless floors, the clean countertops, the dusted blinds on the windows. Looking around at how well she takes care of her home now leads me to believe that she had a stunningly beautiful cow-dung floor, one that gleamed and sparkled as elegantly as any cow-dung floor ever could.

When houses in the *xorio* were built, the rooms were divided with wooden ladder-like frames that were coated with a limestone plaster. Glykeria remembers watching her dad make the plaster by burning wood in an outdoor chiminea and then piling crushed limestone on top after the heat was high, "firing it up for twenty-four hours, the white rocks burn and burn and burn, and asbestos comes out. *Asbesti* we used to call them."

Once the crushed limestone was set aflame, it melted down, "the rocks turn white and it was ashes," she explains. "The ashes fall down, we get the ashes, get mixed up with water and the water turns white and you paint the…paint. You paint the white."

Tom adds that the brush used was "like a broom. Thicker bristles." Glykeria continues, "Paint the inside, outside, whatever you want to paint. It used to stay on for a long, long time too."

"How long?" I ask.

"About a year or so, maybe. Depends how long you take care of it. Because you are turning the fire up, the smoke, it doesn't last too long, you know." Oil lamps, candles, and the fireplace marked the walls with soot each time they were used. "We used to do that once a year. The inside, the outside, around the windows," she adds.

Tom tells me it's the same method they use to paint the Greek island buildings that are always photographed. "You see those pictures of the islands? That's all they do."

Every room in their house is painted white, and always has been. I remember Lambros telling me that when he was a teenager his dad told him he could paint his room any color he wanted, as long as it was a shade of white. They do not ever consider deviating.

"Do you think that's why you guys only want white walls now?"

"Maybe," she chuckles, before deciding that the color of her walls is no joking matter. "Yeah, but white is rich. The white you can see better. It's a nice color."

BONUS! YIAYIA'S BAKED BUTTER BEANS RECIPE
Gigantes

<u>You will need:</u>

Gigantes: Giant lima beans. Giant butter beans. Those are synonyms. Make sure to purchase the dried kind, not the fresh kind (dried are beige in color, while fresh are green). 1 lb (papou wants 5 lbs)

Olive oil: Enough. A cup.

Onion: Yellow, minced.

Parsley: Finely chopped. ½ cup.

Garlic: Whole cloves, peeled.

Celery: Very finely chopped.

Salt & Pepper: To taste

Tomatoes: The type of tomato doesn't matter nearly as much as you might think. Yiayia usually uses 2 tbsp tomato paste mixed with water.

<u>You will do:</u>

1. Soak beans overnight. Drain and rinse.

2. Place beans in large pot and cover with water. Bring to a boil and then reduce heat and simmer until tender but not fully cooked. Maybe ½ hour-ish? It's fairly hard to screw this up.

3. While the beans are simmering, saute onions and garlic. Add tomatoes near the end and combine.

4. Add tomato and bean mixture to a casserole dish and stir. Season with salt and pepper to taste. Bake until tender and sauce thickens—about 1 or 1½ hours. The tomatoes should gently coat the beans (covered, but not soupy.

5. Top with parsley and stir.

Beans are delicious hot or at room temperature. Always serve with a side of feta.

THE VILLAGE
A homespun blanket

In Glykeria's home, one room was used as a storage area, and in the winter time this included storing their sheep. It was common for people in the *xorio* to house their animals in their homes during harsh winter weather and in spring when the goats and cows bore their young, since the babies needed extra protection.

The second room was the family's living space. This one room housed the fireplace and was where the entire family cooked, ate, sat, and slept.

"Did you just sleep on blankets piled on the floor?" I ask.

"Yep!" Glykeria says. "*Choli* we call them. C . . . h . . . o . . . ," she turns to Tom, "How you spell that?" I'm surprised she tries to spell it to begin with.

Tom just laughs and shakes his head. "It doesn't matter." I think he's embarrassed to admit some of this stuff. But he gives in and spells it for her and then provides more information, in an offhanded kind of way, his eyes still glued to the soccer match he is watching on television.

"A blanket. A goat's hair blanket. It was rough. Kind of thick. Goat's hair." Then his voice raises a few decibels as his guard lets down a bit and he accidentally speaks fondly of his house in the village. "But it was WARM. They never wore out either. Boy!"

Back to playing it cool again, he lowers his voice and adds, "Yeah, they had them all over the floor there."

In the Skoutelas household, Yiayia Athena often slept closest to the fire, with her back near the flames for warmth. Papou Lambros didn't get as cold at night, so he generally preferred to sleep in the corner of the room, away from the fire.

Glykeria remembers her mom and dad sleeping together against a far wall with all the children fanned out, encircling the fireplace in a loose ring in summer and packed in tighter around their sole source of heat in winter. In the morning, everyone picked up their *flokatis*, the equivalent in function to comforters, and stacked them up neatly on a table.

Initially, I am confused about the difference between a *choli* and a *flokati*. The first time I hear about how they all slept, *choli* is the term they use. The next time it is *flokati*.

I ask about this, and Glykeria takes me to the basement, where she has homemade blankets and linens from the village packed away in old suitcases piled up in the corner. She partially unzips a light blue suitcase, circa 1970 or so, and tugging a bit rougher than I would have, pulls out several items. She grabs a rug and shows it to me.

"You made this?" I ask.

"I made it all! The yarn and everything."

Every time I am able to touch something that came from the village, I am in awe. It's like a museum piece has been handed to me. What I'm seeing is something made in a time and place and through a process that is completely foreign to me. It is something I know needs to be preserved, handled with care, and not lost or forgotten.

I touch it, I stare at it, willing my eyes to become magical lenses that allow me to get a glimpse of how my in-laws used to live. I stare at the rug that used to be a sheep Glykeria took care of, whose wool she cut, spun, dyed, and ran through a loom.

It looks just like an ordinary rug. Except, it's not. This rug is a present-day artifact. A vestige of a life she used to live, decades ago, living like most people in the States lived centuries ago.

For a minute, it feels like this rug was made by a different person altogether. It's like it's hard for me to imagine someone who had to live like she did being so relatable. Likeable. Intelligent. Sometimes when I hear about people living in the past, before this or that technology, my mind makes a brief false assumption that when people had less, they were less. This rug is a reminder that that couldn't be further from the truth.

Glykeria tells me that the rug I am looking at was constructed the same way as a *flokati*, except this was a smaller, narrower version that was used more like a hallway runner. The sheep wool is clearly visible, the nap long, the shaggy hair poked out and clumped up a bit in spots. It looks pretty much like a section of shag carpet.

Okay, I think to myself, I think I've got it now. A *flotaki* was made from sheep, with the shaggy fur. A *choli* was made from goat, and the hair was more tightly coiled.

The *flotaki* she displays is boldly covered with thick red and black stripes, shockingly vivid compared to what I had imagined these rugs might look like. This is another example of how it is sometimes difficult to really imagine what life in the village was like. It's like I need constant reminders that people in the *xorio* were regular people who lived in color, and not in shades of sepia or black and white.

She shows me the other items from the suitcase. Among them are several blankets made of wool that she had washed, shorn, and spun by hand. Her family then sent the thread to the closest city, about 40 miles away. "They had a big machine over there," she explains. "Professional loom."

They are beautifully woven blankets, with luxurious earthy shades of golds, reds and dark chocolate browns. And they looked brand new.

We head back upstairs, bringing a few of the blankets she made with us, and Tom continues trying to explain how a *choli* is different from a *flokati*.

"The *choli*, we use it for floor covering and it's kind of smooth. And, you know, when goats, when you do the loom, it doesn't leave the hair coming out like the sheep do."

"No, I didn't really know that before," I admit. I've pet the goats at the zoo with the girls. I rack my brain trying to remember if I have ever in my adult life touched a sheep.

"That's the difference," Tom exclaims.

I glance at the blanket on the top of the stack we carried up, which was now sitting on the coffee table. It has short fibers, no shag, and the yarn seems relatively fine. I try to impress Tom, show him what a quick learner I am. I already have a mnemonic. Shaggy = Sheep. Grouped = Goat.

"So, that's goat?"

"No, that's sheep."

Damn it.

He tries to explain (again) how I should be able to tell the difference. "Goat's hair is real course. More like a painting brush than this."

"Hmm. It seems hard to tell."

"Oh, you can tell."

Clearly. So, I'm just an idiot.

He does make me feel a bit better when he all but tells me this is basically a trick question. "But this, that's why I said, that yarn, that is *so fine!* You can't even see the yarn! Not every woman could do that!" He's yelling again. If you didn't know him, you'd think he was angry, but I know that his yelling right now is a display of excitement.

Ah ha! So, my mother-in-law was just too good of a yarn spinner. It's like instead of spinning thread into gold, she spun sheep hair into goat hair. In the village that would have been worth its weight in gold, I'm sure. Oh my goodness, maybe that daughter in the Rumpelstiltskin fairy tale is based off of her. She's THAT good.

I look at the blanket and back at Tom and make a casual-sounding attempt at asking a serious question.

"Did you know from the beginning that you won the jackpot with your wife? Or did it take you a while to figure it out?"

He just looks at me quizzically.

"She's pretty good at everything she does," I prompt.

He doesn't bite.

"Yeah, but everyone over there was. Everyone did the same thing."

"You just said not every woman could do what she did with spinning the yarn."

"Some were better than others, but I never paid attention to that."
He pauses a bit, and then adds, "If I was over there, I'd probably care." He waffles. "But, I don't think so."

I know he's proud of her. His ability to hide it is an impressive art. His love for her is swathed in satire, coated with comedy, and draped with dismissive tones. It's like he can't bear to speak of his adoration out loud.

Maybe it's like when you don't want to say anything, because you're so worried that once you do, the cosmos will hear you and decide to take it away from you. Like, you never really want to say out loud, "Man, the kids have been so well behaved lately!" because the minute after the words leave your mouth, you turn around and find toddler graffiti covering every square inch of the kitchen cabinets, the stainless steel appliances, and the hardwood floors. With permanent marker.

Maybe he's so afraid of how much he needs her that he can't say one thing out loud about how much he admires her.

Even after a lot of explanation and viewing of old photographs, it is still really difficult for me to understand how exactly the spinning was done in the *xorio*.

"If I buy you that tool you need to spin yarn, will you spin some for me so I can watch you?" I ask Glykeria.

"Where you gonna get the sheep wool?" she asks me back.

"Oh, I'll find it."

Glykeria nods. "I don't need you to buy anything. I can get the branch off the tree," she tells me.

"Yeah. I want to see that." Glykeria ripping off a tree branch with her bare hands after shearing a sheep and making beautiful yarn by hand is pretty much the epitome of how I picture her in my mind, anyway. With a pita cooking in the oven. It'd be pretty cool to see that played out in reality.

Tom looks at me and says, "You need a . . ." and he can't think of how to describe it so he starts miming the motion of a person spinning wool into yarn. Even though I still don't have a perfect understanding of the process, I've heard them talk about this enough to at least know what he's miming.

He comes up with the words. "You need a *roka*, *adrahti*, and *sfondili*," he tells me. Sometimes he forgets that I don't speak Greek. Not that I would know what the names of all the parts of an old-fashioned spinning apparatus was in English.

"Wait, wait, wait, I have no idea what you just said in Greek," I say, as I pull out my computer. I ask him to tell me again and I find out that the *roka* is the forked stick that held the sheared wool in place. "*Adrahti*, that's actually a Turkish word," Tom says. "I don't know the Greek word." He explains that it is "the stick that you put in the yarn. It's like a candle, a tall candle. Thinner than my finger. Thinner on top, then wider in the middle, then thinner on bottom."

Finally, he describes the *sfondili*. "And the bottom has a round cone. You put that with a cone in the middle. Picture it upside, with the hole in the middle. For weight."

He starts snapping. He keeps snapping. Glykeria starts snapping. They are laughing and snapping, and I give up typing for a minute, figuring I'll never really understand this process without seeing it so I might as well just enjoy their little show on the couch.

Tom explains to me why the person spinning would snap their fingers around the yarn. "So it can twist around. Once you spin it once, because of the weight in the bottom, it keeps going. It works sort of like a yo-yo. But you have to pull the wool on it."

Snap. Snap. Snap. That's really all I understand about spinning the old fashion way.

"Your wife said she didn't need anything to show me how she spun wool," I tell Tom. She doesn't need any of those fancy things I can't pronounce. "She said she could get a branch off of a tree."

"You need *sfondili*," Tom insists, still snapping. But he turns his head to address his wife. He tells her she at least needs the heavy weight that pulls the thread taut.

"I'll use a *crimidi*," she responds. An onion.

"Or a *patata*," he suggests. A potato.

"That would be fun to see somebody spinning wool. Hahaha!" Tom looks at her with amusement. "You never even spun wool by hand, did you?" he teases.

"Yes, I did!" She immediately gets defensive.

"I tried. I couldn't do it," says Tom.

Glykeria looks at me and says, "My mother send my *sfondili* over one time. My mother-in-law brought it to her daughter and never gave it back." She raises her eyebrows and nods, indicating that she hasn't forgotten about that.

She describes her *sfondili*. "Fancy on top, they all wood cover . . . cov . . . ," she struggles to find the word she is looking for, ". . . carving," she sounds it out carefully. "With designs on it. My papou used to make those." No wonder she hasn't forgotten about it.

Tom says, "*Kala*. We used to make a lot of those thing. We didn't have anything else to do so we . . . what do you call it when you take a knife and chop on wood?" He makes a motion that looks similar to using a screwdriver.

"Whittling," I remind him.

"Whittling! We have nothing else to do, so keep wiggling." He twists an imaginary knife around an imaginary piece of wood on his lap. "Just need a piece of wood and a little knife."

About half an hour after we finished our conversation about spinning,

Tom laughs. Clearly he has been thinking to himself. "Haha, what is a *sfondili?* You go to most places in Greece and most people won't know."

Even in Athens, people usually bought their shag rugs from a store. They didn't make them by hand out of the animals they owned.

"I'll look up what it is in English," he says. "And the word comes from, uh, what's on your back there, *spontilos*, that's where that comes from. I can't think of the word. From one disc." He points to the vertebrae along his spine. "Each of them is a *spontilos*. That's where the *sfondili* comes from. Because what it looks like, and it has a hole in the middle."

Another few minutes pass, and Tom snaps again. "That's how they learn how to snap fingers when they dance," he says, joking about how the Greek folk dances always involve the snapping of fingers. "It's natural there." He tips his head back and laughs deeply before sighing and taking another sip of his coffee.

I enjoy watching him sit and snap almost as much as I enjoy watching my husband Greek dance. They have the same contented smile on their faces, the same graceful wrists.

Glykeria visited her son-in-law Tom's family farm and while she was there she sheared off some wool from a sheep. She sits down next to me on the couch and turns to Tom, who's been sitting in his recliner, talking my ear off for quite a while.

"Are you done?" she asks him. She's been waiting to show me this. She pulls a handful of cream-colored sheep wool out of her pocket. "That is your *malia,*" she says. Hair. "I washed them. See?"

I pick up the wool and smell it. I figure it will smell like wild animal or like perfumed detergent, but it doesn't smell like anything at all. It's like fuzzy air. "What did you wash it with?" I ask her.

"Just water. We always wash it with water."

She holds onto a hunk of the wool with her left hand and starts tugging on the wool with her right, separating the fibers and making them thinner and thinner and thinner. "Machine we used to go through and make it fine just like that," she tells me.

"What kind of machine was it?"

"Little square with needles, like a comb. You see how a comb is? You see the brushes with the long things? Like that," she says.

Once the fibers are stretched out and the hunk of wool is transparent, she starts twisting it between her thumb and index finger. "See?" she says to me. "We go like that and twist it like here. Twist and twist it and twist it."

The fluffy ball of wool is slowly transforming into a strand of yarn. "If you have them all like that and pull it the right way it's not that hard," she says.

I take the wool from her and start pulling and pulling and then twisting and twisting. "See? You can do it; you don't even know how," she says to me. "Easy. So now you know. You don't need all those other things."

It occurs to me she might be trying to get out of spinning the old-fashioned way. Maybe she's nervous because she's so out of practice. Since making yarn with just your hands is still pretty old fashioned, I guess this will do.

I envision the skeins of yarn I've purchased for her and consider how long it would take to make that much. One year we bought her twenty-five skeins, all different colors, as a Christmas gift.

"Well, yeah it takes forever." It's like she read my mind. "This sheep is different, the ones we have, they have long hair. These sheeps have the short hair. All different kinds of sheeps."

THE VILLAGE
An earthquake

I grab a piece of *kouloukithopita* from the pan sitting on my in-laws' stovetop and carry it over to the couch. Pumpkin pita is the perfect combination of sweet and salty and sometimes it just hits the spot.

"What do you remember about the earthquakes in the *xorio*?"

My in-laws lived in earthquake-prone aresa that shook the Balkans regularly.

Tom remembers he was picking cherries from a neighbor's tree once when he felt an earthquake, and he saw a corner of their house come loose.

Glykeria jumps in with a story. "Me, my mom, my sister, and my friend—and it was about nine o'clock at night and it was 1962, I believe. 1962, '63. Around there. And all of the sudden we heard a noise goes, 'Whoooooo!' like wind or something, and I heard the neighbor screaming, 'Get out! Get out!' Before we get out the door to check what was going on, we felt the house go back and forth, back and forth, back and forth, and we could not stand. My mom was yelling, '*Exo! Exo! Exo! Exo!*' (Out! Out! Out! Out!) We could not see the door to go out because it was going back and forth." Glykeria moves her hands left and right, left and right.

"By the time we got out, it stopped. Next day thirteen aftershocks, you call them. They was not that big but it was like a train going by. My dad was not there that night. He was out cow shopping," she adds.

Tom laughs. "He was cow shopping. At the mall," he smirks.

"At *your* village," Glykeria counters.

"We had a lot of cows for sale over there. All three of them," he continues to joke.

My father-in-law's dry humor, sharp intellect, and ingenious wit could easily fall under the radar if you placed too much value on the broken English, the thinning hair on his head, his long rounded nose, the deep, criss-crossing lines on his face, or the false teeth that he sometimes lifts and drops back down with his tongue. You'd miss a lot of good stuff if you only noticed his veneer and weren't paying attention to what he was saying.

"Was your house okay?" I ask as I get up and grab another piece of pita.

"Ours was. Had a crack all the way down, but it didn't fall down completely. Our neighbors' house was a little lopside." His broken English knocked the "d" off the end of the word, like an earthquake might send a mountain stone tumbling down into a valley's deep abyss.

Tom wasn't fazed by most of the quakes. "We have a lot of earthquakes and always we get together and go in the little place in the corner. Whole house would shake back and forth."

In 1962, well after Tom was out of the house, a relatively strong earthquake hit. It was probably the one that Glykeria remembers. Tom proudly claims that their house was so well built that it withstood that and every other earthquake that rocked it, claiming, "it never lost a stone." He credits the cedar four-by-fours, lengths of fragrant wood intermittently spaced between the horizontal layers of rock surrounding the exterior.

My sweet tooth is in full force. I get up again.

"Just get a plate, Christine," Glykeria finally comments on my overindulgence.

"I keep thinking I'm going to stop eating it," I tell her.

"Yeah. Right."

She says it a little sharply.

BONUS! YIAYIA'S PUMPKIN PITA RECIPE
Kouloukithopita

<u>You will need:</u>

Pumpkin flesh: 4-5 cups, shredded. You can keep the pumpkin frozen and thaw the night before—just dump any excess water. Once you make this, you will never again waste precious pumpkins by carving them on Halloween.

Eggs: 5, beaten.

Cornmeal: About 1 cup.

Sugar: A heaping handful if you're Yiayia. A 1-cup measure if you're me. You could use less if you wanted.

Butter: 1 stick, melted.

Splashes and dashes: Of salt, pepper, cinnamon, oil and milk. If you think you added enough, Yiayia would say you need a shake more.

<u>You will do:</u>

1. Combine eggs, cinnamon, salt, pepper, milk and oil. If you're like me, you can panic about whether the ratio of ingredients is right, but trust in Yiayia and know that it'll turn out fine no matter what.

2. Add cornmeal, sugar and shredded pumpkin.

3. Layer 6-7 pieces of filo at the bottom of a buttered 9 x 13 pan.

4. Add pumpkin mixture and top with 6-8 pieces of filo on the top, making sure to brush butter to cover each layer well.

5. Add a touch of oil on the top of the filo.

6. Bake at 350 degrees. If you ask Yiayia how long to bake it she will yell, "UNTIL THE TOP IS BROWN" and accompany her yell with the evil eye because she already told you that. If you ask me how long to bake it for I'll tell you 1½ hours, but the Golden Brown Method used by our ancestors is the most reliable metric.

A CONVERSATION ABOUT KOULOUKITHOPITA

"What should we make for dinner?" I ask Lambros.

"I thought you were making *kouloukithopita*," he replies.

"That's not dinner, that's dessert." *Duh.*

"It's dinner."

"What? It's totally a dessert!"

This need to be settled, so I call his sister Athena and ask whether *kouloukithopita* is dinner or dessert.

"Either" she tells me.

"If you put sugar on the top, it's dessert. If you don't put sugar on the top, it's dinner," she says.

THE VILLAGE
A new bed in a new house

In 1965, about 150 years after the Skoutelas home was originally built, Yiayia Athena and Papou Lambros decided that their house needed an upgrade. Despite Tom's assertions about his house, the family feared that another strong earthquake could cause their home to crumble. The new house was built by Tom's brother-in-law, Harithimos, who hauled the stones from the original house to the new site, adjacent to the old one.

Yiayia Athena and Tom's sister Kathy helped Harithimos move over large quantities of sand to be used for the mortar. Harithimos left the basement from the original household where it stood, and placed a tin roof over the top, so they could continue to use that as barn space for the animals.

"He did almost everything himself," Tom tells me. "He stayed there for about a month, tore the old house down, used the old stones to build the new house." To reward him for his efforts, Tom, who had moved out of the house for a job several years prior, paid him about one day's worth of pay from his restaurant job. He estimates it equated to ten or fifteen dollars.

When he was done building the house, they followed tradition. "The boss, contractor, he climbs up on the top with a handkerchief and hangs it on the highest rafter and starts hollering," Tom explains. "Welcome everybody there, and everybody brought a nice handkerchief and hung it up. Tradition, when the house is done. Sort of like housewarming party, wish good luck to the house."

The new house had two rooms connected by a hallway. It was slightly smaller than the original and had no basement. The house had a very low clearance—only about eight feet tall at the highest point. The fireplace at one end of the house was used for baking, cooking, and heating the house during winter months. During the summer, cooking was primarily done outside to keep the inside of the house cool.

In this new house, for the first time, the Skoutelas family obtained a "double bed." It turns out this "bed" was actually nothing more than a wooden platform composed solely of two-by-fours. In my mind, a hard wooden platform does not equal a bed, but apparently they thought it did.

At the time the bed was built, they didn't have a mattress, so they put woven material and blankets on top. When I question Tom about how comfortable this could possibly be, he tells me they laid a thick blanket made of goat hair across the top of the platform.

"That goat hair is the best thing for insulation. You don't get wet. You put it on the floor and no cold penetrates up to you. It keeps you warm." He continues to tout the fine qualities of such a blanket, and then makes one concession: "It's a little scratchy at the beginning, but you get used to that."

During another conversation, he says, "Nobody slept there. My old man maybe when he was home. Or Kathy for a few years before we came over."

When it comes to any discussion of the new house, Tom speaks from limited experience since he had moved out by then. "I probably spent two or three times there. Over the summer a couple days here and there."

From everyone's recollection, Yiayia Athena continued to sleep close to the fireplace, her back toasty from the flames, while Papou Lambros slept on the opposite end of the floor, with their babies lying between them. Tom explains, "Mom slept here close to the fireplace." He holds his hand up, indicating her location. "It was always on, she liked warmth. The rest of us, by age. Baby, baby, baby, baby." His hand slides to the right as it moves up and down a few times. "Under one blanket, until we grew up a little bit and we moved to the other side of the floor."

I ask why he thought they all slept together, instead of spreading out and using the bed. "We were all small though, we didn't need much room anyway. My older sister got married before the younger two were born, so even though we were seven people we were never there at the same time. My older sister got married when Effie was like three, four months, I think."

I'm visiting Tom's sister Effie one day and while the girls play with toys on her plush living room carpet she laughs and shares a memory about sleeping on the floor near the fireplace. "When I was young, I was a very light sleeper. If Dad would be at the coffee shop, I could hear his footsteps a mile away and I knew to unlock the door. If the cat wanted to go out, they went to the door and I let them out."

If she could hear footsteps a mile away and her cat's paws padding along the dirt floor, you know that in such close quarters she could also hear the sounds of intimate moments between her parents.

Her memories reveal that Papou Lambros didn't always sleep so far away from his wife. She laughs deeply as she recalls not understanding what the sounds meant, and how hearing the unknown noises frightened her. "For a kid to hear the parents . . . you know . . . and not to know what's happening. I thought my father was killing my mother." Effie is the queen of the phrase "you know" and she gestures and raises her eyebrows to make sure I really get her drift. She is the master of nonverbal cues.

She shakes her head at her own innocent ignorance, and tells me how she used to wonder how the people in the *xorio* had so many kids when even the most basic information surrounding reproduction was hard to come by.

"Of course parents never talk about anything like that. Never ever." She eventually caught on. "It took years for me to figure out what was going on. Even in a two room house, usually you don't see your parents sleeping together."

Tom and Effie's sister Kathy might not have had the same sense of hearing, but she made up for that with street smarts. She remembers wondering, "I don't know how the parents make the babies. My friend Chris and I, we wonder." She giggles. "That one, I learn a lot from her. Her mom was so open with her."

So while she learned the mechanics behind the baby-making, she wondered about the logistics. "We wonder how, because she has two younger brothers, and we always talk about how. We never see them. We never see anything suspicious."

The pair searched for an explanation. "One time, me and her, we says they probably go to another room. We said we're going to put some empty cans behind the room to see if we can hear when they open the door. But doesn't work."

Both Effie and Kathy hint, when they share their stories with me, that they aren't as close of siblings as they would like to be, and it becomes apparent that even then, the two of them didn't work together as much as they could have to solve this life mystery.

Glykeria's family didn't have any beds until the mid-1960s either. Glykeria remembers when her dad fashioned their first bed out of wood when she was around twelve or thirteen years old. The bed is still at the house now, sitting outside on the covered patio. It is simple: four straight legs, a base, and a short headboard made of raw maple. A few years after the bed was constructed, her mom made their first mattress.

Most of their clothes were made out of home-spun wool, and when the items were washed at the water mill, a thick coating of lint would separate from the clothes. The lint was much thicker than the fluff we are accustomed to removing from the vents of our dryers. Glykeria's mother saved this material and, when she had enough, stuffed it between two blankets and sewed the edges together by hand.

As I'm hearing about this I flash back to the bed I had when I was in elementary school: a full-sized heated water bed that was covered with a million stuffed animals and a comforter bed set that had diagonal stripes in primary colors.

In the 1970s, my mother-in-law's family acquired an aluminum bed frame and a store-bought mattress. That bed is still in the house now, in the kitchen. I remember seeing it when we visited Greece during our honeymoon. By 2007, the family had added to the house, and there were a couple of bedrooms, so it didn't make much sense to me for a bed to be in the kitchen. But now, hearing how they all used to sleep in the kitchen, near the fire, I get it.

Yiayia Athena moved to the States in 1967, and Papou Lambros came over in 1970. Yiayia Athena's brother had moved to the States as a priest, and he started bringing over whatever family he could. He knew there was the possibility of a better life than they had in the village.

Papou was in the States for only five or six months before telling his family he was heading back to Greece to die, which he did only a few days after his return. "He did not want to die here. He never liked it over here very much," Tom says.

Once he was gone, the Skoutelas house in the village was empty, so an older couple, Niko and Kalliope, moved in. Up until that point, they had shared a run-down shack with Niko's brother. Yiayia Athena gave them permission to move in and, according to Tom, "they had an agreement, probably verbal, to prevent squatters rights after living there for twenty years or whatever you get it."

Every summer, Yiayia went back home to Greece and stayed with them in her old house when she wasn't staying with her children.

During our honeymoon, we visited the Skoutelas house, where Kalliope and Niko were living. We knocked on the door, and the old lady answered. There aren't many unknown visitors in the village, so it was certainly a surprise. She looked at me, Lambros, and Theio Giorgo, and then back at Lambros. She told him he looked familiar. Lambros told her he had never met her before. Theio Giorgo then told her, "This is Lambros Skoutelas." She shocked us by immediately starting to sob.

She wept large tears that rolled down her wrinkled, weathered face and dripped down her chin, as she repeated his name, "Lambros Skoutelas! Lambros Skoutelas!"

Lambros had reminded her of the other Lambros Skoutelas, she said, the one he was named after. His papou. Kalliope opened the door and led us inside the dark house and pointed to a lone photograph centered upon the mantle above the fireplace. It took a moment for our eyes to adjust and see that the photograph was of Papou Lambros. Every day they paid homage to the man who had given them a home. She gave us a tour of the modest place. It was made completely of stone.

What made it so dark, other than the combination of the low ceilings and lack of windows, was that it still wasn't hooked up to electricity.

Tom remembers how his father would get up in the middle of the night and turn on the kerosene lamp when he couldn't sleep. "The only light we had in our house was a little lantern. We'd put in some fuel oil with a wick on top."

He adds wryly, "Try to do homework with that thing! That little light. We couldn't do it before because we were doing work outside. I don't know how we didn't go blind!" Then he chuckles and adds, "Well, probably because we didn't go to school that long."

The old couple used that kerosene lamp until a few years ago, when they both passed away. Other than the fireplace, the only other remarkable feature in the house was the large, white, two-gallon refillable plastic water tank, called a *yeptira*, that sat supported outside, about six feet above the ground, hanging from a tree. The spigot on the underside of the *yeptira* gave access to the water it held within. It was used as a faucet and shower since the house did not have indoor plumbing.

"My dad's house still doesn't have electricity or plumbing, but the whole village has WiFi now," Lambros points out, shaking his head at the irony.

THE VILLAGE
A universal timepiece

For the most part, the members of the *xorio* didn't have watches. Tom's dad had a pocket watch I remember hearing about, but I knew he didn't use it much and I figured my in-laws knew what time it was based on the sun. I was close. "Went off the North Star," Tom says.

Right idea. Wrong star.

"*Avgerinos.*" Glykeria tells me the Greek name for the North Star as she nods her head in confirmation.

"I never would have thought of telling time with any other star but the sun," I say.

"Yeah, it's the same, with the stars and the moon!" Tom says. "But, the skies were clear there. No light to pollute it. You lay on the porch up in the village, you look like you can touch the stars. It seems so close if the sky is clear."

"Yeah, I'll bet it's beautiful."

"A lot of people working like that at night, with the moon." It was often bright enough to work in the fields with the light from the stars and the moon, something that wasn't possible with their kerosene lamps alone.

"Oil lamp, like one candle, you can't see much with it. You know how we were going over there from house to house?" Tom asks me. "With a torch," he answers. "A wooden stick lit on fire. Just a branch, until flashlights came along. Sixties. Then we had flashlights for a few days until battery died. When battery died, back to square one." Tom shakes his head. "Years later, they got those gas lights you put the fuel in and then pump it, nice flames. Bigger ones. More light in other words."

"How exactly did you use the North Star to tell time?" I ask, trying to get him back on track.

"You looked up, you see it, time to get up."

That doesn't really do it for me, so I ask him to explain a little further.

"You just look up and see phases. In the morning it's in the East, and you tell time because three o'clock, it's rising in the horizon. If you see it midway you know it's one hour, two hours, whatever. Close to it. You know what I mean."

Sure.

I think I was in middle school before I finally mastered reading the hands on an analog clock. I wonder if he thinks it's ridiculous that I don't know how to tell time by gazing at the stars, just like I'll think it's ridiculous if my girls can't someday write in cursive or tell time on a clock that isn't digital.

"Just guessing, I mean," Tom continues. "Some guys, they look at the shadow going off of the mountain, where the shadow is the shade, they could tell time from the sun. 'Oh, it's three o'clock or so.'"

"What if you had to know what time it was, exactly?"

"We didn't," he says, matter of factly.

Well then. I guess that would solve that problem.

"*We* didn't, Christine. But the rest of them, they have clocks," Glykeria says pointedly. The city folk were different.

I shook my head as I continued typing, trying to catch up, long after they had quieted. "I can't believe you used the North Star to tell time."

"So hard to remember all of this stuff. It's so much," Tom says. "I know. We need to do this more often, all these things come out!" I reply.

"Yeah. What else would make me think of when I was getting up in the morning?" Tom asks me. We grin at each other, he sips his coffee and I keep clacking the keys.

BONUS! YIAYIA'S BAKLAVA RECIPE

<u>For the stacked layers, you will need:</u>

Walnuts: 7 cups, chopped.   **Cloves:** Whole. Lots.

Butter: 1 lb, unsalted and melted.

Filo dough: 1 package, thawed overnight.

Cinnamon: 1 tbsp.   **Sugar**: 2 tbsp

<u>For the stacked layers, you will do:</u>

1. Combine walnuts, cinnamon, and sugar. and 1 tbsp cinnamon.

2. Butter the sides of your pan. Layer 6-7 sheets of filo on the bottom, buttering between each layer. Press filo down with pastry brush to remove air bubbles.

3. Alternate nut mixture and 1 sheet filo dough until walnut mixture is gone. Butter filo layers lightly. Don't neglect the corners.

4. Top baklava with 6-7 sheets of filo—make sure to butter these completely.

5. Use a paring knife to cut into diamond shapes and secure each piece with a clove. Cloves are technically edible, but eating them is totally regrettable. Remove before eating.

6. Bake on the bottom rack for 350 degrees for about 1½ hours, or until golden brown.

For the syrup, you will need:

Water: 4 cups.   **Honey:** 1 cup.

Sugar: 6 cups. You didn't think this was healthy just because it contains honey, did you?

Cinnamon sticks and whole cloves: If you're Yiayia, you dump both in until the aroma is abundantly fragrant, but not too intense. If you're me, you measure out 3 sticks and 10 cloves.

For the syrup, you will do:

1. Add sugar, water, cloves and cinnamon sticks in large pot. Bring to a boil and then reduce heat so syrup slowly simmers. Panic that too much water will evaporate and you will accidentally make sticky baklava candy.

2. Add honey and stir occasionally.

3. Yiayia says you can tell when it's done when it sticks to your fingernail and doesn't pour off. Or when it sticks to the bottom of a spoon when the spoon is turned upside down. If Yiayia is available, have her tell you when it's done because none of that makes any sense.

4. Scrape the gunk off the top before pouring syrup evenly over the stacked layers. Tilt the pan to the sides several times to help syrup reach the upper layers.

IMPORTANT! Stacked layers should be at room temperature when pouring hot syrup on top.

THE VILLAGE
A dirt road

There were no roads in the *xorio*. If people wanted open pathways they would have to clear their own brush and dig their own trails. More often than not, people simply trampled through the bushes, perhaps chopping down brush with a machete, particularly when they were meandering through the mountainside herding their animals. For larger community projects, whoever lived in the area would pitch in to get the jobs done.

Tom and I are talking in the living room while Glykeria is in the kitchen. He gives an example: "When something needed to be done, everyone would get together, and say, 'Let's fix something. Let's fix the road.' The whole village would work together. They called it, like, personal days you had to put in. Community work. There was no one else to do that."

He tells me there were no roads in the village but then tells me they worked together to fix the roads. I have to clarify everything because sometimes they tell me one thing when they really mean something else. Or they use words to try to relate their experience to something they think I'll understand, but by doing so it warps the reality of what their experience truly was.

"I thought you said there weren't roads in the village?"

"Not a car road, just a little walks type thing. The mules or us walking around. Clean it out, wash it out. Goat trails, in other words. Fix them up once a year. You know how they were doing that."

The workers would band together, bring their pick axes, shovels, and other supplies, and the work would be continuous for one or two days until the task was completed.

Tom tells me how when he was young, "When they were close by, I'd take them food every day. One time they were building close to our village, and my mom made some *spanakopita* and said to take it to my dad for his lunch." Halfway down, "the cloth unfolded, and I lost the pita on the ground."

Tom, only five or six years old at the time, panicked. Food wasn't something to be wasted, and he was worried about getting into trouble for his carelessness.

"So, I picked it up and wrapped it back up and took it to my dad." His dad bit down on the pita. CHOMP! Tom remembers him letting out a little "uh!" Something in the pita hurt his teeth. Tom watched his father. "He handed it to another lady, who was also working, and she didn't have a problem with it."

Later, Tom's dad asked him about the pita, and Tom had to confess about dropping it in the dirt. About the lady who ate the pita, Tom says with a laugh, "The girl was young, in her twenties or so, and she was hungry." His laughter turns from a rumble to a roar. "She ate the whole thing!"

Tom has told me this story dozens of times, and each time he laughs so hard he has to wipe away tears. Sometimes I ask him to tell me the story of the dropped pita just because I love hearing him tell it so much. There is something powerful about hearing someone laugh until their sides ache.

"Tom, tell me the story about how you dropped the *pita* in the dirt."

"*Plasto*, not *pita*. Don't overdo it, now. We didn't have *pita*."

This is why I need to hear the stories over and over. I need them to correct me when I repeat back to them what they told me the first (or second, or third) time. *Plasto* is basically the same as *spanakopita* except instead of filo on the top and bottom, a cornmeal dough is used. Filo requires white flour, something their families rarely had. Plasto is the poor people's version of *spanakopita*.

I am obsessed with *plasto*. It is one of my favorite foods my mother-in-law makes. Every time she makes a pan, I devour it. Tom shakes his head whenever he watches me eat it.

"You're eating village food," he says, with a tone indicating that *plasto* is the equivalent of bologna and mayo on Wonder Bread. White trash food. *Aspro scupidia fageto*. For some reason I know how to say that in Greek. Three of my vocabulary words out of the approximately twenty-five I have mastered.

The bologna might contain more hydrogenated fats and excess sodium, but both have the same amount of stigma. My mouth is too busy chewing for me to answer, so I happily nod, even though it is apparent that he wasn't complimenting my diet.

After making his important correction, he retells the story. "Haha, oh yeah, I dropped it on the way there. In the gravel. Put it back in the napkin thing. I take it there, my old man takes a bite." Tom grimaces and sticks out his tongue. "She was sitting right next to us, he just took one bite and left it there. She must've been starving. She probably swallowed it whole. He didn't want to say anything. I don't know if he didn't want to embarrass me or because the lady ate the whole thing.

"Later on he said, 'What happened?' I said, 'I dropped it!' He knew it right then, I dropped it someplace. I was what, like six? Ohhh, it was funny." He laughs deeply and wipes the corners of his eyes.

I'll never get sick of hearing him tell that story.

During the late 1970s and early 1980s, when my parents were finishing up high school in the suburbs of Detroit and moving on to college life at Michigan State University, the first bulldozers were brought in by the government near my in-laws' ancestral homes to break up the hard rocks and construct some proper gravel roads. While my parents traveled back and forth along I-96, the neighbors in the *xorio* fought bitterly about the exact locations of their new roads.

Each family had a small parcel of land, and everyone was worried about losing acreage. The arguments would become so fierce that the road construction would be halted until arguments about whose land the road would cut through were resolved. Eventually the conflict would be ironed out and the road building would continue. Some households chose to forego road access in favor of keeping all their land.

Glykeria's father forfeited some of his land for the road. He had a decision to make since his home was on a slope. His choice was to lose the land above his property or the forest just below it. He decided that it was to his advantage for the road to wander up and around the house instead of below and in front of it.

Glykeria says he did this so he could roll goods from the road down the hill to his house instead of carrying the goods up to it.

Even with the construction of the roads, driving along them was somewhat treacherous, as gravel roads along a winding mountainside tend to be unstable.

"One rain, they wash away," Tom says.

In 2005, the main road winding up the mountain was finally paved, while the rest of the lanes and offshoots are still made of unpaved gravel, including the section closest to the Skoutelas house. The gravel road never made it all the way up to it, so there's still a bit of a trek through unpaved land to get up there.

THE VILLAGE
A phone call

Lambros has to go out of town for work for a couple of days, and since it is summer and I don't have to work, I am able to go with him. When you're a teacher and a mom and a bit of an introvert, there is no better vacation than sitting in a hotel room in beautiful silence by yourself.

We leave the girls with his parents, something we can always count on, unless they are already watching one of his sister's kids. We've joked, in a sort of serious way, about needing a joint calendar so we know when Yiayia and Papou are available. They are always watching someone's kids.

We get back from our trip and head to their house to scoop up the kids. We visit for a bit and then head out. On the way out, Glykeria asks if we want to take any food with us. We try to say no, but we end up leaving with a container of spaghetti and a half platter of *yemista*. Stuffed peppers.

"Thank you!" we say as we give them a hug and kiss goodbye.

"For what?" they reply. "We didn't do nothing."

We're very lucky that they are our family. We're VERY lucky that they are our neighbors too. My in-laws talk about having had nothing in the *xorio*, but by doing so they downplay how much it means to have family nearby. A close-knit family provides more support than the strongest brace or buttress.

Houses in the village were widespread. Unlike the next-door neighbors my husband and I had in our first house—we could literally reach out and touch one another if we both opened up our kitchen windows—next-door neighbors in the mountains were miles apart.

Effie tells me, "If it wasn't for the mountain, we couldn't communicate. We went up to the mountain and called."

Tom explains that this was exactly like it sounded. "Sometimes one person on one side of the mountain would yell, 'Heeeeeyyyyy,' and someone else would come out on the other side of the mountain and yell back. They could do this all day long, and since there weren't many people, you always could tell who the person was that was yelling."

Starting in the late '60s, the first phone was introduced. This crank phone was located at the coffee shop, so if you needed to make a phone call you had to go there.

"What if someone wanted to call you?" I ask my mother-in-law.

"They make an appointment," she says.

"Who did they make an appointment with?"

"The phone company did that. They would notify people that someone was going to call you on the phone."

"How did they make an appointment with someone if they didn't have a phone in their house?"

"They just told whoever had the phone."

". . ."

This is not the first time I just stare blankly in response to something they tell me.

"The person who had the phone was responsible for letting the person know," she adds, in response to my blank stare.

"That sounds pretty unreliable."

"You could call and just see if they were there. Like Tom's dad was at the coffee shop a lot so sometimes he'd just call and see if he was there. If not, no biggie. But, if there was something important like I need a birth certificate or somebody got sick or whatever, then make an appointment."

"So, how'd you set an appointment time if nobody had clocks?" I ask.

"Oh no, no, no. Approximately," he says. He gives me an example: "Okay, I'll call at three in the afternoon. So, maybe you go early. Might be two o'clock. Or an hour later, or whatever. So they just keep trying until you're there, in other words. Doesn't matter."

As a high school teacher who lives by the bell, I account for each minute. And as a mama who carts her kids around to innumerable appointments at specific times, I have a hard time relating to this.

"Most of the people spend most of the time in the coffee shop anyway," he adds. He keeps trying to explain: "Wasn't like make an appointment for the quarter to three. We didn't have doctors, we didn't have lawyers. If you wanted something, you just call across the mountain. 'Heeeeeey, Giorio!'" He cups his hand to his mouth and pretends to yell to his friend George across the mountain. "The voice carries across those little valleys. Most of the time, we did that." He simulates a typical conversation: "'You want to meet someplace? I'm going up tomorrow.' 'Oh, okay.'"

Oh, okay.

From what I can gather, the most common method to reach someone was to call the coffee shop and tell whoever was working there, or whoever happened to be sitting there, to inform the person they were trying to reach. Then they would call back in a half hour or so to give whoever they were trying to call enough time to walk there. I guess whoever was there yelled across the mountain to tell them to head over.

This whole appointment thing wasn't just a village issue. Even in Athens, most people didn't have phones. "Call Athens, call a kiosk. Little kiosk where they sell newspapers and cigarettes," he explains, to make sure I know what he's talking about.

"See, that's the thing, you didn't have the phone right there and somebody would answer it. You had to call a store or a kiosk. The kiosk, the guy was busy all day. Call out, literally yell out, 'Hey barber! Hey neighbor! You have a phone call!'"

I laugh and shake my head. I can remember a time before cell phones existed, when everyone wasn't attached to their phones and it took a considerable amount of effort to get ahold of someone. I mean, not nearly as much as he's talking about, but much more than today.

"To get a phone in Athens, even in the '60s, took two or three years. Even nowadays. I'm not talking the 1900s when we didn't have phones. Even three, four, five years ago."

He gives me an example of how those conversations go, "'I want a phone.' 'Okay.' 'When?' 'Whenever they get here.' Not like here, you call and they come hook you up in what? Couple hours?"

This aligns with everything I've heard about Greek customer service compared to the American version. He shakes his head. "I don't know why they got used to that over there."

Tom doesn't know exactly when phones started showing up in his area, because he had moved out before they got one. There wasn't a *caffeneio* in his neighborhood, so phones were put directly into people's houses. Tom's parents were the first in their village to get hooked up with a crank telephone, so for a while it served as the entire neighborhood's phone.

Effie explains that the "phone line was placed in our house first because our house was central. People passed by it to go to the other village."

Even when the rest of the neighbors received phones, there was still only one phone number for everyone, and everyone could listen in to everyone else's conversations. "The phone was connected to a party line," Effie adds.

When my in-laws moved to the States, their first phone was connected to a party line as well. Glykeria remembers calling over to the village from the U.S. once and she listened in for a while as the ladies in Greece were talking to each other, idly chit-chatting about what they ate and what they did that day. She says that none of them knew she was listening. "Tried to call my mom. I heard those ladies, I knew those ladies, but they couldn't hear me."

"Did you call your mom a lot?"

"Not a lot, once in a while. It was expensive, Christine. About ten dollars a minute."

She must've been feeling nostalgic to waste a few of those minutes just listening to idle chit-chat.

Phones clearly weren't the primary mode of communication. Yelling was. But for people who were out of shouting distance: "Lot of letter writing. It would take a week or two to get there. At first we did," Tom says, nodding to his wife sitting on the couch across from him. "Before she came here."

This was news to me.

"Do you still have them?" I'm very curious about what they might have talked about.

"Oh, I don't know," Tom says dismissively.

"I have them, I have them," Glykeria nods, sure of her answer. "I have them all."

"You don't have to answer me now," I say, "but if you want to share them, I'd love to read them. But just talk about it and think about it," I say, trying to be polite.

"Oh, I don't know where it is," Tom says, before teasing me, "I'll edit them first, Christine." He laughs and tosses his head back against the couch cushions. He looks at his wife, "What? One? Two? Three letters?" He turns his head back toward me. "Mostly about the paperwork anyways," he says, referring to the government papers required to bring over his bride.

"I have to search in the basement somewhere," Glykeria tells me.

"You want them now?"

"No, no," I tell her. "Just think about it, and if you find them . . ."

"Next time you cleaning the basement you look for them," Tom says to her. "Christine can't read them anyway, what you worried about?" he laughs. Obviously, they were written in Greek.

"That's the last time I probably wrote letters," he says after a pause.

"I wrote letters," Glykeria says. "The last letter I wrote, I wrote my dad. Never wrote a letter after that."

"Why not?" I ask. I love handwritten cards and letters.

"Well, now we have the phone. It's so easy now, whether it's the phone or computers or whatever," Tom says.

I nod. It's so easy nowadays.

BONUS! YIAYIA'S STUFFED PEPPERS RECIPE
Yemista

This one is written how Glykeria and Tom tell it.

<u>You will need:</u>

"One pound ground beef." Glykeria tries to tell me the recipe the way she knows I like to hear it. She even has her recipe book out for reference, to make sure she doesn't forget anything.

"*Kala*," Tom interrupts. He is sitting in his recliner and he looks up to share a bit of wisdom. "Depends how much you make."

Glykeria rolls her eyes, sighs and gives him a glare, which he ignores.

"Onion. Yellow onion, chopped up. Two tablespoons parsley, salt, pepper, oregano." She waits for me to finish writing this down before she continues.

"And the important one—MINT. Always have to have mint that one." She looks me square in the eye, making sure I've heard her. "And garlic. Two, three cloves." She reads over her recipe for a minute and is just about to speak when Tom interrupts again.

"In the *yemista*, you need mint. That's the main ingredient," he yells.

"I just said that!" Glykeria admonishes him. She looks at me and shakes her head. "He drive me crazy, Christine. Okay, I think I said it all," she says, meaning she has listed all of the necessary ingredients. She moves on to the directions.

"It depends how many peppers you want to stuff. Let's go four or five peppers. Or tomatoes, either way. Or mixed." She usually makes a pan filled with half stuffed peppers and half stuffed tomatoes. Sometimes she stuffs a few zucchini flowers too.

"That's what I didn't say. Olive oil. Did you get it? And tomato paste. Melt it in water, about a tablespoon full."

I add tomato paste dissolved in a tablespoon of water to the ingredient list.

"Or, if you want to, put more. Less. Whatever. You can do that," Glykeria adds, referring to how much water you can mix with the tomato paste.

<u>You will do:</u>

1. "Chop onion and sauté with garlic and then add meat. Sauté for that—brown it. And then you put the rice in." She waits again for me to catch up on writing down what she says. "Add tomato paste, salt, pepper, spices. You put it all in."

2. "Slice the top off the tomatoes and clean them out," she continues. "Cut the top—you know how we do it." With her hands, she mimes slicing horizontally through the top of a tomato.

She often assumes I know things I don't. In this case, though, I actually do know what she means.

3. "The peppers the same way," she adds. "But, if you want to put them in the rice and the meat, you put them in there." She refers to adding the flesh that was cleaned out from the inside of the tomato right into the filling mixture. I look at her and nod appreciatively. I hadn't thought of that.

"That's right! Chop them up and put them with the rice and cook them for a little bit."

4. "And then stuff the tomatoes and bake it. Put a little water on top. Yeah, so it'll cook. Put another cup of water in there with another tomato paste around the pan. Let it cook at 350 for an hour or so."

"Ah, a little bit longer." Tom chimes in again from across the room. "Until the rice."

"Yeah, the rice needs to cooks!" Glykeria yells in his direction as she rolls her eyes and waves him away with her hand. The rice needs to cook until it is soft.

I giggle because I find the way they interact to be hilarious.

"It's not funny, Christine. Oh my God, every day he doing that." She says it under her breath, as if he can't hear her from a few feet away.

"It's kind of funny." I try to get her to crack.

"No. He drive me crazy." She takes a deep breath before adding, "An hour fifteen minutes, maybe. Depends on your oven."

"Did you tell her to put the covers back on upside down? Tom asks?

Yiayia and Papou

Without waiting for a response from his wife, he tells me to place the tops of the tomatoes upside down after I have filled them.

"Turn them upside down, so the rice and the meat—if you overstuff them—not to come out. Glykeria nods in agreement at Tom's latest contribution.

"That's all I'm doing. I don't do any different." She thinks she has told me everything I need to know about making *yemista*.

"How much rice did you put in?" I ask.

"A cup! I told you a cup!" she says accusingly.

"I'm going to write this in the book exactly as you told it to me."

"Oh, come on, Christine! I said it! I said a cup!"

AN ADOPTION

"I never met my father's side," Tom tells me. "They died when I was born. But the grandparents on my maternal side, they lived a long time. I was in my 30s when they passed away. My dad was adopted anyway, in the first place."

"Was he?" This surprises me. It wasn't like they had adoption agencies in the *xorio*.

"I met one of my uncles. I was in grade school, like ten, eleven years old, and I met him but not my other uncle."

"There were three siblings?"

"Three that I know of. I think they had sisters too, but I never . . . they never talked about . . . because it . . ." Tom stammers a bit, trying to think of how to explain it.

"I don't know, they kinda, people are crazy you know?" he finally spits out. "They are strange over there. They were ashamed to not have kids and to adopt kids. Other kids were adopted, they didn't have kids and so went out and get somebody," Tom says, explaining that adoption happened in the village just as much as anywhere else, even if it was never openly discussed. "They didn't tell anybody. They wouldn't talk about adopt kids. They just didn't want to talk about it for some reason."

"What's wrong with it?" Tom wonders out loud.

"Your dad's adopted," he remembers hearing. "In school some of the other kids started calling us these names, we heard rumors. We didn't know exactly, but we knew he was adopted." Tom says. "So that's when we find out. We didn't know until we were older kids, five or six years old, and the other kids start teasing us."

It was then that Tom started questioning his parents about his dad's lineage. Even before the school ground teasing, there had been suspicions. One of his dad's biological brothers came to visit.

"He comes up and visited for ten days. He was a city boy, well dressed, groomed, polite," Tom tells me. "We called him Theo Taki. They had different last names," Tom says, referring to the last names of his dad and uncle. "We start wondering. How can they be brothers if they had different name? So, everyone knew, just no one talked about it. Somehow you always knew it."

Tom didn't think much of it. "Okay, we didn't think it was anything strange or whatever. But no one talked about it. And they still don't! I don't know why."

He shakes his head and stares into space for a few minutes while he takes several sips of coffee.

"After he grow up, my dad found his brothers, his family, and was visiting them a lot. But nobody was coming up where we were, except my uncle. For visit. So we knew who he was." He never met Taki's other brother, Peri.

Effie shared one of the juicy tidbits about how the adoption transpired when I was visiting her one day. "My dad's mom, we don't know her name, was engaged to this guy and she got pregnant while they were engaged. Back then, that was unheard of."

It was out of the question for the couple to keep the baby and admit their indiscretion. His parents didn't want any association with the scandal, so after giving birth, she left the baby, Papou Lambros, with her parents, who raised him.

"She went off, married the guy, and created another family," Effie said. "And I think she had two more boys."

It took me a long time to wrap my head around this. A couple decide they are in love. They get pregnant and have a baby before the wedding. They give the baby up. They get married and have a couple children who are full-blood siblings to the first child, but the first kid is never welcome in their family.

So, Papou Lambros was technically adopted, but by his own grandparents. If I had lived in the village during this time, I would've been in the exact same boat. I was born two days after my parents were married.

Papou Lambros was given his mother's maiden name, Skoutelas, while his brothers, Taki and Peri, were given her married name.

Tom's grandfather took a liking to Lambros, the bastard. "As a kid, he took him under his wing," Tom says. "My grandpa had seven daughters, and he liked Lambros so much he said, 'Let's marry him off with Athena.'" So that's how Papou Lambros and Yiayia Athena were arranged.

In the 1970s, their biological uncle Peri sent Tom and Glykeria a letter and asked them to send money because he needed an operation. Tom and Glykeria were new to the States and didn't have any money to send. "If I had the money, I probably would have sent some," Tom says. "In fact, if he contacted me today, I probably would send him something."
Knowing their generosity when it comes to family, the fact that he didn't send anything speaks to how little they truly had at that point.

I try to dig deeper about the family history. "So, was your dad named after his biological grandfather?" I wonder, since that is the tradition. But this circumstance was different.

"Well, I don't know," Tom says. "We don't have that many on my dad's side around. I don't know anything before that. I tried to go through. Can't go farther than that. Can't find anything. We should have done that when people were still alive."

I nod. Seems like we all think that same exact thought at some point in our lives.

ANIMALS
A goat with a bell

Each and every one of my relatives by marriage has a large soft spot in their heart for *katsikia*. Goats.

Every time I am gleaning stories from one of them, goats somehow sneak into the conversation. Curse of the goat herder, I suppose.

I hear more praise for the glorious goat from Tom than from anybody else. I have heard him say a million times at least, "I love goats. I still love little goats!" At some point during each of our interviews, he invariably takes a protective stance surrounding the topic of goats, defending them from trash talk from invisible goat haters. *I'm* certainly not hating on goats. I'm just nodding and typing.

He gets so worked up, his voice raises a few decibels. "I have no idea where they got the goat stinks and eats everything. I don't care what people say, goats don't smell! They are clean animals! The only time they smell is if they are in rut, but otherwise, they are great animals." His coffee almost splashes out of the metal cup that seems permanently attached to his fist, as he swings it around during these recurrent rants.

"I had one goat. When I was born my parents gave it to me," Tom tells me when we are in the car together one Sunday afternoon, driving home from church.

We don't love the Greek Orthodox church where we live, since they don't let kids sit in the pews; they banish them to the back behind a pane of glass, which results in all of the kids acting like caged animals. We prefer to attend the church in Saginaw that my in-laws have been attending since they came to the States. Every time a kid screams there the priest says, "That's okay. That's the best noise ever. That is a sign that our church will continue."

It's an hour-and-a-half drive each way, but it's worth it for that kind of rational kindness. Plus, every time we go I have my in-laws trapped in the car for three hours of story time. We bought our minivan in large part so we didn't have to take two cars when we're all driving the hour and a half to and from that church.

"They would give us each an animal when we were born," Tom continues from the back seat. "I had an old goat, a female. From that female goat, from the time I left school, I had thirteen of them," he gushes. I'm sitting in the passenger seat, angled a bit so I can see him nodding his head with pride as I type.

Goats were valuable commodities. They could be traded for goods, used toward a dowry, or, of course, eaten. But, Tom says, "we never ate the goats. We sold them for money. We never ate them unless one was sick or something or unless there was a wedding or something."

Goats were special. They weren't just thought of as valuable or edible. They were legitimately *liked*. "We would rather go a whole year without eating meat before eating our goats," Tom says.

Goats, I've been repeatedly told, have amazing personalities. "Goats, though, they do what they want, they run wild. The kids play and bite and chew and are friendly like dogs," Tom tells me.

My in-laws and their families tended to their goats and sheep daily. They herded them up and down the mountain to make sure they pastured on their own land and not the neighbors', and to keep them safe from injury or loss.

Over the years, I've heard quite a bit about one particularly rebellious goat. "I had one goat in my herd that would always leave and find a garden to get into and eat something. Every day! I could not stop that goat! Every day, that goat would go out and leave the group," Tom shouts from behind me.

Even though this goat obviously made Tom's life harder, you can tell he was more impressed than annoyed. "We ended up putting a huge bell around the goat's neck. A huge bell! That goat . . ." His narrative about the goat is punctuated with laughter, and he starts to laugh so hard he can't make a sound.

When he pulls himself together, he continues, "That goat learned to pick up its neck, so that the bell would hang flat on its neck so you wouldn't know she's in someone's garden again." He demonstrates, craning his neck until the back of his head hits the headrest behind him. He laughs and shakes his head at his goat's ingenuity. "She was a good goat. She had lots of babies."

Somehow during that trip I never asked an important question. A few days later I call Tom and ask him, "Tom, I have a question for you. You know your goat with the bell?"

"WHAT? I can't hear you."

"YOU KNOW YOUR GOAT WITH THE BELL?"

"Oooooh," he starts chuckling, "yes, yes." I can't see him, but I can tell he's smiling.

"Did it have a name?"

"Hehehe. Oh man." He pauses, sounding slightly embarrassed. "Mouska," he finally says.

"Does that mean anything?"

"Eh, it's for the color. Like, a gray." He laughs again. "Ahhhh, you're reminding me of that."

He normally hates talking on the phone, but it sounds like he wants to keep chatting about Mouska. Man, he loved that goat.

Effie confirmed his goat story when I chatted with her another time. "Tom's goat with the bell was the leader of the pack. She learned how to jump the fence without ringing the bell. After that goat was gone, her daughter had the bell."

The daughter goat was the one that paid the price for its mama's unruly behavior. "She eventually got struck by lightning," Effie explained. "Poor thing."

We're still in the car, but we're getting closer to home when Tom starts telling a story I've heard many times. I eye my full coffee cup sitting in the cup holder. We stopped through the drive-thru immediately after church, and I haven't had a chance to drink any of it yet since my fingers have been busy taking notes. I wonder if I can sneak in a quick sip and not miss too much, especially since I've heard the story before.

Somewhat reluctantly I decide not to risk it and, with a concentrated effort, I refocus my attention to his tale since this is the first time I'm writing it down. Everyone knows writing can be difficult, but no one warns you about the inability to consume caffeine when you're frantically transcribing family history.

"One of the goats had a baby," Tom begins, "so we brought the baby into our room, so it would be close to the fire. It was really cold out and we couldn't leave it outside."

"Did your parents know about the baby goat in the house?" I interrupt.

"What else you going to do with the goat? It was winter!" Tom shouts, his tone indicating he can't believe I asked such an inane question.

Of course you had to bring the newborn goat inside your home. Silly girl.

"Not only did we live with that goat, I loved that goat!" He's yelling. He doesn't only profess his love for goats often, he professes it *loudly*. His love-yell sounds a lot like normal people's hate-yell. It's a Greek thing, I've learned. His voice reverberates off the walls of the minivan.

"That same night, my mom had my sister Romi. We knew she was pregnant, but none of us knew she was delivering the baby in the middle of the night. We woke up the next morning and there were now TWO new kids." A human kid and a goat kid.

The morning of the deliveries, a family friend, Theo Hari, popped by. He frequently visited and stayed for a bite of pita or *psomi*. Bread. Yiayia Athena entertained the visitor even though she must've been completely exhausted from birthing all night. She did not want him to know she had given birth, and was hiding the baby.

When I talked with Effie, she explained why Yiayia Athena was being so secretive: "You aren't supposed to say anything until the priest came to bless the child. If you gave birth at the house, someone had to go to the priest and get holy water. If the priest was available, he would come on the day the baby was born and again eight days after birth. It was customary for people to keep the baby out of sight until the baby was forty days old."

The children were instructed not to tell Theio Hari about their new sister. Tom's little brother, Andy, couldn't hold it in. He kept curling his fingers into an "o" shape, and placing them in front of his mouth, creating a little megaphone with his hand and saying, in the deepest voice he could muster, "We have a baby!"

"What did he say? What is he talking about?" Theio Hari asked.

Yiayia Athena quickly responded that they had a new baby goat.

Effie laughed and remembered Andy repeating, "We have a baby . . . we have a baby girl . . . we have a baaaaby!"

Tom shook his head, "Andy couldn't keep the secret."

ANIMALS
A goat for dinner

Tom and Glykeria took their three kids on a family trip to the *xorio* in 1988.

"My dad passed away April and we go back July, I believe," Glykeria says, as she sits perched on the edge of our brown leather sofa. She's holding a small glass of cabernet. In her tiny hands, the stemless glassware looks comically large.

She starts telling me about two goats her mother had that caught the Skoutelas family's attention. "My mom has the one mama goat and one little one."

She describes the young goat, a black kid with a splotch of white on its forehead and a smidge of white around its mouth.

"Oh my God, Christine, it was so cute," she tells me, her voice getting even higher pitched than usual. Her arms bend at the elbows, and she tosses the hand not holding her wine into the air. She looks off to her right, as if she can see the goat standing by her side. She leans her body toward me a bit and continues, "It was a cute little baby goat, and it likes to play a lot. He was too friendly and excited."

She reminds me a bit of a child swinging their feet and bouncing up and down. Her feet touch the ground though. Barely.

She explains how the goat was continuously running and jumping, prancing and playing on the mountainside. The goat ran up the hill toward its mother, and instead of stopping when it got close, it jumped up onto the mama goat's back, running along her spine, from tail to head, before leaping off and running back down the hill.

Lambros, then ten, decided to try to catch the goat, chasing it as it ran. At first, the goat was unsure of this stranger, the skinny boy with pale skin and black hair following him around. It ran away from him, its agile body easily weaving and bobbing through the uneven landscape of rocks and brush.

But the goat must have sensed that the boy meant no harm, and before long the goat and the boy were chasing and playing, the tiny goat climbing up the boy's back, as it had its mother's earlier in the day. When the goat ran away, it turned its head every now and again to make sure that the boy wasn't too far behind.

"Then they went back and forth. That's all Lambros was playing, that's all he did the whole time we were there." She sways her arm, the one holding the wine, back and forth, back and forth. All that wine sloshing around above my carpeting might worry me if I didn't know what a strong grip she had. She is very small but not at all frail.

Lambros's sisters, Athena and Voula, also became enamored with the goat, and the young trio called their pet "Mbailo." Glykeria pronounces it BYE-Oh. Everyone loved Mbailo, but it was Lambros who loved the goat most of all. For a full week, Glykeria tells me, "anywhere the goat's going, Lambros is going."

After that first week of their visit came to a close, Glykeria's mother, Stavroula, went to feed her goats and sadly discovered the kid was no longer able to support itself on its legs. Glykeria remembers her mom explaining the problem the goat had in this way: "He was a baby, he was not eating grass or anything yet, just milk. If he drinks too much milk, the milk stays on his legs." Her mother could tell it was not good news for the little goat.

While her medical explanation may be far from accurate, there is no doubt in my mind that Stavroula knew it was over for the goat, and that any efforts to heal the goat would be in vain, not only prolonging the suffering, but also reducing the chances that the goat's valuable meat would be edible. The week did not end as well as it started for Mbailo.

"She killed him, cleaned him, and roasted him in the *gastra*."

The week did not end as well for the children, either. They sat down at the dinner table and were shocked when they saw their friend on a platter next to roasted potatoes and sliced and salted cucumbers.

Oh, no. I'm morbidly fascinated.

"They were all crying," my mother-in-law tells me. "They hollering, 'There's no way we're going to eat Mbailo with potatoes!'"

She places her hand firmly to her chest. The corners of her mouth tremble a bit, and she adds, as she pats her chest, "I still have that in here." She blinks several times and takes a sip of her wine.

I ask my husband about what losing the goat was like from his perspective: "Tell me about the goat you played with that you had to eat."

"I didn't eat it. I don't think any of us did," he says, referring to himself and his siblings. "Just my aunts and uncles and my mom."

"Tell me what you remember about that time."

"I'm going to bed."

My husband has a very difficult time talking about loss, or death. I used to think it meant he didn't care, but now I know it means he cares so much. It's not that he doesn't have the feelings, it's just hard for him to express them.

ANIMALS
Quite probably a rabbit stew

Other than a few fish, and Mbailo the goat for that week, the only other pet my husband had growing up was a rabbit. I forgot this until I asked him about it after Glykeria told me about poor Mbaio.

"You only had fish, right?" I ask him as I sit down on the couch and open up a bag of potato chips.

"We had a rabbit."

"Oh, yeah. What happened to the rabbit?" I offer him the bag. He declines.

"The rabbit died."

"Did you eat it?"

"I didn't eat it."

"Did your mom cook it?"

"Probably not."

Probably. I know she loves *stefado*. Rabbit stew.

"How old were you?"

"Old enough to remember."

I was hoping to have a more entertaining conversation with my snack, but since I can't get anything out of my husband, I curl up the top of the chip bag and put it back in the pantry. When it comes to any sort of discussion that involves emotions, his lips become sealed tighter than a vault.

I ask my mother-in-law about the rabbit the next time I see her. "Between Lambros, Athena, and Voula, never let the bunny walk," Glykeria tells me, explaining how the kids loved that rabbit so much they were always holding it.

"What happened to him?"

"He started chewing the plastic shoes. We took him out one day and put a chain around his neck and let him run around outside, back and forth outside. We found out he ate the shoes. He ate a whole flipflop. Chewing it. We buried him in the garden."

"So you didn't eat him?"

"No, I don't think so we eat that one, because he's a pet."

I don't think so, she says.

Whether or not they ate the rabbit seems uncertain to me. It's also a good litmus test for determining whether my in-laws were at this point still goat-herding yokels struggling to survive, or if they had begun their conversion into bona fide, blue-collar, wage-earning Americans that could afford to waste the meat.

ANIMALS
A stolen sheep and a murder mystery

I mostly hear about the goats, but there were other animals around the *xorio* as well: sheep, cows, chickens, horses, donkeys, pigs, and the like. For the most part, the villagers raised their animals to survive on. They would sell them for money, trade them for goods, use them to meet their nutritional needs, and use each and every part of the animal, never wasting anything. All of the Skoutelas siblings, at some point, had firsthand experience watching over their herds.

"So, did you get up when the sun rose and go to sleep when the sun set, or what?" I ask, knowing they didn't have electricity.

"Well, we got up a lot earlier than that," Tom laughs at my ignorance. "Animals don't wait for the light."

Wait, what? They don't? Doesn't the rooster get up the moment the sun rises and wake up the rest of the farm? Apparently my vision, the cartoon one of a golden, circular sun and a confident, smiling rooster acting as a rustic alarm clock is a total sham.

"Sometimes it was like three in the morning."

"How did you know you needed to get up if it was before dawn?"

"You know. They're ready to go, you can tell watching them."

He's starting to sound a lot like my mother-in-law trying to explain when the baklava syrup is done cooking. Like, you can tell it's done by looking at it and seeing when it's done. Whatever that means. Plus, wasn't he sleeping? How could he be watching them with his eyes closed?

He gives me something a little more useful, telling me that the animals would "bleat . . . move around." This let him know they were hungry and wanted to go find something to eat. If the noises the animals made didn't wake him up, "They go by themselves. They aren't locked up. Then you go find them."

He elaborates: "When they're ready to go eat, they want to go graze. When the sun comes up they don't like that, they want shade. When it's hot they don't come out. Especially the sheep. It's too hot for them because they have the hair, you know. The goats, they go up far, they don't care because it is higher up in elevation. Cooler."

In the spring and summer the animals grazed, often high up the mountain where vegetation was plentiful. Families that owned large herds had no choice but to bring their animals higher and higher up the mountains each spring, so they could access ample nutrition. A lot of animals had to be moved around the mountain so they could eat.

"You couldn't get around back then, there were thousands," Tom says. "You look up at the mountainside from our house, it was full of animals." Some households had only a few animals while others had hundreds.

Each fall, as the weather began to chill, the herds were migrated to lower altitudes to escape the barren cold that crept in from the top of the mountain and spread downward. When spring arrived again, the herds were migrated back up.

"We didn't have that many animals, so we kept ours indoors during the winter," Tom tells me. Families that owned a large number of animals had to make a biannual trek up and down the mountain each year. The kids assigned this task bore a semblance to migrant workers and missed a lot of schooling because of the amount of time it took to travel between the fall and spring sites. They might attend school for a few months in one locale and then attend at another location later in the year if they had a friend or family member to stay with.

I ask Tom how many sheep he kept indoors during the winter, and he says there were thirty to thirty-five sheep in that room at any given time.

"We just lived with them."

"Oh, you must have some good sheep stories."

"No, no, they were quiet, we never had a problem with them," Tom insists.

Seriously? Sheep are boring, apparently. They're no goats.

The animals trekking up and down the mountainside moved slowly, constantly pausing to munch or sip. This isn't to say one could daydream idly during the expedition, Tom explains.

"You would see a line of animals all down the valley below us, alongside the river, sometimes people would hide in the ravine and grab and steal a sheep."

"People would steal sheep?"

"Oh yeah. A lot of times. For food. They didn't have any food. Especially during the civil war. They grabbed anything they could to survive. Sometimes you had to give them one. They come up with guns, 'Give me a goat' . . . just take it. You didn't have any choice. That's a part of the situation. The war.

"But this one guy, yeah, kept on going after things calmed down, when we have some kind of organization he kept doing that."

I think I remember hearing about this guy. Large black moles spattered all over his face.

"Spotted Pavlos?" I ask, making sure I have the right person in mind.

Tom nods in confirmation and picks up his coffee to take a sip. "Anything. Didn't matter. He wanted to steal anything."

He swallows his hot coffee and exhales the steam through his teeth. "I think that guy was a kleptomaniac though," Tom says gently. "He always had to steal something. He was imprisoned for three years, after stealing a cow."

Tom's posture changes when he gets into the storytelling. He sits up straighter, he speaks louder, he puts the Kindle down and gesticulates with his hands instead of using them to clutch his treasured book. I always get excited when he puts the book down.

"He went to steal a sheep for a wedding reception. He went with another guy, his friend. I remember that exactly. And I remember the people who were getting married," Tom says.

I knew there had to be a sheep story.

"We always took something to the wedding reception: some food, meat, pastries," Tom explains. "So, he wanted to give them a lamb for the roast. But he didn't get one of his own." My father-in-law shakes his head.
"They had close to a hundred, that family. He just wanted to steal somebody else's. That's the thing."

He sighs and raises his eyebrows to remind me that Spotted Pavlos had the stealing disease. The little klepto.

"They were ready to go to the wedding reception. His brother was looking all over the place, checking all over the mountains," he puts his hand over his eyes and mimes peering up at the mountain top. "Finally, he didn't show up. Wedding over and no Pavlos. Nobody knew what happened to

Pavlos."

"Well, what *did* happen to him?"

"Finally they found a sheep tied up, waaaaaaay over on a different mountain tops. It was tied there, but alive." They found evidence of Spotted Pavlos's thievery, but it was unclear why he would be so far away.

"Hmm. What was he doing over there? Way off, different village, different mountains. After we couldn't find him, they call the police and they start the investigations. And that's how it went."

The main suspect in Spotted Pavlos's disappearance was his close friend, the one who had set out with him looking for a sheep to steal prior to the wedding. "And the next thing, the cops had grabbed the guy. In other words, his friend killed him."

Spotted Pavlos had been murdered.

"Oh my God." I am actually saddened about the loss of a guy I've only met through my in-laws' storytelling.

"We never found his body. We looked all over," Tom said.

"So, how do you know he was killed?"

"Well, he goes up with the guy and then ends up MISSING. So, WHAT HAPPENED IN BETWEEN??" Tom shouts at me loud enough to make my eardrums burn. *Come on, Christine. Don't be so naive.*

"So after a while they grabbed the guy's partner, and asked, 'What happened?'"

The guy confessed that he killed Pavlos, but he kept changing his story about how and where. "The other guy: 'Oh, I burned him up.' . . . 'Where?' . . . Okay, you go there and couldn't find anything. Then he says, 'Oh, I pushed him off a cliff.' But you never see anything."

Somehow, Tom got roped into helping with the murder investigation.

"All that summer I showed that guy around. Policeman. Because he wasn't a local guy. He was from a big town. A big shot. Not a cop we had in the village, he came especially for the investigation."

"How the hell did you get picked to take this cop all over the mountain looking for murder evidence?" I was a little worried about swearing in front of my father-in-law but it just came out. He didn't seem to care.

"Nobody knew the area as much. I was spending every day in that general area. With my goats. My father I think is the one that got me hooked

Yiayia and Papou   84

with them. He couldn't do it himself or something, I can't remember. He told me to take that guy there, you know what I mean."

I look up at him and raise one of my eyebrows. *I've never been asked to help a cop look for body parts, so no, I do not know what you mean.*

"So I got stuck. Who's gonna take him up there?" he says, indicating there were no other options. "We went all over the place."

Tom and the detective walked through the mountains for hours at a time, for a couple of weeks, but they never found anything. Spotted Pavlos's friend had confessed, so he was convicted anyway. "The other guy went to jail for twenty years. He got hard labor, so he was out in ten."

"How old were you when you were helping this cop out?" I knew he had to be quite young.

"The year I finished grade school. June of '58." Tom had just finished the sixth grade.

Tom enjoyed his time with the police officer. "We walked for hours at a time, so we talked. He knew I knew everything about school work, so he told me, 'Oh, you gotta go to high school.' So, I came home, told my old man, 'He said I got to go to high school, no matter what.'"

Tom tips his head back and squeezes his eyes shut as he laughs, remembering his dad's response. "Ahhhhh, he looked at me like I was crazy."

Something isn't adding up in my mind. "Wait, that guy that killed him. He was a friend of his?" What was the motive?

"Ahhhh, so many rumors. My dad said stealing the sheep had nothing to do with it. Don't put this in there," he instructs me. I stop typing and he tells me the reason he heard.

You don't get to hear the reason, but it sounds like probable cause to me.

Tom, having ended his story, picks up his laptop and starts scrolling through his wife's Facebook news feed. He won't create his own account, but he uses his wife's all the time. We can always tell who is posting what though, since she shares recipes and knitting patterns and he shares political rants.

A few minutes later he yells out "HAH!" He tips his head back and his eyes shut as his mouth opens wide. He laughs loudly from the back of his throat. "You know what we talking about, where that sheep got tied up?"

"Yeah?"

"Someone just posted a picture of that place on Facebook!"

"No way! That is crazy!"

"I KNOW!" This is one of the few times that I can say with complete certainty that his yelling is due to excitement and not anger.

He's still laughing as he runs his laptop over to me and points to a picture of a huge bluff covered in pine trees. The top of the trees look like they're touching the clouds.

"This is the road I used to walk when I went to go visit my sisters. We made it in four hours one time, but usually took six or seven."

"Shut up! Someone just posted that?" I'm shocked that someone posted this obscure place on Facebook, and also that he can so readily recognize a location where the only landmarks are rocks and trees.

I don't know why I keep using the expression "shut up" to express surprise. I definitely want him to keep talking. I'm also a little worried that I offended him by telling him to shut up. Again, he doesn't seem fazed.

"I know!" he repeats, shaking his head. "I can't believe it!" he laughs. I laugh with him. It's just the two of us in the living room, but with all of the yelling it sounds more like a dozen.

I love when coincidences like this happen. They make life so much more interesting and wondrous and hilarious. It's why we look for those things, why we find patterns and grab onto them. They illuminate how amazing the everyday is.

As if to prove his point that the photo is indeed the location he was just speaking of, he expounds on the area: "They call that bluff *Papas Piedema*. The Priest's Leap. We have a monastery up there that a lot of people claim that they performed miracles, in other words. Healed some deaf, some blind, some lame, and they walked and all that stuff. You know how myths are going from mouth to mouth."

He tells me how the bluff was named: "So this priest, he was tilling the land with his oxen and his plow and he fell off the cliff - him and his animals. They found his animals but never found him. This seems a little over the top, you know what I mean. But it's going around forever."

He sits back down with his laptop and exhales loudly as he continues shaking his head. He can't wipe the grin off his face.

ANIMALS
A lot of uneaten cow

Tom's family had goats and sheep, but usually they didn't own cows.

"They ate so much," he says. "For one *agelada* - one cow, for wintertime, you feed thirty sheep. Goats didn't need anything. Very seldom you feed the goat."

Another reason to love goats, I suppose.

"We always have cows," Glykeria says. "Two at the most. If it had babies, we grow up the babies and sell them and get money."

"They didn't eat beef anyway," Tom says as he supervises Lambros replacing a light socket in our kitchen.

"No. We didn't eat beef," Glykeria confirms. "We couldn't kill the cow. The cows we only had for the milk and to make the cheese. In the village no one ate beef. Thought it was gross because no one ever ate it."

Tom continues: "Nobody liked beef up there. We didn't think it was edible in the first place. But then, after the Americans kept sending us canned meat, we found out it's beef and we ate that. Eh, beef, it's okay. We didn't mind. But they used to send us a lot of it. As help. Canned food."

Zap! I didn't see the electrical arc, but I heard it.

"Oh my God, are you okay?" I ask.

"Hehehe," Lambros giggles. "That's how you know you've got the right wire."

"Aren't you supposed to turn off the electricity when you do that?"

"Ehhh, it's just a little zing," Tom defends his son.

Glykeria and I look at each other, roll our eyes, and hope neither of our husbands get electrocuted to death.

One of the Skoutelas neighbors had a cow that broke a leg, and the family was forced to butcher her. The other neighbors all pitched in and agreed to buy some of the meat, so that the neighbor would have enough money to purchase another cow. Everyone except Papou Lambros, that is.

One day, when I'm over at Effie's house, I ask her questions about the *xorio* and she confirms the familial distaste for beef.

She tells me, "My father gave [the neighbor] some money, but he didn't buy the meat. He knew we wouldn't eat it."

Effie recounts with horror a memory of eating beef: "I remember my aunt cooked a large roast beef. We used to all gather together to eat on Sundays."

She grimaces, shudders a bit, and continues.
"To this day, big chunks of beef disgust me. You cut it, and it's fibery and stuff." She explains that she isn't always a picky eater: "I mean I'm not one to turn down anything, but the meat was so dark. We never ate it." She shudders again.

The talk about strange meats invokes one of her memories. "My father, in the army, they ate donkey. Some Italians eat that today in the delicatessen. It was not like the armies now, with all kinds of food and stuff." She laughs. "But, you know, you just aren't used to it, so you don't want to eat it.

"Even when I started eating deer, venison, it took me a long time to eat that. And there isn't a difference really. It is all about what you are used to."

She's spot on. Pretty much everything in life is about what you're used to, what your version of normal looks like. It's hard to imagine anyone else's version, even when they explain it to you, but everyone's normal is unique.

There are simultaneously infinite versions of normal and no such thing as normal.

This conversation reminded me of the time Lambros was talking about how he was planning on making homemade pastrami.

"I never eat pastrami," Tom says. "They told me it was camel."

"Who told you it was camel?" I demand.

"The guys that were selling the pastrami!" he says. "Dried like sausages and things like that."

"Where was this?" I am not convinced anyone trying to sell pastrami would claim it was camel.

"In Athens. In Athens in places that is all they sell. Dried or smoked stuff. Their specialty. And they said, camel meat, camel meat," he insists. "I said, 'No, I don't want it.' A lot of people pay for it. Eat it with appetizer with ouzo. Like salami. Slice it. Never eat a sandwich out of it like here," he says.

"Yeah, it is. The pastrami is camel," Glykeria says.

"No, it isn't, that's just what they say," says Tom.

He contradicts himself, so I'm not sure what his official take is on the whole "pastrami is camel" controversy.

"It's smoked corned beef," Lambros tells his mother.

She shakes her head.

"If you eat a Reuben, that's what you're eating," Lambros says. His mother loves Reubens.

"You know what they say. If the hooves are split, you can eat them," Tom says.

"Do they?" I ask.

"Don't they?" he asks back. "Don't eat the animal if the hoof is not split up. No, no, no."

I shake my head. All I have to do is listen.

Back in my kitchen, as we watch the men work on the light socket, Glykeria tells a story about a time their family raised a cow to be sold: "I remember one time we have the baby cow, like I said, and we feed it and special care so it get bigger and fatter, so we get more money.

"One night, a person came to see and give us a price, how much they give us for baby cow. We didn't agree on the price, my dad said 'No'. My sister Ismini went in the morning to feed the baby cow, she found him on the floor, he couldn't stand on his feet. Shaking.

"My dad went there and he could not get the baby cow to stand on his feet. So, what they did, my dad and my uncles came, they took the cow and cut the neck."

She thought maybe she would get a chance to see what beef tasted like. "Said, 'I wanna try,' but they didn't give it to us because it was sick and they didn't want to give us any. "Disease on the head," she says as she shakes her head back and forth.

"Mad cow?" I ask, throwing out the only bovine disease I could think of.

"Yeah. Goes crazy or whatever." She bobbles her head around in a circle, her eyes rolling around in her head. "They thought we'd get like that."

This family appears to have nothing but extremely negative

experiences with cows. Glykeria describes an unpleasant memory from when she was twelve or thirteen: "One time they sent me up to wait for the cows, and I went up there, and I saw where the cows were. But I started playing with the other kids and got distracted and I forgot about the cows."

The cows had migrated into a neighbor's farm and were munching on their crops. The neighbors were upset and started yelling about the crops being eaten. They were screaming at Glykeria, telling her to get the cows off their land.

Glykeria retrieved the cows and brought them home in the evening. When she got home, her father had already heard what had happened and he started questioning her, asking where the cows were and why they had wandered onto their neighbor's land.

She tried to explain herself, but, she says, he didn't listen and became so angry that he slapped her. This was the first (and last) time her father struck her.

"I didn't want to go in the house, so I went to the barn to sleep. I hid in the hay, and my mom came around and was begging me to come home," Glykeria says.

She was crying and was worried about getting hit again. Her mother promised her that wouldn't happen. Mentally and physically drained, Glykeria "went home and just went to sleep. I didn't eat any dinner that night."

ANIMALS
A dowry accepted and a dowry refused

Lambros and I are sitting in our living room, chatting with his parents. I offer them coffee, but my mother-in-law declines and my father-in-law just raises the styrofoam cup full of Colombian Supremo that he picked up from the gas station on the way over. They very rarely drink the coffee I make. Somehow we get on the topic of dowries.

When Tom's older sister Eftehia got married, the family gave thirty-five goats as part of the dowry. Later, when his other sister, Chrysanthe, got married, they gave even more. It took a while for the Skoutelas clan to build their stock back up.

"Did you have a dowry?" I ask Glykeria. I didn't remember ever hearing about her family giving his family any animals.

"No," she replies.

"How'd you get out of that? Didn't everyone have one?"

Tom answers: "That's one thing I said before, I don't want anything." He asserts this before answering my second question: "Yeah, they do. They still do. It's an old custom."

"But before then, you were negotiating." Tom tells me about how the dowry was agreed upon. "Goats, sheep," he lists a couple of common dowry items. "How many gold sovereigns, the English gold coins," he says.

I hadn't heard that mentioned before. "The richer people," Tom clarifies before I get the chance to ask him about it. "Or if they were like us, we never seen one, so nobody asked," he laughs. He takes a sip of coffee and continues explaining how the dowry negotiations went. "Let's say the brother-in-law asked for forty golds. They might give him twenty. Or everything my sister made, when she got married she took it along."

He's talking about handmade knit blankets, crocheted tablecloths, and the like.

"And other things," Tom continues. "Whatever you had to give them. Some parents might give a grove of trees that they had. Oh, okay those ten acres or five acres. Will them. And the grooms, some of them took advantage of it. They took everything from some people!"

I look up at him and wonder how much of an impact it had on him when his older sisters married and their family gave up so much of their herd. He shakes his head at the injustice of it all. "If she wasn't a little pretty or they had a hard time, they would give anything."

"Give more to get the girl away," Glykeria clarifies.

"I was against it," Tom says firmly.

I look at Glykeria, raise my eyebrows, and shrug, telling her telepathically that she lucked out on that one. She shrugs back at me and says, "He didn't get *anything!*" and telepathically tells me back that she sure as hell did luck out.

Tom continues his rant about how unfair it was to expect a dowry. "Especially people have five, six girls. They have a hard time. Then they have nothing."

Then he switches gears a bit.

"I don't know how it is nowadays. Kids just live together and don't get married. Or they get married after twenty years or whatever. It's not like the traditional marriage. They go to the court now. Some they go to church afterwards, just because they want to baptize kids. Now they don't even need a marriage license anymore to baptize kids!"

"Really?" I ask.

I try to remember if we needed a marriage license when we baptized our kids. I have no idea because that isn't so important to me. I do remember that my husband wouldn't live with me before we got engaged. Engaged was close enough, I guess, one generation removed from the *xorio*.

"It's a mess now, Christine, that's what it is," Glykeria says.

"And they keep their names," Tom continues. "They don't even have, in other words, to take their husband's name. It's just like living together, that's it. Eh, things change. I don't think anybody gets married, like arranged marriages, anymore. I don't know."

Tom and Glykeria were arranged.

Tom turns to his wife and asks her if she has heard of anyone having an arranged marriage recently. He speaks in Greek, but I still understand. I don't always need to know the words they utter to understand what they're talking about.

"I don't know. I never hear anything. I don't know," Glykeria replies in English.

Tom adds, "Before, you didn't meet your fiancé until the day you got engaged. We didn't meet until two days before, but at least we met! I saw a picture though."

He's told me the story before about how he was given a picture of Glykeria and encouraged to check her out while he was on a visit home from the States. "Theio Gregory gave me a picture. 'Ah, I want you to go there and meet this girl.' I think her dad sent it to Father Gregory."

"He wasn't going back for me, though," says Glykeria, raising her eyebrows.

"No. I wasn't," Tom freely admits. He does that thing again where he raises his pitch at the end of his sentence, almost like he's asking a question, but really he's just emphasizing his point.

"Yeah, I remember you were going back to Greece for someone else. Soula, right? But you decided not to marry her," I say.

"I didn't. Because . . ." he trails off.

"You said 'because.' Why 'because?'" Glykeria presses, glancing at me from across the room before looking back at her husband.
When I'm interviewing them, she gets to ask him questions that he probably would never answer if it were just the two of them.

Tom pauses for quite a while. He holds his breath and closes his eyes before exhaling and opening them again. He takes a sip of coffee before he begins.

"She was a highly educated woman. I never finished grade school. We're not going to live together very long. That's the only reason. Nothing else. Nothing else." He repeats himself and then rests for a moment and regroups.

"I just decided," he states firmly. "It was okay when we were friends and stuff. But that wouldn't last very long. You know how it is. I was working at a fountain." Tom worked at a restaurant called Mr. Hotdog when he first arrived in the States.

"Think now, working at a fountain, married to a lawyer. Know what I'm saying? Different lifestyles. Let's say that."
I nod and think about how my husband and I are pretty much aligned in our

thinking about how much we want to spend on furniture, how often and where we go out to eat, what we want to do in our free time, how we want to raise our children . . . . our ways of life match up. It's important.

Tom snaps out of his serious rant, and a sideways grin appears on his face. "And they had dowry too! Could've gotten a house in Pirio, a few acres. I threw it all away!" He looks at his wife and laughs at this last bit.

Glykeria laughs in return. "You busted! You didn't get nothing! Oh boy, I feel sorry for you!"

They laugh together for a while.

"I probably wouldn't have taken it anyway, even if I was with Soula," he throws out.

I have a lot of questions running through my mind. I wonder if Tom, a lover of goats, a penniless *vlaxo* from the village, would really ever turn down thirty-five goats as part of dowry.

I wonder what he thinks about Soula —if he thinks about her—now. I wonder what Glykeria thinks of her, too. I wonder if she's a little jealous of this other woman, or if she's envious of the freedom her husband had that she never did.

I will never get the answers to those questions, but that's okay. I don't need them. My in-laws are perfectly suited for one another: a beautiful, complementary team. They are a perfect arrangement.

BONUS! YIAYIA'S GREEK SALAD RECIPE
Salata

You will need:

Lettuce: If you're Yiayia, you use only iceberg. If you're me, you include kale or radicchio or you use a spring mix. Yiayia doesn't approve of these other greens, which is surprising, considering how she plucks and eats wild greens of all kinds off the side of the road. Yiayia doesn't always make sense.

Cucumbers: If you have them. Sliced and quartered.

Tomatoes: If you have them. Sliced into wedges.

Onion: Any kind. Yellow. White. Red. Green. Chopped.

Garbanzo beans and/or beets: If you're feeling really fancy.

Feta cheese: Crumbled.

Olive oil: A lot. Greeks don't eat salad to lose weight.

Apple cider vinegar: A little.

Spices: Salt, pepper, oregano, and garlic powder for sure. Fresh chopped parsley is optional. A bit of crushed red pepper, if you like that sort of thing. You need WAY more salt than you would ever think. Just keep shaking that shaker. Most people can't recreate this dish because they can't imagine the amount of salt that truly goes into it.

You will do:

Combine ingredients and toss with dressing right before serving.

FARMING
A wooden plow, a woven sack, and a worthless donkey

Spattered across my in-laws' village were many small farms. Each family had their own plot. Tom estimates that the Skoutelas plot was a little less than an acre. Glykeria estimates hers was smaller, about a sixth of an acre or so. Tom qualifies the size of the plot: "You have to remember, it wasn't flat at all." I can't get a truly accurate judgment for the size of the lot. We'll just have to go with the idea that it was not large.

The mountain was steep, so horizontal sections were prime acreage, while the vertical sections couldn't be used. Tom says they would periodically have to "build a little wall to even it out and make it flat," to use as much of the land as possible. Corn, wheat, beans, potatoes, onions, apples, cherries, and walnuts—Glykeria points out that there were no carrots or celery—were grown wherever they could be sown. Every square inch that could be used, was. It was necessary in order for the villagers to grow enough food to feed their families and their animals.

Springtime planting began in March. By then the snow had melted, and the sun shone vibrantly through cloudless blue skies, beating down enough to warm the earth and soften the thaw, but not so much to scorch and harden it. New life budded, flowers sprouted, and by April the planting was done. By June, harvesting began. Tom compares this to our Michigan spring, which borders on winter in April and smacks into summer in June. He says, "Weather is earlier in there."

Planting was done using cattle-drawn wooden plows. I'm sitting on the couch as Glykeria pops a batch of blueberry muffins into the top compartment of her double oven. She explains that she was often the one dropping the seeds, "the corn or beans or whatever," into the freshly carved rut made from the plow her father handled a few yards ahead of her.

As hands-on as my mother-in-law is, I always pictured her wielding the plow. I imagined her strong, stout hands gripping worn-out wooden handles, indents under both thumbs from so much wear. I pictured her calloused fingers holding tight, the tendons in her forearms pulled taut, all the muscles in her body clenched so she could control the depth of the plow. Too deep, and the plow would get buried in the dirt. Too high, and it would skim only the top of the earth, cutting a trench too shallow to properly prepare for planting.

Tom turns away from his crossword puzzle for a moment to explain why Glykeria was typically the one planting the seeds instead of steering the plow.

"It was usually a man. Could be the neighbor, cousin, uncle, whoever was available." The villagers helped one another out. "They had teams. Today they did this field, tomorrow they do their field, and go around." Tom explains that this was not done out of a sense of neighborliness but rather because "a lot of people didn't have animals, so people would take turns."

Once I knew she was the one dropping seeds, I wondered if she held the seeds in her dress, or maybe an apron. I asked her what she used to carry them in.

"A sack. Little bag on your shoulder, put your hand in it and every foot you drop one."

"What did the sack look like?"

"Homemade bag, like this." She points to one of my daughter's books on her coffee table, and aligns each of her hands with the narrow ends of the book, palms facing each other, thumbs pointing up towards the ceiling, and then shifts them over, creating a rectangle with her hands, indicating that the sack was about the same size and shape as the book.

"What was it made of?"

"Wool, little bag. Stripes, sew it on the bag, put a string on top and put it on your shoulder."

I process pretty slowly, and I was trying to put together what she said. Did she knit strips and sew the strips together to make the sides of the bag? Did she knit one solid bag, but use different yarn part of the way through to create the stripes of color? Did she not do either of those things, and do something else I wasn't thinking of?

I wasn't really sure. I just stared blankly as these questions meandered around my head. This happens a lot when I'm gleaning stories from them.

Pretty much every story they tell me, we rehash over and over. The stories get retold in all different venues. Sometimes we're sitting on the brown leather couches in our living room littered with toys. Sometimes we're in their navy leather recliners. Every now and again we're sitting at our dining room table (which used to be their dining room table). And then there's my favorite venue, where it all began: sitting in one of our cars while driving somewhere together. We have to go over everything several times, between them not being able to articulate every detail and me not being able to ask all of the right questions as I'm frantically typing.

Often when I'm trying to process what they're saying and my thoughts haven't moved on yet, my fingers hover over the keyboard and the absence of my usual clicking produces a very loud silence. My eyes stop blinking and my lids open wide. I get a very creepy-looking blank stare. Tom notices my eerie eyeballs.

"It's a BAG!" Tom shouts, looking up from his puzzle again.

His tone screams, *Just what the hell do you want from us, Christine?* But then he lowers the volume of his voice and calmly adds some vocabulary his wife cannot: "A carryall bag. A tote bag."

I snap out of my trance and continue my questioning while my fingers resume clicking the keys. "Did it have a flap or a closure on top, or was it just open?"

"Little square thing, rectangle bag, nothing on top," Glykeria adds, nodding, proud to offer up a needed detail.

Tom may have been getting a little annoyed with all of my pestering.

"A HOMEMADE BAG!" he shouts, even louder than before. He yells this at me like people do when they are talking to someone who is blind or who is a non-native speaker of English. You know how people do that? They speak like the person they are talking to is going deaf, like shouting the same thing over and over will do the trick, instead of just being more patient or giving better descriptions.

I find this slightly ironic coming from Tom, since I imagine people have barked at both of them like this, being non-native English speakers themselves. But I could be reading too much into this. The Skoutelases always sort of sound like they are yelling, so it can be pretty hard to identify the intent behind their tone.

Glykeria comes up with the word for this type of sack: "A *trova*, we call it."

"*Kala*," says Tom, waving his hand dismissively. "That's a Turkish word," he says out of the corner of his mouth, a toothpick poking out from the other side.

"Well, I know, but that's what we call them, so . . ."

"That word is gone. Gone with the Turks."

Glykeria clucks her tongue. "Tom," she says quietly.

Tom looks at me and reminds me, "We had Turks over there until 1912. Our grandparents were speaking Turkish." I've heard about the Turks. Greeks, in general, do not like Turks.

Tom gets up, grabs his Kindle, and heads out to the garage to read while he has a smoke.

Glykeria takes the muffins out of the oven and sets them on a rack to cool. Then she runs to the spare bedroom closet and returns with a sack. "Here's my *trova*." It is much larger than my daughter's book on the coffee table.

Tom is back from the garage. "You gotta have one of them," Tom says, not referring to me but referencing the fact that every villager carried one. "You put everything in that," he says. "You start going someplace, you put a piece of bread and some cheese, or whatever you had, and that's what you needed."

Glykeria is proud of her work. "Handmade. First you get the wool, spin it; as fine you spin it, the finer it is, the smoother."

"Did you use a loom?" I ask.

She nods a confirmation. "Used a loom." She points to her bag and adds, "Stripes, blacked and white," in her imperfect English, she indicated that she used the loom to make the pattern. She points to the strap: "It's like a *cochita*," she says.

"A *cochita*?"

"A braid!" she says, sounding disappointed. Apparently I was supposed to know that word. "Sometimes add a pocket with a color, cross stitch on it. But that's fancier, that's not for working."

"Men and women both used these?" I asked.

"*Neh.*" Yes. "Everyone had one. Men, women," Tom nods his head.

While Glykeria's family generally plowed with their cows, Tom's used a team of donkeys or mules. Tom tells me, "We never had cows. They cost too much to feed."

"So, the Economou's were way richer than your family, huh?"

He raises his eyebrows and purses his lips as he tilts his head a bit to the side, indicating *yeah, in that sense maybe they were.* Richer poor folk, at least.

His wife, proving she's worth a million bucks, hands him a fresh blueberry muffin on a small plate. Her muffins are the best: always made from scratch, using some of the massive amount of blueberries she picked during the summer and froze.

Tom explains the dynamics of using a wooden plow system while he chews.

"Need a team of oxen. You need two." They usually used mules because a mule "pulls better than an oxen" and compared to a cow is "faster, it is more agile." Tom chuckles and jokes that maybe he just thinks this because of the cows the villagers had to work with. "That was the cow you were milking every morning. It was nothing special."

He goes back to his original point that two oxen were ideal. "The system, the yoke, it's for two."

Glykeria shows me a picture of the wooden yoke that is still at her parents' house, next to the butter churn and the wooden barrels that were used to store cheeses. It's a simple, hand-carved piece of wood, crudely cut into the shape of a bow, with two arches to fit around the necks of the two animals and small holes, drilled out by hand, for connecting a rope. It looks archaic, a relic from their childhood that easily could have been a prop at a museum celebrating the pioneer days.

All this talk about plowing reminds Tom of something: "After the war, the Americans came over as part of the Marshall Plan organization from the United States, helping rebuild Greece." The village as a whole received clothing, foodstuffs, animals and other aid.

"We ended up getting a bull," Tom snickers. "Not sure how we ended up with it. I mean a HUGE bull, one of the ones you'd use over here for breeding." Prior to coming to the village, "I don't think that bull worked a day in his life!" he cackles. The bull was out of its element in the village.

"In order to plow with animals, we had to have a pair," he reminds me. He goes on to explain that since they had only one bull, and couldn't afford to purchase a second one, they were unable to actually use the bull for plowing.

"We couldn't do much with the one bull." The bull was so big, Tom explains, that "he wouldn't fit in anything we had. Didn't have harness, yoke, that big. Our family didn't have any big animals like that."

So even if they had owned a pair of bulls, they still couldn't have used them to plow with. He recognized the ridiculous irony in receiving such a beast: "They tried to help us out, and we ended up getting a HUGE bull."

He breaks up completely, his face scrunching up, the lines on his cheeks diving far deeper than I usually see them, and he shakes his head, as if still not believing their luck. "He was HUGE!" he bellows.

After keeping the bull as long as they could, Tom's dad, Lambros, decided he needed to get rid of it.

"My old man, he went and found an old donkey, and traded the bull for a *donkey*," he says. Tom understands that a donkey wasn't a step up, and that this was almost as ridiculous as getting the bull in the first place. It was just more practical; they couldn't afford to feed a bull that wasn't pulling its own weight. "Couldn't do anything with that bull. Couldn't afford to feed it," Tom explains.

It makes me think of people who win a car or a house on a game show, and then lose it because they can't afford to pay the taxes on such an expensive item.

Unfortunately, the particular donkey Papou Lambros chose ended up being a dud. "Everyone was teasing my dad for getting that useless animal. It was an OLD donkey. It couldn't do anything," Tom hoots.

He can hardly speak now, he's laughing so hard, and his voice is getting hoarse. "This old lady who lived nearby, she kept saying that the donkey was on his deathbed. 'Oh, I saw that old donkey, he is going to be executed in the morning,'" he says in a high-pitched falsetto. "Everyone was teasing him because the value was like ten to one," in favor of the bull. It turned out that old lady was right. Not long after trading for him, Papou Lambros had to decide between letting the donkey die a slow, miserable death or just shooting the thing and putting it out of its misery.

Tom wipes tears from his eyes, and I'll be damned if he doesn't slap his knee in amusement. I'm pretty sure this is the first time I've ever seen anyone actually do this.

"So he shot him. Vultures came down and started eating that donkey. He didn't last very long." He grips the arms on his recliner and tips his head back. "Ahhhhh!" he shouts.

The same old lady who had teased his father was irrigating the corn in her field not too long after the vulture attack, and she shrieked when she discovered a single hind leg stuck in the water trench. There's your executed ass, lady. That's what you get for all that teasing.

FARMING
A garden

Every summer we grow peppers, tomatoes, onions, cucumbers, and copious amount of basil in our backyard. My mother-in-law usually helps us plant. First we clear the land, and then we till the dirt.

And by we, I mean her.

The first time we planted, "we" had to clear out a space to make room for the garden, and my mother-in-law ripped a tree from the earth with her bare hands.

I saw her do it. I watched her pull out a tree taller than she was—a five-foot maple with a trunk several inches in diameter—with her uncovered fists. The root system stuck out the bottom, comically intact. She momentarily held the tree horizontally, like a weightlifter holds a barbell. She reminded me of the rhinoceros beetle: so much stronger than one could fathom, and so cute on top of it.

When she was through wrestling the tree, dirt was smeared across the front of her shirt, soil coated her bangs, and a line of mud streaked her forehead from her dirty palm sweeping across her brow. Her bangs were parted unevenly and matted with sweat.

This may have been the moment I realized my mother-in-law pretty much ruined my chances of ever really impressing my husband with my work ethic. She is far too much of a badass.

Our gardening adventures go well, for the most part, but invariably during this season my husband complains that I don't weed or water the garden enough. He can be a real nag about it, to be honest. Here's my stance: In nature, food just grows. Nature doesn't weed. Nature waters all by itself. It pretty much has been proven to work, right?

Could we get an additional three tomatoes and five red peppers if I paid a little more attention? Probably. Am I perfectly content with whatever bounty we end up with? Absolutely. We always have enough to make a salad, or to pluck a ripe tomato or cucumber off the vine and chop it up, douse it with salt, and devour it. *We have enough.*

Even though I really love homegrown produce, I know that if we don't grow enough vegetables to satisfy our hunger for village salads, the worst-case scenario is that I will have to take the twenty-minute drive to my favorite produce store, which incidentally has a free coffee bar with dozens of coffee flavors, cream choices, whipped toppings, and sugary syrups.

As if that wasn't amazing enough, they recently added a cash bar near the meat department where you can purchase a pint of beer or a glass of wine to sip on while you shop. Could I subconsciously be trying to not grow enough tomatoes so I have an excuse to go there? Perhaps.

My point is that we aren't in the *xorio* anymore. *We have enough*. We often have too much. We don't need to maximize the growth in our garden in order to properly nourish our children. We aren't going to starve if I don't maximize the yield or weed our garden. In fact, we're doing this more for pleasure and fun than for necessity. We have the luxury of doing things as a hobby, and hobbies are supposed to be enjoyable. My husband has inherited his mother's mentality of gardening as if his life depends on it. He reminds me when I'm not measuring up.

"My mother has grown enough spinach and onions to make four *pitas*," Lambros tells me.

"She got a lot from your Aunt Kathy." I get defensive.

"Look at the side of her house. She's got a ton of *horta*." Greens.

"Well, she's better at it." I try that excuse.

"It's not better or worse. It's that she does what she's supposed to. She waters it and takes care of it."

"Yeah. I know." I shrug my shoulders. *Meh.*

Even though I consider throwing a shoe at him and telling him to weed and water it himself, I have to admit that he's right. I'm a horrific gardener, and incredibly lazy about it. I usually don't weed it until my view of what's growing behind the fence is obscured by sprouting wild greens that make it impossible to tell if my tomatoes are ripe or my peppers are ready to pluck. Or if they're even still alive in there at all.

But still. I hate that he compares my gardening with his mom's. She's a super gardener. A super human. She's one of those people who could survive if she got stranded on a desert island with nothing but her bare hands. *Waah. Waah. Waah.* Sometimes I just want to be lazy, okay?

When we moved into our house, we transplanted an oregano plant from his parents' house, which was originally transplanted from the village. I'm not sure how that originally made it through customs, but it did and we've never had to buy oregano from the store, ever.

We keep the dried oregano we get from his mom in an old glass jar that is wider at the top than the bottom. It sits, precariously perched, threatening to fall and shatter to pieces every time we spin the Lazy Susan or take it out and place it on the countertop.

For a while, every time I opened the oregano I cut my hand because one of the glass handles broke off long ago, leaving behind a jagged reminder that a curved arm once existed in that spot. It has an ill-fitting metal lid—one I'm not convinced was originally the jar's mate—so screwing or unscrewing it is a dangerous act, due to the aforementioned broken handle.

The oregano is *really* good, though. It is earthy and sharp and has about a trillion times more flavor than any store-bought herb. It's worth the potential finger gash.

When we first moved in together, I suggested we get a new jar to replace this broken one, and Lambros said, "No. That was my yiayia's." The way he said it made it clear. This was one of those non-negotiables that married couples just have to work with.

He has a hard time talking about how much he misses his loved ones who have passed away. But something like this jar, that he can hold and touch, something he uses regularly that she used to hold and touch, that she used for decades to feed his parents—he needs that to be near him. It's gestures like this that show how you can express how much you miss someone without ever saying a word.

The first year we had our garden, the oregano in our yard just died. I mean, it turned out that it wasn't all the way dead, but we weren't able to get anything that was worth drying. We thought we had killed it.

The following year, it started to thrive a bit more. The year after that, we harvested our first real batch of our own oregano, via the *xorio*, by way of Saginaw. We dried it out, crushed it up, and added it to our jar. It was a lighter, brighter color of green. It smelled good, but not quite identical to the other oregano.

Why is that?

"Soil is too rich here. Needs to be more dry and dirt," says my mother-in-law.

The oregano that is grown in her garden is always dark green. Kind of funny how a different environment or a little different care can make the exact same plant taste different, smell different, look different.

It's hard to describe exactly what is different, but there is no denying the differentness. The further this oregano plant gets from hands that were raised in its homeland, the more it deviates from its original form.

Sometimes it's not only my gardening that doesn't measure up. Sometimes it's my memory.

I'm making grape leaves, and partway through I realize I don't have any mint, a key ingredient. So I call my mother-in-law and ask if she has any to spare. When Tom stops over, bringing me the goods in a plastic baggie (which could have looked slightly suspicious if you didn't know any better), Lambros asks why I didn't just pluck some fresh leaves from the side of the house.

"We have a ton," he says.

"We do?"

He just shakes his head.

Once he mentions it, I vaguely remember watching my mother-in-law planting it a while back. But clearly I hadn't thought of it since. So even though our oregano is floundering somewhat, I did accidentally manage to keep the mint alive. More than alive.

I walk outside and see the giant bush and discover that it is THRIVING. The possibility exists that this is due to the absence of my touch.

If some people have a green thumb, I have a necrotic one. I have the Grim Reaper of thumbs. Add that to the list of reasons why I'm not all that concerned when I neglect my garden for a few days.

I pluck some fresh leaves, rinse them in the sink, and plunk them into a glass of ice water. Delicious. I won't put it all in my water, though. Now that I know it is there, I will dry most of it and save it for future grape-leaf making. The mint is essential for delicious *dolmades*.

All the Greek women I know have gardens that thrive, but Tom's sister Kathy wins the prize for most extensive. Her backyard is so beautiful that a landscape professional would be impressed, but what is even more stunning is the sheer bounty of roots, herbs, and flowers she grows back there.

Lettuce lines the entire perimeter of their privacy fence; onions grow in bountiful fragrant rows; dill and parsley and basil flourish magnificently in every crevice. The other day, I walked by eight large bunches of dill hanging upside down in the garage on my way into my in-laws' house. I didn't have to ask. I knew the aromatic bundles came from Kathy.

There have been times that Glykeria has complained to me about having to make too much *spanakopita* because of all the greens Kathy gives her, on top of the ones she grows on her own. I nod and pretend I can relate to her misery as I shove the *spanakopita* in my face, glancing at the pan and wondering how many more pieces I can eat before I really appear rude.

FARMING
A bale of hay

My mother-in-law is making her homemade *tzaziki* (cucumber yogurt sauce). She mashes twelve cloves of garlic with the side of her chef's knife and chops them finely. She adds the garlic and a one-pound container of plain Greek yogurt in her glass mixing bowl, and then scoops in the shredded cucumber. Greek *tzaziki,* if it's made right, is so garlicky that when you eat it your tongue feels like it's being bitten by a million miniature piranhas and the odor continues to emit from your pores a week after it's been consumed. It's deliciously bitey and incredibly pungent.

    I remember my mother-in-law telling me once that she got called into the back office at McDonald's, where she worked for years, because her manager was worried about the strange odor she was emitting that day. "Are you drunk?" they asked her, in an attempt to explain her aroma. She was forced to throw light upon her excessive garlic consumption. Her coworkers clearly weren't Greek. Glykeria adds the lemon and the salt and puts the *tzaziki* in the fridge to chill.

    While she's working in the kitchen, I pull out my laptop and start asking Tom to elaborate on what they've already shared about the process behind planting, growing, and yielding crops in the village.

"I never did any farming at all," Tom says.

    I know by now that "never" never means never. I had to wait for approximately seventeen seconds for his admission that he did, in fact, farm. "Ahhh, I helped my mom once in a while. When they had the water, irrigated, I help her watch it or fix the little channels where we bring the water in, sometimes they break. Eh, I was taking care of that." Those were the jobs he didn't mind doing: the fixing, the tinkering. Things he still seems to enjoy. Glykeria listens to him and looks at me as she leaves the kitchen and enters the living room. With her eyebrows raised, she says, "I did A LOT of that, Christine," referring to farming.

    "I was a terrible farmer. I was the worst farmer in the family." Tom chuckles, the twinkle in his eye hinting that he's joking, but Glykeria just nods and confidently asserts, "I was a much better farmer than he was."

She expounds on her farming expertise: "I did the rolling, like you see that," she points outside, and I understand that she's indicating the rolled hay that we see as we drive by farms.

Tom translates anyway: "Bales. You did the bales."

"In '68, '69, '70, my dad was in Athens. He used to go work for money," Glykeria continues. When he was gone, the family needed someone to help with the jobs he usually took care of, like cutting down the hay. "Hay, clover, grows up to here," she puts her hand near her forehead, "and has little purple flower on the top. You get the seeds. My dad's brother supposed to cut it. Use a little special . . . *coshah* . . ." She can't think of the English translation for the tool they used to cut the hay down with, so she looks at Tom and asks if he knows how to say it: "*Pos les coshah?*"

"Ahhhh, what's it called?" He grimaces. "I can't think of the word." Tom, the voracious reader, the obsessive crossword puzzler, hates it when he can't think of the word. He pulls out the Greek-English dictionary that lives on the coffee table next to his recliner.

She continues, "So, my uncle, he was so busy he didn't have time to come and cut it. So my mom says, 'Why don't you go try?'" The hay was taller than she was at certain points. "It was so big, you couldn't see me there." I giggle a bit to myself thinking about how when we go shopping she's so short that I can't see her behind the racks.

Glykeria successfully cut down the hay. This doesn't surprise me one bit, so I can't believe that her mom was even close to being amazed, though Glykeria insists, "My mom came and said, 'I don't believe you did it!' She was so excited. So after that I did it all the time. Then my uncle was supposed to come and help me with the rolling. The *BALL-ayes* we call them." She looks to Tom to translate the Greek word that sounds like *BALL-ayes*.

He shakes his head, looking annoyed. "Bales. It's the same thing. BALES!"

He makes fun of her for not realizing the word was the same, with the exception of where the accent is placed, especially since he just mentioned it moments earlier. He finds the word in his dictionary that neither of them could think of previously. "SCYTHE!" he yells out in triumph. She cut down the hay with a scythe. When it comes to gardening, I have the Grim Reaper of thumbs, yet my mother-in-law is the one who actually wielded the scythe.

Glykeria is used to him clarifying language for her, so she nods and continues to tell me about how she made the bales: "Pack the hay in a wire bin, step on it, pack it down, tie them with wires. Packed like squares." She shaped bales into rectangular packages made from flat layers of cut grains.

"What did they smell like?" I ask, trying to be a good investigative journalist.

"That didn't have smell," she says. Her Greek accent creates an unnecessary contraction as she adds, 'It's smells like weeds."

I have no idea how to investigatively journal. I ask the next question that pops into my head: "Was it hard?"

"It was hard, yes. Because you have to tie it with the hands. We didn't have fancy stuff so we have to tie it with the hands tight, so it doesn't go away—split!" She pushes her hands apart, fingers splayed wide, demonstrating the wire giving out and the hay becoming uncontained. Unbaled. Pop!

"How long did it take you to make the bales?"

"For a whole day," Glykeria says.

"Sometimes two. Sometimes three. Sometimes one. Depends how much you have," Tom adds.

"Then we have to carry them with our backs and put them in the barns and store them in the barns until the wintertime. Cows, sheep, goats ate that in winter." Glykeria and Tom are quite good at piggybacking off of each other's stories, when they're not arguing or talking over one another.

"How often did you have to do this?"

"Spring until fall, once every other week or so. Regularly."

After our discussion of the plowing and the *trova* and the bales, I know that there are so many more questions that I should be asking to get a greater understanding of what their life was like in the village. I want to know every detail, every piece of information that seems like it should belong to someone else—someone who maybe isn't a real person, a made up character out of a history book, perhaps—but instead belongs to this ordinary couple sitting right in front of me. This real live couple experienced all these things!

Learning about their experiences makes me wonder what narratives are hidden inside all of the other people who look so ordinary on the outside. Everyone's got their buried gems, but we hardly ever take the time to unearth them. Maybe we're all too embarrassed, too lazy, too focused on ourselves, but whatever the reason, we hardly ever dig the good stuff out of the rough.

After cutting down hay, wheat and other grains with the scythe, they allowed the wheat to dry. "You let the wheat dry for two or three days?" I confirm when we are going through the stories one day.

"Ah, more than that," Tom says.

"How long then? You said two or three days," I remind him.

"Well, depends on the weather."

Okay, so *depending on the weather*, they'd flip the grains over with a pitchfork and keep rotating the wheat until it was thoroughly dried, for two, three, *or more* days. The dried grains were transferred to a large, flat, circular arrangement of stones, about forty feet in diameter, that her father had constructed close to the house.

The wheat was dumped onto the stone floor called an *aloni* and one of their donkeys would stomp atop the grains all day long, crushing them to remove the seeds from the chaff, exposing the nutrition trapped inside. A frayed rope was tied around the donkey's neck, connecting the animal to a vertical post standing at the center of the stone floor. The donkey walked the circumference, the rope got tighter and tighter, until it was too tight for the animal to turn anymore, and then it was sent off to circulate in the other direction. Crunch. Crunch.

I think about the common cook in the '50s and '60s idly opening cans of chicken noodle and cream of mushroom. Picking up a loaf of manufactured white bread so processed it hardly resembled a proper loaf. And then there's my in-laws—their "processing" being done by the hooves of a donkey tied to a pole.

If they had a donkey.

If a donkey wasn't available, the work was a little more violent. "If you didn't have one of those, you started beating it. You got clubs and you beat it until it separates."

"You do the same thing for rice," Tom says. "For everything. For all the grains."

"I can just picture you both wielding clubs." Lethal, those two could be.

The grains had to be flipped over periodically, in order to ensure that the all of the seeds were reaped. Both Tom and Glykeria explained the tedious act of using a pitchfork to flip the grains high into the air so that the wind would ferry the lighter pieces of hay away and leave the denser seeds to fall heavily in the middle of the stone circle. On a calm day, the separating of the hay from the seeds was impossible, so they'd have to leave the grains on the ground and wait it out. Glykeria explains this by saying, "You needed the air."

"That sounds absolutely horrible."

I get impatient waiting for the dishwasher to finish cleaning my dishes for me.

"It was, Christine. I used to cry for that."

Unfortunately for her, a breezeless day didn't result in a day off. She remembers being stuck there standing guard "forever" in the baking sun, preventing the birds from eating the seeds, waiting for the wind.

BONUS! YIAYIA'S TZAZIKI RECIPE

<u>You will need:</u>

Greek yogurt: If you want it to be healthy. 1-lb container.

OR

Sour cream: If you want it to be tasty. 1-lb container.

Cucumbers: 2, plucked straight from Yiayia's organic garden. Or from your grocery store, covered in fingerprints and carcinogenic pesticides.

Garlic cloves: 15 or more if you don't mind garlic oozing from your pores for days. 10 if you like an authentic Hellenic bite. Way less if you can't handle garlic but love the idea of cucumber flavor in a sour cream sauce.

Apple cider vinegar: Because Greeks don't use other kinds of vinegar. About two splashes.

Olive oil: 2 heaping spoonfuls.

Salt: 2 heaping spoonfuls.

<u>You will do:</u>

1. Use a mortar and pestle to completely mash the garlic into a paste. If you're like Yiayia, this will take about 3 minutes. If you're like me, it'll take closer to 15. Add olive oil and vinegar.

2. Peel cucumbers and cut lengthwise. Scoop out seeds. If you're Yiayia, plant the seeds in your garden. If you're me, toss them.

2. Grate cucumber. Toss with salt and let sit. Squeeze out excess water.

4. Combine cucumber, garlic mixture and sour cream (or yogurt).

5. Add salt and vinegar to taste.

A CONVERSATION ABOUT TZAZIKI

"Maybe you can make gyros this week," I suggest.

"Yeah, then ask my mom to make tzaziki," Lambros replies.

"I can make tzaziki." I give him the eye.

He doesn't notice.

"Have my mom make it."

"Don't you want me to learn how to make tzaziki?"

"Yeah, you can make it. But have her come over and make it with you."

He wants me to learn her recipes, but he doesn't really want to have to eat my my not-quite-right foods while I make my way up the learning curve.

She comes over and "helps" me make it. It is delicious.

FARMING
An ear of corn

Wheat was one main grain they farmed, corn was another. Glykeria explains this process to me: "Corn, peel it, clean it out, let it dry."

"Where did you leave it to dry?"

She shrugs her shoulders, raises her palms up towards her ears, the corners of her mouth turn down as she speaks: "Eh . . . in the room, lay them out outside, on the porch, the sun dries it. Sometimes you leave them on top of the roof. Someplace out of the way."

It didn't matter where the corn was stored, or for how long, really. Tom told me that they often stored their ears of corn in the unfinished second floor of their home "kind of like an attic." He continues, "We had kind of parties when it was time to harvest the corn. They take turns: today your house, tomorrow their house, peel that, store it, save the husks for animals," he says. "For the cows. Use the cobs for fire, they burn those. I mean, they used *everything*." Nothing ever went to waste.

Glykeria went up to the village recently, during a trip to visit her family. She showed us pictures when she got home and pointed out dumpsters that were sitting next to the road. "They have garbage now." This is the first time any sort of trash removal has existed there.

This prompted me to ask, "Oh yeah, what did you guys do with your trash?"

"We didn't have any trash! What we have, Christine?" Glykeria reminds me sharply.

"Huh. Yeah." I hadn't really considered that before. I think about how many bags of trash we toss each week. How much we waste. It's pretty gross, really. Sometimes I think becoming so-called "civilized" has made us far less sophisticated.

"Even if we had a little piece of plastic or a bag or something, we used that."

We get back to the corn.

Once the corn was dried, the kernels had to be removed from the cob.

"Sometimes store it up there until Christmastime and then we'd do that," Tom says.

The first time I heard about this, I asked Glykeria how getting corn prepped for the mill differed from what needed to be done to prep the wheat. I hadn't heard anything about drying out the cobs yet. This is what she told me: "Put it in a room and then go with a stick. Boom! Boom! Boom! Boom! Boom!" With each exclamation she raised her arm high and then swiftly lowered it, making a chopping action with her arm. "Until it comes of the . . . what you call it? The stick."

"The cob," Tom corrects her. He adds, "You get one, or couple people, you get a nice big bat and start beating it until it starts to separate."

I picture them beating corn cobs to death with a bat. "Do you ever feel like your life is crazy?" I ask.

Tom doesn't hesitate for a second. "No. It was normal."

"Do you feel like *our* life is crazy? Do you think we're the laziest people ever?"

"Yes, Christine. Exactly," Glykeria says.

If you didn't know any better, you might think my mother-in-law just called me lazy. And I'm not saying she didn't. But knowing her for the last couple of decades now, I think she's also saying, in her Greek mother-in-law way, that *she* feels lazy living the modern American lifestyle. And for her, feeling lazy equates to feeling bored. This is not an exact translation, I know, but trust me on this one.

She reminisces about the good times in the village: "We're drinking and singing and dancing and making fun jokes, making fun of each other, and we working at the same time. That's what we're doing."

"Ah, women were getting together for knitting," Tom says.

"We had fun. Here is boring, I can't stand it," Glykeria laments.

See? I told you. She's bored here.

"We didn't have TVs, we didn't have anything else. That's all we had, that's all we knew. I didn't see a car until I was twelve years old." Tom's getting amped up and starting in on one of his usual spiels.

"I was twenty years old!" Glykeria shouts back. "Here, I come here and you tell me I don't know nothing. How am I going to learn any of those thing?" Some of her pent up frustrations emerge. "But, anyways." She pretends she can dismiss years of being viewed as an ignorant woman here, when she was such an expert at all of the tasks required to survive in the harsh *xorio*. For now, at least, she sets her resentments aside.

Once the corn or the wheat was ready to be ground into flour it was taken to the mill.

"How often did you go to the mill?"

"Once you get a sackful. Every couple of weeks, maybe. Sixty, seventy, one-hundred pound bag, you take it to the mill. Carried them in a sack. That would last you a month or so," Tom says.

"What kind of sack was it?"

She can't think of the word, but she knows how she can describe it to me. "Like the one Athena got for Alexia's bridal shower last year," Glykeria states. I picture the burlap runner and the dozens of small burlap bags decorating the tables, which held the bottles of flowery-scented hand soaps we gave away as favors. Rustic elegance.

"A burlap sack?" I ask her.

"Yes. Burlap. Or a cotton sack," she said.

"And you'd carry that?"

"Oh yeah. Sometimes when you don't have the animals you'd carry it on your back." It took about twenty minutes or so to walk to the mill.

"So, if you used a donkey or whatever to carry the grain, what did you do, tie it up?"

"Yeah. You ever see how the donkeys carry things with sacks on both sides?"

"Yeah, I've *seen* it," I say. "But I've never *done* it." I wanted more info.

"Saddle," Glykeria says as she puts her hands together in front of her chest and makes a large rainbow shape in front of her. "Not for riding but for carrying. Put the sack on, sitting there and you hook the string, what's it called, the rope! And tie it around each side," Glykeria explains.

"Nothing scientific about it," Tom tells me. *It's not rocket science, Christine.* He gets impatient with my naiveté sometimes. He is probably annoyed that I'm interrupting his reading with questions I should know the answer to. Luckily for me, he always resumes his composure and answers my questions. "But, the thing is, if you didn't have any help you had to do both sides at the same time." He explains how doing this by yourself could be tricky, since you couldn't add the weight on one side without adding equal weight to the other at the same time. He explains how they got around that difficulty: "Had a stick-like thing to hold one side up, and then go around to the other side and tie it up." If the stick came out of position before the second bag was added to the saddle the first bag would fall off.

"How often would you take grain to the mill?"

"Well, depends on how quickly we ate the bread. Weeks sometimes." Then he points out, "Sometimes months, because you didn't have any wheat to mill."

A local family owned the solitary mill in the village. "Everybody goes there, not just us. And we have to pay for it, give them corn." A balance scale sat in the corner of the mill, and once the flour was ground it was placed on one side, and weights were added on the other side until it was balanced. A fraction of their flour was given to the mill owner.

Cornbread was one of their biggest food staples. A typical meal featured cornbread as the centerpiece. Cornbread is one of the only village foods Glykeria never makes. Whether or not they had ingredients for spinach pie or salads depended on the season. Glykeria explains, "Whatever we grew on the farm, that is what we were eating. We didn't use no chemicals. It is like organic they call now."

Tom adds, "During the summertime we had vegetables, springtime no problem." Green beans, zucchini, and *horta*, wild greens, were some of the typical vegetables consumed in season. He says the corn was "nothing like the sweet corn we had here." Then he points out that they never really ate corn on the cob like we do here, boiled or grilled: "Well. we never cut it fresh either. We couldn't afford to just eat fresh corn. If we eat it, it's gone! We need it for flour, to save it for future wintertime. That's the only thing we had for flour, it had to last for the rest of the year. But still, it was different though." Even so, "we liked it," he says.

"Well, we didn't know better than that," Glykeria points out.

"It's not like here, all soft and juice. It was rough and dry. Like they grow for animal feed," Tom tells me. "There you ate an ear of corn and it filled you up," Tom continues.

"The kernels were big," Glykeria gives me a visual by creating an "o" shape, the size of a quarter, out of her thumb and pointer finger.

"Do you think it filled you up because you were just not used to eating that much?" I asked.

Tom snorts and nods his head at me. "We were hungry all the time. We had to save some for winter, otherwise we'd have nothing. If we ate some every day, we'd never have anything left," he says.

FARMING
A bunch of weeds

We're sitting at my in-laws' and my mother-in-law takes a pan of beautiful *plasto* out of her double oven and places it on the counter. It's like spinach pie but with corn meal instead of filo: the poor man's version. It doesn't matter how full I was before, once I see her *plasto* my stomach rumbles. There is always room. Tom gets up and scoops a large piece onto a plate and goes back to his armchair. "Mmmmmm," he says, shutting his eyes and enjoying his wife's cooking.

"I thought you didn't like *plasto*?" I said to him.

"Why you think that?"

"I don't know, for some reason I thought I remembered you saying you didn't like it," I tell him. Maybe I'm thinking of how he made fun of me for so loving their white-trash village food. "Why did I think you didn't eat *plasto*?" It's bugging me. I swore he said he didn't like it before.

"I couldn't eat my mom's *plasto*," he admits.

I smile. *That's it.*

"She was picking wild greens. They were so bitter. You take a bite and ew! But the butter she put on the top—mmmmm. I only liked the crust," Tom explains. "But here? The garden stuff?" He nods his head to tell me that he thinks this is divine. "The only thing missing is goat's butter. Mmmmmm." He takes another bite.

My husband told me that when she lived in Saginaw with them, his Yiayia Athena would sometimes make them pull the car over on the side of the road so she could pick edible weeds. I picture her in my mind, a robust seventy-year-old, dressed in her thin, black cotton frock, her strong calves poking out below the hem, bent over on the corner of a busy intersection pulling up greens mildly infused with exhaust.

I imagine the drivers passing by, watching her bent over in the bushes that were growing not too far from a 7-Eleven, her long gray hair pulled into a tight bun at the nape of her head, her wrinkled hands deftly pulling up the comestible herbage. She couldn't bear for that *horta* to go to waste.

When I asked Glykeria about this, she admits that she did the same. "Sometimes you drive the road and see them and you stop and pick 'em up."

Tom is, as always, reading his Kindle in the chair next to us, and without glancing up from his book he clarifies what it was Glykeria often picked up: "Chicory."

Since they lived in Freeland, a relatively rural area, there was a lot of farmland near their house. Glykeria would see wild growth and couldn't bear not to salvage it, apparently even just a few years ago. If she saw someone when she stopped, she would ask permission. "I asked, 'Can I pick some?'" According to her, they always obliged and told her, "Take them all if you want it." She admits she was a little bit embarrassed to want what essentially were farmer's scraps: "In the beginning, I would tell them we have a bunny we would feed them." This was even when they didn't have a bunny. She got to know some of the farmers from her frequent visits and eventually became more comfortable and she admitted their chicory consumption: "After a while, I said, 'we eat those sometimes.'"

"What is chicory like?" I ask. I sacrifice my pride to get an answer to the question.

"It's like dandelions. Weeds. They sell them at the store now."

"'See even those old people know that the chicory or the dandelion would be good for salad.'" My father-in-law mimics someone younger than him, who used to find their ways weird but now thinks they're hip.

"See, now they are figuring out that these old people know what they're talking," Glykeria adds. She knows there is value to all of the knowledge that she possesses.

Glykeria continues her story of how she used to get free chicory from the farmers. She says that sometimes their response was an incredulous, "'You eat thooose?'" She laughs at how she must have looked to the farmer: the strange foreigner eating the weeds. She laughs also at the American farmer's naivety, at his wasting of all that precious nutrition.

BONUS! YIAYIA'S COOKED GREENS RECIPE
Horta

You will need:

Greens: Pretty much any kind you want. Even the kind growing on the side of the highway. Just be sure to rinse really well so you don't crunch down on gritty dirt.

Lemon: Probably 1 is enough. I heard somewhere that if you roll the lemon back and forth on the counter a few times you get more juice out of it once you cut it. I don't know if that's true or not, but it is sort of satisfying to roll it back and forth on the counter with my palm so I do it every time.

Salt: More than you think you should add. The salt is what gives the bite—not the vinegar. This is contrary to what most people think.

Vinegar: A little. See note above.

Olive oil: Don't be stingy when it comes to the price of the oil or how much you add to the greens. When in doubt, add another splash.

You will do:

1. Boil a pot of water. Add salt.

2. Add greens to pot. Cook until greens are wilted, but not mushy. Drain water if needed.

3. Dress with fresh lemon juice, olive oil, and salt, to taste.

These are good warm but in my opinion are even better served at room temperature.

FARMING
A Greek gift

"Do we have anything to eat?" Lambros stares into our fridge.

"I told you if you wanted me to make something to tell me what you wanted and I'd make it."

He asks me to heat him up some frozen buffalo chicken tenders, so that they're ready when he gets back from taking Penelope to dance class. I stay home with Daphne.

Glykeria and Tom come over while he is gone. My mother-in-law hands me a dish covered in foil. *Yesssssss!*

"I brought you a surprise," she tells me.

I unwrap the foil and peer inside the dish. *Dolmades*. Grape leaves. It's like Christmas.

I immediately open them and pop a few in my mouth, one right after the other. I know my husband will be thrilled to have some home-cooked food when he returns home. I think Glykeria helps out our marriage a lot, feeding him the way he wants to be fed, without ever being asked. She's always bringing over food. That, or she calls and tells us to come over because she's been cooking and has more than enough for her and Tom. Even if she doesn't call and we just pop over to say hi, she feeds us. She's always feeding us.

The other day, she brought over a spinach pie. As usual, it was delicious and I ate a large chunk of the pan. While chewing, I detected a taste that was unfamiliar. It was a sort of crisp, fresh, slightly bitter taste in the greens. It was good, I just knew it wasn't something she usually put in the pita, so I asked her what I was tasting. She told me, but I couldn't understand her. She said it again. I still didn't understand. Lambros translated, "Swiss chard." She said it a third time, this time pronouncing it correctly. Almost.

"Ahh, okay. Yum," I replied. Later on, I was reflecting on this encounter, since I can usually understand what she says, and I asked Lambros, "What did your mom call the swiss chard today?" I wanted to know how she had pronounced it.

"She said 'Swiss chard.'"

"No, but I mean how did she say it?"

"She said 'Swiss chard.' You just didn't understand her."

It started to feel like we were arguing about what she said. My husband and I have a gift - we can simultaneously love each other unconditionally and drive each other crazy. "Well, she didn't exactly say 'Swiss chard,' otherwise I would have understood her. How did she pronounce it?"

". . ." He stared at the computer screen and ignored my question.

Communication is tough. Even when you both speak the same language.

BONUS! YIAYIA'S STUFFED GRAPE LEAVES RECIPE
Dolmades

You will need:

Grape leaves: Freshly plucked off of an overgrown vine at a random house that Yiayia spotted. (Don't get caught!) Or, pick up a jar at the grocery store.

Ground beef: 2 lbs, seasoned and sautéed.

Egg: 1.

Rice: 2 cups, uncooked. Yiayia swears by Uncle Ben's.

Onion, Garlic, Parsley, Dill: Enough. Chopped, minced, chopped, chopped.

Salt, Pepper, Oregano, Garlic powder: The usual suspects. Yiayia doesn't tell you these spices are in her recipes anymore because it is a given that they should be included in EACH AND EVERY RECIPE.

Lemon Juice: ½ cup or so.

Olive Oil: ½ cup, give or take.

You will do:

1. Snip the ends off of the grape leaves, boil for 10-15 minutes – using a plate to keep the leaves submerged. Leave in water until cooled.

2. Combine beef, egg, onion, garlic, spices, herbs and olive oil. Mix well.

3. Add rice, 1 cup at a time, and combine.

4. Wrap a small amount of mixture in each grape leaf, folding like a burrito. Yiayia says that the shiny side of leaf should be on the outside.

5. Stack rolled grape leaves tightly in the bottom of a pot. Yiayia's grape leaves fit perfectly in her pot. Yours probably will not. Know that if you have a layer of grape leaves that do not extend to all sides of the pot, some might come unrolled. Try to find a pot that fits your grape leaves perfectly. This will take trial and error.

6. Cover the stacked grape leaves with olive oil, fresh or dried dill, garlic powder, and lemon juice. If you're Yiayia, just eyeball it. If you're me, add ½ cup olive oil, 2 tsp dill, 16 sprinkles garlic powder (yes, I counted Yiayia as she shook the powder over her pot one day), and ½ cup lemon juice.

7. Cover grape leaves with water (add as needed during cooking to keep grape leaves submerged).

8. Bring water to a boil, then reduce heat and simmer for 2 hours. Keep covered, but with the lid cracked so steam can escape.

FARMING
A forbidden fruit

In the *xorio*, each day was spent tending, reaping, harvesting. Toiling. All centered around survival. Food.

Sometimes stomach rumbles outweighed integrity. My in-laws have a lot of stories about stealing food to fill their bellies.

Tom and some of his friends were plucking walnuts from a neighbor's tree and shoving them in their pockets. Euclid, the neighbor that was losing his walnuts, caught them in action and chased them all the way home. The boys scattered in every direction. Tom made his way home and Euclid followed him right into the house, screaming like a banshee.

Yiayia Athena, who was cooking dinner at the time, didn't appreciate being barged in on in such a manner, so she told him to leave or she'd bash him over the head with her pan. Tom tells me the literal translation was something like, "Euclid, get out of here. If you don't, I'm going to blacken you with the bottom of my cast-iron pot." Tom chuckles mischievously. "In my family, we didn't steal. We weren't like that," Tom says, seemingly contradicting what he just admitted about the walnuts. Tom pauses, and then admits, "I stole once in my life".

"The walnuts?" I ask.

"Oh, no, no, no, that doesn't count." He shakes his head. He justifies the walnuts and other edible theft. "You grab anywhere you went, it was just open. Food was not like in an orchard, it was just out in the wild, just happened to be in somebody's property."

I'm trying to wrap my brain around any valid distinction that might exist between acceptable pinching and outright hooligan-style thievery. I'm starting to become convinced that my in-laws were hungry hooligans.

"When I was ten or eleven, I beat up an old man over cherries," Tom tells me.

Hooligan confirmed. I raise my eyebrows and keep listening.

Tom and his siblings were always going back and forth from their house to this guy's house. He was about forty years old and, like many of the elders, they simply called him *Barba*. Uncle. Tom says, "He wasn't all there." According to Tom, "He was always chasing us and wouldn't let us steal anything."

So far, he sounds pretty sane to me.

Tom describes his elevated status as a fruit thief: "I was a little older then, so I knew what I was doing. I was on top of the cherry tree and I was breaking branches and dropping them down to Andy and another kid." *Barba* came out and stood at the base of the cherry tree, trapping Tom up top. Tom, clearly culpable, didn't want to come down. *Barba* was screaming and hollering. Something had to be done to end the situation, so Tom jumped down from the tree, on top of him. He says he figured that his brother Andy and his friend would help him out if he got into trouble, but he figured wrong. Instead of helping him, they ran.

Tom says he hit the guy a couple of times and then went running off, heading home. *Barba* followed him straight into the house, shrieking and wailing, saying to Yiayia Athena, "He killed me, he almost killed me! I'm going to call the cops, I'm going to sue!" Lucky for Tom, Yiayia Athena talked him out of it. Tom says that after this encounter *Barba* "was always chasing us and always wanted to beat us up, but he never caught us."

"We used to steal a lot, you guys, because we were hungry and we didn't have anything," Glykeria explains, excusing her husband's behavior. "Fruit. Cherries. Plums. Apples. Pears." She shares a tale of a stealing stint of her own. One of her neighbors was highly protective of her plum tree, so periodically she would go outside, face the trees, wave her arms wildly, and scream "Ahhhh!" in an effort to chase away any hungry birds who happened to be sneaking around.

When Glykeria was about thirteen, her older sister Ismini hatched a plan. As most plans go, the person who thought up the plan didn't actually implement it. Ismini told her, "When it gets dark, you climb up and get some plums." Once nightfall arrived, Glykeria snuck up to the plum tree while Ismini stood watch. She started yanking plums from the tree. As if she could sense her plums were in danger, the old woman came outside, and waved her arms and yelled to shoo away any pests. Glykeria climbed further up the tree, where she was hidden from view. The old woman didn't see her and went back into her house. Glykeria finished plucking as many plums as she could. The next day, the old woman went outside and realized there was no fruit left on the tree. The girls could hear her yelling and hollering in dismay. She never discovered who stole the fruit from her.

Then we get back to Tom's story about stealing. Not the walnuts. Not the cherries. Not the plums. The other stealing story. The real one. When Tom was in the third grade, he traveled across the village to an old neighbor's house. Tom stopped by and chit-chatted with the older man. The old man asked how school was going and two exchanged pleasantries.

"I went inside the house and inside he had a little pocket knife. I kind of liked that knife, so I turned around and put it in my backpack. I snuck it in and took off. I went home like nothing happened."

Later in the afternoon, Tom visited one of his friends, Vasili. While there, he saw a thirty-page notebook filled with lined paper. This was a rare item and one that Tom coveted, so Tom traded the knife for the notebook. Later in the day, the old man realized that Tom had taken his pocketknife. He went to Tom's house and said to his mom, "That devil stole my knife." According to Tom, even though he called him a devil, the old man really liked him and said it lovingly. As lovingly as one could call someone a thief, I guess. Yiayia Athena turned around and glared at Tom. She didn't raise a thief. "We weren't stealing, we weren't like that," Tom repeats his earlier claim. "She goes to me, 'Where's the knife?'" Tom admitted that he gave the knife to Vasili in exchange for the notebook. Yiayia Athena took care of the problem immediately.

"She grabs me, we go for an hour walk to the kid's house and gave him the notebook and got back the knife. That was the last time I stole anything."

"Even fruit?"

"Fruit doesn't count. We stole that all the time."

CLOTHING
A pair of knit socks and unheard of pajamas

Each year on Christmas, my husband used to get two pairs of hand knit socks from his yiayia. The chunky wool thread made it easy to distinguish each knit and each purl. They were thick, a tad bit itchy, and kept his feet warm as hell. Most of the socks she gave him were two-toned: a colorful stripe on the toes and at the top of the body, a complementary color in between. His favorite pair has a light blue body and is banded on both ends with navy. The tan pair, lined on each end with red, is a close runner-up.

When she died, he stopped getting those homemade socks, so as a gesture I usually stuff some store bought socks into his Christmas stocking. It isn't the same, but he needs to put something on his feet and it's the best I can do. He doesn't wear the ones she made anymore. They sit now in his dresser drawer. He doesn't want them to wear out and be gone forever.

Glykeria knits and crochets all the time. She keeps a little bag next to the couch that holds her yarn and needles and the occasional magazine page she's ripped out with a pattern on it that's inspired her. She makes tablecloths and blankets and gifts for her children and grandkids. My favorite work of hers so far, is a pair of matching cupcake hats she made for each of the girls. One winter she made the two of us matching hats and scarves. They were butter yellow, fit perfectly around our crowns, and were a bit slouchy on top, by design. A yellow puffball added a bit of whimsy. She saw a similar hat on the computer and decided to try it out. They turned out great.

She can't read a pattern, but she can look at something someone else has made and figure out how to copy the design. It's impressive. When my sister saw our matching hats and scarves, she asked Glykeria if she had knit or crocheted them. Glykeria told her they were crocheted, and Tom, who was standing nearby, pointed out to Carla that she knew how to do both. Her fingers are strong, agile, and smart. He doesn't admit it often, but he's proud of her. She's talented.

When they were younger, my in-laws, like the rest of the village, grew up without the luxury of almost any store-bought clothes or linens. Almost anything they had that had been professionally made they acquired through donations. Most of what they wore was handmade. Even the wool was "made" by hand: shorn from their own sheep, washed and spun into thread, knit into clothing or woven into blankets. For young children, the standard garments were unisex.

"What kind of clothes did you guys wear growing up?" I ask, knowing most of what they wore was homespun.

"We wore dresses until we went to school, because Yiayia couldn't make pants," Tom replies.

"So, what did you do when you went to school?" I ask.

"Oh, she made some pants then," he says.

This is how most of our conversations go. Half the information in this damn book could be completely wrong, because they say one thing and then something comes up and they completely contradict what they said the first time. This happens all the time.

Let's be clear here—if anyone claims any part of these stories is full of shit, don't blame me, blame the storytellers. I'm just documenting.

As for the clothing, Yiayia Athena "used to make them all the same for boys and girls." Tom explains that all the kids had one "dress." These dresses were simple hand-sewn garments, consisting of a sleeveless top and an A-line cut of material extending down far enough to cover the knees. He chuckles and says, "It's kind of hard to explain. Make a bag with a hole in it and you have a dress." He assures me that all of the small children in the village wore this type of outfit, and that it was "very rare you'd see a child under five with pants on."

Pictures I've seen of my parents and their siblings when they were toddlers, taken during the '60s, scroll through my head. Matching blue button-down collared shirts and black dress pants on the boys. Pleated skirts and store-bought sweater sets on the girls. In these images, one of my grandmothers has her dyed hair pinned up in a fashionable beehive and sports a great deal of liquid eyeliner. The other has her hair "set" in curls and wears cat-eye glasses.

As far as I know, every day of her life Yiayia Athena wore her hair tied back in a braid at the nape of her neck, and she owned only a couple of cotton dresses—even when she lived here in the states. Maybe she wore color before, but since I met her after her husband had died, per Greek custom, she only wore dark navy or black. That's why all the old Greek ladies you see in photographs always look so severe - they're eternally mourning their dead spouses.

For the rest of the family, Yiayia Athena made all types of clothing: pants, coats, shirts, underwear, knit sweaters and socks. She didn't have the time, energy or fabric to make many of them, so each person usually had one outfit. Once that wore out, a new one would be made. My father-in-law's sister Effie tells me that as a teen she had two dresses, one for winter and one for summer. "I had two outfits. Two! Little dresses."

"What did your dresses look like?" I ask.

"I remember a little flannel one, plaid. Black and red plaid. I loved that dress. The other one, can't remember."

For some reason, picturing her in the black and red plaid dress surprises me. In my head I had been subconsciously picturing all the childhood moments they were sharing in black, white and gray. It's like I pictured their lives being lived on film reels, as old-fashioned movies that were interesting because of their antiquity. It's easy to forget that their lives did, in fact, exist in color. Maybe it's because all I'm really able to capture is snapshots. Vintage clips of a flick that is no longer playing.

According to Tom, people in the village slept in their one outfit, and there was no such thing as pajamas. "No one had even heard of that," he says.

I ask Glykeria how many outfits she owned growing up. She looks at me and doesn't answer right away. She scrunches up her face, like she doesn't want to acknowledge how little she had. She makes a circle out of her thumb and pointer finger. "Zero." She amends her answer: "Just one." A second later, she revises it again: "Maybe two."

She's certainly no clothes horse now, but she has a closetful of elegant suits and dresses. When the two of us go shopping together, at some point we both pick up the same shirt or sweater and are reminded that we have very similar taste. On more than one occasion the two of us have purchased the same pair of shoes. There have been several times that we have wanted to, but they only had sizes available for either her teeny feet or my large ones, but not both. It's hard for me to reconcile this version of her, the one that I know, with a vision of her wearing one single dress for months at a time.

One of Glykeria's earliest memories, from when she was five or six years old, was when her parents took a trip to the nearest town and left her with her Papou. She smiles when she remembers them returning. "I was happy, I saw them come home with some material." It was "burgundy, with yellow diamond patterns." She made a dress out of it, which she was very fond of.

There are two dresses that she remembers having as a teenager. One of the dresses was sewn from another piece of fabric. "But, I don't remember, my sister sew that for me? My mom did? I don't remember who sew it. It had patches all over it. That is all I remember when I was little."

The family purchased new swatches of fabric about once a year, and the clothes were stitched by hand until Glykeria was in her late teens, when her sister Ismini enrolled in a sewing class. The class was offered in the village next to theirs, and was about a half-hour walk away. An instructor from town was brought in to teach the sewing course to the village girls. Ismini learned how to use and operate a sewing machine, as well as how to follow paper patterns. She wanted to purchase a sewing machine for herself, but the family didn't have the money to buy one.

Glykeria and Ismini begged their parents to let them work, so they could earn some money and purchase a machine. They wanted to work for a farm several miles away picking cotton. It was too far to walk on a daily basis, so the girls would both have to stay there for a month in order to raise enough money for the machine. Ismini had worked at the farm in the past in order to earn some money, but Glykeria's parents had never let her go because she typically had to tend the sheep. "But this time they let me go. I was so happy to go."

On the way to the farm, seventeen-year-old Glykeria saw an automobile for the first time in her life, a pickup truck. She and her sister walked part of the way and then the truck picked them up, along with a few others, and drove them the remaining distance. Glykeria and Ismini earned a combined five thousand drachma during their month's work. "We came back with the money and gave it to my dad and he went into town and picked out a sewing machine for my sister."

I'm a direct beneficiary of those sewing skills. I keep a stack of blouses, sweaters and pants that have tears along seams, stitches that have come undone, or buttons that have fallen off. Every so often I'll bring her the pile and sheepishly ask her to fix them for me, which she does—expertly, in record time, and without complaint. If she were the type to judge, I imagine she'd scoff at my lack of skills or my overabundance of clothes. Or, she'd just ask me why I didn't use my own sewing machine, the one sitting in my art room that I use solely for hobbies, instead of anything actually useful. Pretty much all I've used that thing for is making zippered bags, some baby blankets, and once I made a furry bear hat with ears as a joke for a coworker. I might have also hemmed a couple of curtains once, before declaring I would never do that again. Thankfully for me, judging is not generally her style.

She tells me about the other dress she had.

"The other one, my sister made. She knit the dress, she made it for me."

"Tell me about it." She and her sister were very close. I imagine she loved the dress simply for the fact that her sister made it for her.

"She knit it and she made the dress."

". . ."

I give her an expectant look, my fingers hovering over the keyboard. I'm working on my give-me-more-information look. Based on their responses, I clearly haven't perfected it yet. "What did the dress look like?" I'm forced to ask.

Glykeria continues, "She knit it and she color it with the walnut." She tilts her head and looks at me through her periphery, her eyes squinting a bit, and says, "You never see a walnut outside . . ."

"The green thing?" I ask, picturing the light green orbs I see being carted across my backyard in the mouths of the many black and brown squirrels we have in our neighborhood.

"Yes! The green thing!" She sounds shocked to hear that I know that walnuts have green outer coatings.

"Take the walnut, clean the inside the shell, separate the nut from the shell, get the green shell, put it in water and boil it and take the shell out then put the material or yarn or whatever in there, and put salt in it and take them out and let it dry and it was ready."

"What else did you use to dye material with, other than walnuts?"

"The rest of them we used to dye with regular dye, but that one we used the walnut."

"One color. Walnut brown. We didn't have any choice," Tom says, indicating that most of the knits they had were dyed that color. He adds, "Well, we used to buy black dye too, for a dram."

"Wait, was your dress brown or green?" I had assumed that it was green, like the coating of the walnut.

"Brown, brown, the color came brown!" Glykeria informs me.

"Tom has socks still from Yiayia. Oh, I have them!" She bolts upright.

"*Endaxi, mori,*" Tom says, sounding annoyed. Okay, okay, okay. "They're just socks."

"I have in the basement. Dyed with the walnut. Dark brown. Gorgeous." Glykeria ignores him and runs down to steps to retrieve them.

While she's gone, Tom goes off on a tangent about walnuts. "Oh, they used that for everything! If you had sore feet, not calluses, but if your feet had . . . what you call it . . . fungus or stuff like that, you rub on it walnut shells," he chuckles. "Man! But then you have brown feet for a while."

"Did it work?"

"Oh, who knows?" he replies, before another memory surfaces. "Every summer we'd get fresh walnuts off the trees, once they started to get hard inside, so our hands were all brown when we started school in September. We had to clean up. They were kind of picky, the teachers, so we had to rub with sand and stones, our hands, to clean our hands up."

I don't have time to question Tom further about the stained brown hands from picking walnuts or exfoliating hands with sand, because a pair of socks is thrust into my face.

"I made this yarn." Glykeria nods proudly and hands me the socks she just unearthed from the basement.

"THIS yarn?" I point to the wool socks I now hold in my hand. They look like they were bought at a high-end camping outfitter. They are sturdy, dark brown, and well-made, the thick yarn twisted into a neat and tidy pattern of stitches throughout the body. A complementing pattern lined the top of each sock.

"Yes, I made this yarn from the sheeps. Wash 'em, dry 'em, spin 'em." She takes the socks from my hand and turns them over in her own.

"Couple holes in the heel," she says, pointing to holes the size of pencil erasers at the base of each heel. "Why they're in the basement. I would sew them up but I can't find the same yarn."

"Heh!" I can't help but let the sound escape from my lips. *Couldn't find yarn that matched? No kidding.*

"Tom used to wear them hunting and to work sometimes. Going in and out of the truck and it was cold."

"I used to wear those things," Tom confirms. "They were so warm!"

"What is the name for these?"

"How about just 'wool socks?'" Tom scoffs before giving in: "Well, it all depends who you're talking to. Our village, *tsourepia*."

"Well, that's why I want to know how *you* say it, Tom," I shoot back.

"That's right, Christine." Glykeria nods her head vigorously, supporting me. I can tell that lately she's been getting excited about this book. I've been interviewing them pretty regularly for years now and she's starting to ask more questions about the final product: how many pages it will be, will it be an actual book people can buy, and so on.

I think she's eager to read it, albeit a little apprehensive about how she will be portrayed. She wants to know what parts of her story will be remembered. I can tell she's been trying to give me everything she can, so her grandchildren will know about her life. She and I both insist that Tom tell us how to spell *tsourepia*.

"I made about forty pairs of socks, with this kind of socks like this," Glykeria tells me. "The girls, when they are not married, they used to make some of those." She explains the purpose behind so many socks: "That is all they have for presents when they go to the man's house. For presents."

"Is this before or after you got married?" I ask. I didn't know if you had to impress them with your knitting before they would agree to marry, or what.

"When you get married, to go give his family gifts."

I'm still not sure if this means before or after they get married. After a somewhat lengthy discussion, what I can gather is that it was customary for the bride to exchange gifts with her new family as a way to welcome one another. I still don't know if that happened before or after the ceremony itself, but I think I'm going to let this one go.

Glykeria lists items that were typically made for this purpose: "Socks, sweaters, handkerchiefs, shirts with no sleeves that you wear inside . . ."

"Undershirts," Lambros says, helping her out. He isn't always around when I interview his parents, or if he is, he isn't always paying close attention. He's heard these stories a million times.

"Undershirts," she confirms.

I already know why socks and undershirts were customary gifts, so I don't need to ask, but Glykeria adds, "they didn't have anything else."

About the forty socks she made, she says, "I remember I make it. What happens? I don't know. I made them for my sister and mine. I don't know what happened to them."

"You never gave them to Tom?" I ask. I immediately feel sorry that Tom missed out on so many great pairs of socks. A good pair of socks can really make your day, and I imagine that these socks had the potential to make one's day exceptional.

"No. Don't know if Ismini gave socks to anyone. She went to Athens and left them at the house. Don't know what happened to them."

"She left them when she went to Athens?" I can't imagine why she would do that. Seriously, these homemade wool socks are amazing.

"In Athens, you can't wear that stuff. You had to go buy stuff in the stores, no homemade stuff," Tom explains. "They'd call you names. 'You old shepherd, you villager, you're not from Athens.'"

"They make fun of you, yes," Glykeria confirms.

"Of course they make fun of you," Tom says. "They call you *vlaxo*. Shepherd. Even the clothes look different. The way you walk. You walk someplace, they know you came from the village."

CLOTHING
Rice falling from the sky and flour-sack couture

One of my favorite clothing stories my in-laws shared with me dates to the early 1950s, post-wartime, when the United States was still sending aid to Greece. Tom talks from our family room couch. It's one of those rare instances when we've cooked and had them over for dinner.

"I was probably six years old. They sent us some flour from here, from America, in big huge bags and they had big stamp that says U.S.A.," Tom says, sipping on a post-dinner beer. He explains that in the beginning, the U.S. sent supplies to the village via airplane: "Every afternoon an airplane came over with both doors open. The airplane flew lower than our houses," he tells me. The planes flew at a lower altitude than their houses, which were so close to the mountain peak. "We'd watch the loads on the airplane before they push them out, go over the valley, drop the stuff, and then take off." Often, the bags would split as soon as they hit the ground. "Half of the supplies we lost because they exploded when they hit. Flour all over the place, rice all over the place."

The villagers were so in need of supplies, he says, that they salvaged everything they could from the ruined packages. "People would try to pick up a pound of rice scattered all over the rocks." He tells me, "They got smarter." To remedy this, the U.S. started adding little parachutes to the supplies to prevent the bags from tearing on impact. Eventually, the government sent materials via helicopters. The first time the Skoutelas family saw a helicopter, "We didn't know what it was. Everyone gathered to see what was going on. He landed on the cemetery. The only flat spot."

In addition to the flour itself, the sacks that contained the flour were used by the family. Nothing ever went to waste. Tom takes another sip and then shouts, "Ask her what she made out of the flour sacks!" He looks at Glykeria and snickers playfully. Before she can answer, he shouts out, "UNDERWEAR!" and tips his head back and cackles again.

"He had underwear out of that too, it wasn't just me!" Glykeria strikes back, pointing in his direction from a couch across the room, her glass of red wine sloshing around a bit. For a minute she looks hurt, until she realizes we aren't laughing *at* her, we're laughing *with* her.

Tom makes sure it is clear what kind of material the underwear was made from: "Not the burlap. Soft cotton sacks. We made other things out of the burlap."

Tom's sister Kathy confirms this when we're over at her house one day. She and her husband live down the street from Tom and Glykeria. "My mom opened that material up and she made us underwears with it, and she dyed it red. But, the black stamp couldn't be covered up, so it was right in back, in large letters across the rear: 'U.S.A.'" Though the letters would mean so much to them in later years, they didn't mean anything to them at the time: "We didn't know what that meant though."

CLOTHING
A pair of shoes

"Don't ask me how many pairs of shoes I had," Glykeria threatens, before answering the question I hadn't yet asked. "One! With patches on the soles on the bottom." She continues, "I remember years later my dad's cousin sent us lots, passed on clothes, and my sister make me a skirt and a jacket out of that. Like a suit. Like a fleece one, you know. And then they give me a white nurse shoes." She nods. "Yup. I used to wear those, too," she laughs. "My dad's cousin sent them to us," she repeats. "Hand downs, you know. Who cares? We didn't know what nurse shoes was or whatever, we just put them on because we didn't have any."

She ends her rant and turns her attention back to the kitchen counter, where she's preparing homemade *pastitsio*. Greek lasagna.

Since the villagers were so needy, their wardrobes were occasionally supplemented with donations—care packages they called them—from churches or other charities. Tom explains that during the civil war they received official U.S. aid, but even during peace times they would receive goods sent over from the States. "Care packages had nothing to do with politics, but just people like us, church donations and such, sent stuff over." He gets up from his chair and rinses out his metal coffee mug. He fills it with an inch of water and drinks it. I notice this because I hardly ever see him drink water. Only coffee.

The donations would be sent to the school and the teachers would distribute items to the local children. "Everyone got *something*," Tom says as he returns to his armchair. He looks at me pointedly, his thick brows raised high. His tone doesn't make the "something" sound all that great.

The school handed out clothing from these care packages two or three times during his elementary years. He remembers one special instance, when he was around five years old, when he was given blue shorts *and* gray shorts. "TWO pairs of shorts!" He couldn't believe his good fortune. "Now I'm kinda rich because I have more than one pair," he remembers thinking. Tom was now faced with the previously unexperienced dilemma of having so many articles of clothing that decisions had to be made. "I had a hard time deciding which one to wear." He says he struggled with indecision, so he used to consult with his mother each morning: "Which shorts should I wear, the blue or the gray?" He laughs.

"I was a little spoiled, because I was the first boy in the family after three daughters." I look at him in awe, typing and staring. He calls himself spoiled, *because he had two pairs of shorts.* Shorts that draped across his small frame, many sizes too large for him. He loved all of his shorts. All two of them.

Tom's sister Kathy recalls one particular shipment: "My father got a yellow shirt and a lot of ties." The shipment proved useful, though in an unconventional way. "Those ties we used to tie the goats and sheep and tie the food up that the goats ate, the branches." I can't help but laugh as I picture blue striped ties and maroon paisley ties and a silly Christmas tie covered with Santas and Rudolphs being used to bundle branches together, or to link a goat to a tree to prevent it from running off. I'm sure whoever donated those could not begin to imagine how their gift would be used.

Glykeria brings us bowls of *toursi*: homemade pickled cauliflower, peppers and cucumbers. We eat it as an appetizer while the *pastitsio* bakes in the oven. She makes five-gallon batches of *toursi* and stores them in her garage. Tom takes a bite and starts talking about one of his most memorable donations.

"When I was in grade school, got a men's top coat. Very good quality American coat. Brown herringbone. It was for a tall man. I used to put it on top of my head and it was still hanging on the ground. I used to wear it a lot." He wasn't picky about the type of clothes he wore. He couldn't afford to be.

A few months after receiving the top coat, he became the recipient of a pure white girls' coat, made out of nylon. "I wore it; I didn't care. It was closer to my size."

I can hardly keep up, typing frantically as Tom continues telling me about the clothes. "Sometimes things lasted . . ." he pauses for a split second and the next thing out of his mouth is, "I went through the winter one time with no shoes once, because I chopped my toe up with an axe. I used to like woodwork."

Really, they aren't making this documenting process easy for me. Because I have some ADD tendencies, at this point I become completely enthralled with the toe-chopping story, and forget all about the white nylon coat he was talking about previously.

And I'm also trying to eat my *toursi*.

"We always carried an axe or a machete of some type. All of the time. I also used to carry a pocketknife to do some whittling. That's all we had: a piece of wood and a knife, or an axe. I wanted to make one of those things that you knead the dough for bread."

Sometimes it is hard to know what question to ask next. There are just too many questions. I often find myself in a "you don't know what you don't know" type of scenario. In this instance, I ask what one of those things for kneading dough is called. Since I personally have yet to ever knead my own dough, I have no idea. Tom fumbles for the word: "A big bowl . . . more oblong . . . like a baby bathtub. Out of maple."

Uh, ok. I figure maybe I'm in too far above my head, so I just take a break and dive into my pickled vegetables.

A Google search informs me that kneading dough in a bowl is, in fact, a thing, and the name of this special vessel is simply 'dough bowl.' No wonder Tom didn't know what to call it. When I search for things related to Tom and Glykeria's story, often I'm led to images and information about antiques, once again showcasing how my in-laws essentially grew up in an area that was decades behind much of the modern world. They're like living fossils.

Tom proceeds to tell me that he cut down the small maple tree to make his dough bowl, but had nothing to split the wood with. His axe wasn't big enough, so he decided to use it to dig out the innards, creating the bowl's hollowed-out center. He hit the edge of the wood at one point, and his small axe fell onto his foot. It "fell on the toe, just the tendon was holding it on. I dropped the axe on my toe, and the toe separated on the joint. You can still see it. I couldn't wear shoes for the rest of the winter." He kept the injury wrapped up for months. He says he can still feel the scar tissue, but it doesn't cause him any pain.

Glykeria, not to be outdone, raises both of her hands and points to her right thumb with her left index finger. She asks me to try to see if I can tell what is different between the right thumb and the left one. She wiggles her thumbs and demonstrates that she can move her left one away from her palm, creating a ninety-degree angle between her thumb and her fingers, while her right thumb can only be widened to about a forty-five-degree angle, at most. It gets stuck and can't move any farther. She recalls a story from when she was about sixteen and she was trying to prevent "a flock of thirty or forty sheep from running into someone else's yard." Apparently her efforts were in vain.

"I slipped and the axe went into my hand." She had the axe handy to chop branches and brush for the sheep to eat during the day. She continues describing the maiming: "It wouldn't stop bleeding for two or three days." Her mother tended the wound, as going to see a doctor wasn't an option.   My documentation was derailed yet again.

"Did you ever go to a doctor?"

"I went once when I was little, five or six, because I have some little red bumps all over, and a fever. Like measles, but it was not. I don't remember what it was. But it was far away. They gave me shots. TWELVE shots. I remember that. I remember my mom told me it was a good thing they came outside, not inside. Then when I was twenty-one or twenty-two, I went to the doctor 'cause I got really sick. Tonsillitis. And when I came here and I had the kids." That is the only times I went to the doctor."

When she is done talking, I look down at her hands again. She makes sure I am able to observe the scar.

I am silent. I don't know where to start. Donated clothing? Machetes and axes? Going through an entire winter without wearing shoes? My brain's processing speed isn't fast enough for me to quickly answer my husband when he asks what I want to eat for dinner, let alone to handle conversations like this. My brain hurts.

This is how the conversations go, though. All of them. From my experience, compiling family stories is not at all a linear process. It's more like a bunch of random facts that come out densely intertwined, a knotted ball of history that somehow makes sense in the oral history kind of way, but takes endless hours to unravel and straighten out in order to make them understandable in any kind of written form.

We get back to the original topic of shoes.

Tom finishes his last bite of *toursi* and hands his empty bowl to his wife as he starts telling me about a time when Spotted Pavlos traveled "some place where the cars were" and returning from his trip with an old tire. Tom shakes his head. "This guy stole everything. He was stealing stuff all his life. I think he was a kleptomaniac. That's how he died, stealing a sheep or something." I nod, remembering the story. "He stole from us, one time. He stole our axe. My mom knew it was him. She went right over there and said, 'Give me that axe!' He said he didn't have it, but it was sitting right there. She got the axe back."

He gets back to telling me about Spotted Pavlos's stolen tire: "He knew though, that the tire was good for soles, so he brought that tire out. A whole tire!" It was several hours walk from "where the cars were." Quite a long stretch to lug such an unwieldy prize. "From that tire, we cut pieces of rubber and put them under the soles of our shoes that we already had. It took me a while, with the old knife I had. It won't cut butter, you know? And then wax the string so water wouldn't get into it, and cut slots so it went in the rubber sole, and then you trim it around," Tom explains. "We would resole our shoes two or three times." Shoes, like everything else, were hard to come by.

"We used nails to hold up the sole," Glykeria remembers. "The nails would stick up into your feet."

Shoes weren't always viewed as necessary, especially for younger children. "Until I started school, I didn't have any shoes," Tom states. Even when they had them, sometimes they were only slightly better than having nothing. "I remember I got a pair of shoes, size twelve. What can I say? It is just sad. That is all we had. I was five or six years old getting a size twelve American shoe. But that's all we had."

Oh, the stories these people have of shoes.

"When I come home for vacation or to visit, I'd send this little kid, Alex—about eight years old, our next-door neighbor—to go pick me up a pack of cigarettes from town. By the time he got back, half the pack would be gone. He would smoke it on the way."

Tom was almost twice his age, so this kid really looked up to him. Tom added, "He looked like John Derek. Good-looking kid." He continued, getting to the part about the shoes, "One time his mom, bought him a pair of shoes. Blue canvas shoes with white bottoms. And that poor kid put them on and they got dirty. So, we go down to the little spring below our house and he washed them off. Then he put them back on and right away they got dirty again!" Tom laughs.

The river bank was muddy, and the moment he stepped out of the water, muck would splatter onto the white edges. Alex wanted to wear them out on the unpaved village roads, but he also wanted to keep them meticulously clean. Tom finally told him, "Don't put them on!" That was the only way to ensure they remained unsoiled.

"We didn't really wear shoes, anyway. We would carry them to church, and then outside of the church put them on and wear them in. Then, once you leave, you take them off and carry them home," Tom says.

I think that most women at church around here probably wish they could do that.

All of the kids in the *xorio* had feet that were leathery on the bottom. It didn't matter what they stepped on, nothing punctured their tough soles.

"We weren't comfortable in shoes," Tom says. This declaration brings another story to his mind. When Tom was in first grade, a new student, Achilles, joined the class. Achilles walked in with a pair of thick-soled boots that Tom describes as being similar to ones he wears today. Tom remembers eyeing the boots. "Hiking boots. Beautiful! We had never seen anything like that. I mean they *looked* nice, who knows what they were really like." Tom laughs, remembering both the reaction of the barefooted students at school, as well as Achilles's response to the peer pressure: "We picked on him at first, this strange kid."

Strange because he was wearing boots.

"So, he started not wearing the beautiful boots, so he would fit in." I imagine the bottoms of his feet were sore for a while before they toughened up. Poor kid. Tom offers up a silver lining: "We ended up becoming very close, once we got to know him." He finishes his story just in time for dinner to be served.

Tom's brother-in-law, also named Tom (seriously, everyone has the same name, right?), his sister Kathy's husband, adds a shoe story of his own when I'm over there visiting one day. Tom went through an entire winter of tending to the sheep and goats, trudging all over the snow-covered mountain, without shoes. Spring finally arrived and the plants on the mountain began to bloom. "Springtime, those animals, they go crazy, they want to go wherever they want to go. They are out of control." He explains the motivation behind the animal behavior: food.

"Like me, I was hungry. They were hungry too. If they knew something was good over there, they wanted to go over there." But often times "over there" meant the sheep wanted to go into someone else's land and eat their beans or grains, which they weren't supposed to do.

After an entire shoeless winter, a neighbor gave Tom his shoes. "He said, 'You wear this, I got a new one.' These were boots, very heavy, and I wore a size five probably, and he wore an eight or nine." Tom didn't flinch at the size discrepancy, and he doesn't make one comment to me about wishing he got the boots during the wintertime instead of after the thaw. He was just thrilled to have had his own pair of boots. He cared more about keeping his feet warm than he did about their size. "I could not lift them but eh, it's fine," he shrugged.

Tom explains that he had the shoes for only two or three days, "and then my sheep run away and go on someone else's property." He knew he would be in big trouble if the owner of this property saw his sheep on their land. Tom tried to run after his herd, but the boots were much too heavy. He unstrapped them and hid them beneath a bush. After retrieving his sheep, he returned to the bush and discovered that someone had taken the boots. "So, then I was left with no shoes again."

In my head, I blame Spotted Pavlos.

CLOTHING
A pair of earrings

"Penelope, can I take you to get your ears ears?" Glykeria stumbles over the last couple of words. "Your earrings?" she tries again.

"You mean my ears pierced?" Penelope asks. At only four years of age, she's pretty damn sharp.

"Yes, *koukla*. Do you want me to take you to get your ears pierced?"

"No, thanks."

"Why not? You afraid?"

"No."

"Daphne, how about you? You want Yiayia to take you to get your ears pierced?"

"Yeah!" Daphne yells.

"You can take them whenever they ask to get them done," I tell my mother-in-law. "I don't mind them getting them done, but I want to wait until they ask for it." I look at her ears, which are pierced. "Did your mom pierce your ears?" I ask her.

"Oh yeah, she did. With the needle."

"We never cleaned anything. A needle. We never cleaned a knife," Tom shouts, without looking up from his book.

"No, she cleaned it! She clean the needle. She put it in the fire and burn the needle and then she put it in there." She points to her ears.

"Didn't that hurt?"

"It hurts. I don't remember now, but I'm sure it did," Glykeria replies. "She had a pair of earrings, I think, hers. I think I lost it or something. Then I remember she put in oregano things." She mimes putting something in her ears.

"You put oregano stems in your ears?" I ask. I know they love oregano, but that seems a little ridiculous.

"Mmm hmmm," she says. "I remember it get alllllll infected."

I grimace.

"*Scarfi*," Tom corrects. "You put *scarfi*," he directs this towards his wife. "A wild plant that has hard stems, real small, real fine. They used that one because it's, what they say, it's like poison when you taste it. They put the little bitter stick in. That's normal," he schools me about ear piercing, *xorio* style.

"I remember my mom put the oregano," Glykeria insists.

"*Scarfi, scarfi.*" Tom wasn't there, but he is sure he's right. "They put a little rope type thing. Thread, yeah, thread. Put it there. And they kept moving it so it doesn't get sticked up. Little piece of thread. That kept it open in other words," he adds.

Maybe I'm wrong, but I don't think I'd be so open to my mother-in-law piercing my daughters' ears if we lived in the village.

CLOTHING
A white dress

It's wedding day for Lambros's cousin Alexia. Penelope is two and Daphne is only a few months out of the womb. I take the girls over to my mother-in-law's in the morning and we get ready for the pre-wedding photographs there. Glykeria eyes Penelope's flower girl dress, which is hanging over the door.

"Let me iron it, Christine."

Shit. Was I supposed to iron it?

I hadn't thought about that. I look at it more closely and try to gauge the level of wrinkledness. It doesn't look horrible to me. Even though I'm worried about time, I let her take the dress. Now that she's said something, I assume Bob's sister Athena has neatly pressed her daughter Nina's identical dress and I don't want my daughter to be the one looking like a hobo in comparison. I'm embarrassed that my not thinking about this resulted in more work for Glykeria. Tom and I sit upstairs and I guiltily pour myself a cup of coffee while he cuddles with Daphne.

Glykeria is downstairs for quite a while.

I get anxious about the time, so I leave Daphne with Tom and head downstairs. She's still ironing, even though the dress looks perfect. I'm surprised by how much better the dress looks now than it did when I brought it over. It's gorgeous.

I watch her hands deftly iron the dress for a bit. She keeps moving the iron back and forth, finding new crevices to put the point of the iron towards, new lines to neatly crease. My eyes move up from her hands to her face and I'm taken aback when I see tears.

"I'm sorry I'm taking so long, Christine," she chokes out. "I'm sorry," she apologizes this time for crying and wipes a tear aside.

"It's fine, it's fine!" I say. "What's wrong?"

"It's silly."

Clearly, it's not silly.

"What is it?" I press.

"I just . . ." She takes a deep breath. "I treating this like her brides dress. I might not be here for that, so . . ." She starts crying again and this time I cry with her.

"I'm sorry, I'm sorry," she says again, watching me wipe mascara from my cheeks.

"Oh, stop it," I tell her and I squeeze her arm. I head back upstairs and let her iron the dress as long as she wants. It turns out absolutely beautiful.

I sob the entire car ride to the photography session. Lambros calls me while I'm in the car and when he hears my voice he asks me what's wrong. "It's just hormones," I tell him, even though it isn't. He's not the only one who has difficulty talking about his feelings.

Throughout the wedding, I keep noticing how beautiful my daughter looks in her dress and I try to ignore how puffy my eyes feel.

FOOD
A batch of freshly baked cookies

One day, we take the girls over to my in-laws' after work. We stop over there a couple of times each week. Penelope has been really into watching cooking shows on television lately, so the timing is right for her to get her first hands-on tutorial from her yiayia. Today she's learning how to make *koulourakia*: a braided cookie made from a butter-based flour dough. Glykeria grabs one of the wooden chairs from the dinette set and pushes it up against the black-and-white-flecked granite counter. Penelope washes her hands and lets me pull her long hair back into a tight bun before hoisting herself up, standing on the chair so she can reach. The chair gives her the perfect boost, her belly button is now at counter-height.

    Glykeria adds egg whites into the metal mixing bowl, then shows Penelope how to lift the handle and raise the bowl towards the beaters that poke down from the top of the stand mixer. Pep giggles with glee when she turns on the mixer, sliding the button over one click at a time. Her eyebrows raise higher and her smirk grows wider as the beaters spin faster, whirring louder and louder.

    "Huhhh?!" she says. Her dark eyes widen and the corners of her mouth crinkle as a bit of egg splashes out of the bowl.

    "That's why we wear an apron!" Glykeria explains. Penelope grins and drops stick after stick of unsalted butter into the bowl. She pours in the sugar, followed by the milk.

    It's a good thing she has Glykeria to help teach her these things, because I could probably count on one hand the number of times I've made cookies from scratch in my entire life. Maybe on one finger. "I want to eat them after I make it," Penelope says.

    "Of course we will, that's why we making them," Glykeria assures her as she pauses the mixer and drags her dough scraper around the circumference of the bowl. Penelope is enthralled with the whole process and can't stop gasping and giggling and doing little dances on her chair as she watches. As the dough mixes, Glykeria lets her know that cooking requires patience. "We going to wait a while for that," she informs her.

Glykeria removes the bowl from the stand mixer and uncaps a small cylindrical bottle, adding its contents to the dough. Lambros walks through the kitchen moments after she does this.

"Oh, it burns!" he says, coughing. "It burns just like regular ammonia." He coughs again.

I look at the white label on the bottle. The black text blandly reads, "Cooking Ammonia." I've never heard of cooking ammonia, so I do a quick Google search and discover that this was apparently developed as a chemical leavener before baking powder existed.

Yet another example of my in-laws using technology that was utilized by people who lived during the 1800s. I wonder if they would have used wood ash for this recipe in the *xorio*. If they even made these there. White flour and sugar were so hard to come by.

Glykeria pulls out a large, white, airtight bucket, which originally housed thirty pounds of sliced strawberries but now contains an excessive amount of all-purpose flour. She transfers the dough from the mixer into an enormous metal mixing bowl. She lets me know that she could have halved the recipe, but she figured she might as well make a full "Yiayia-sized" batch of cookies that she can freeze, replenishing her stock. The bowl and the bucket are both so large that she and Penelope are forced to move from the countertop down to the kitchen floor so that Penelope is able to reach.

And maybe Glykeria too: she's pretty short as well.

"Don't put this on Facebook, Christine!" Glykeria instructs, embarrassed at the thought of someone seeing her cooking on the grey ceramic tiles, immaculate as they may be. Penelope repeatedly dips a one-cup measuring cup into the bucket of flour and stands there, waiting to add it, until Glykeria—who is sitting on her knees, using her hands to combine the flour with the rest of the dough, tells her she needs more. I watch, impressed with Penelope's impulse control, impressed with how well she is following directions.

"Wow, Penelope, you're doing a great—"

My words are cut off by a hollow banging sound as the plastic measuring cup in her hand hits the floor and detonates, an eruption of white dust forming a mushroom cloud in the air. Glykeria and I can't help but laugh, even though we try not to. We both hold it in as much as we can and make that snorting sound that adults make when a child does something that they think is hilarious but that they certainly don't want them to do again. I immediately turn to grab a wet rag to clean up the mess.

"That's okay, Christine. That's kids. We'll get the vacuum later."

The two continue their work. While Glykeria is finishing up kneading the dough, Penelope sits on her knees and leans in. The bottoms of her feet are coated with white powder.

"I'm doing great?" she asks me.

"Oh, yes," I confirm.

She kisses my arm at the same time I kiss the top of her head.

"We both kissed," she says to Glykeria, before starting to create shapes in the flour on the floor with her finger. Small white footprints mark the gray tiles. After the dough is ready, she hops back on her chair and helps her yiayia roll out the dough into ropes that are then twisted two or three times, into the classic *koulourakia* shape.

"Like this. Soft. Not hard, not push 'em down." Glykeria demonstrates transforming the ball to a thread and then folds it in half. "See? One, two, three!" she sings as her small fingers twist the strands one, two and three times.

Penelope copies her sing-songy voice: "One, two, three!" She rolls out her dough. "Lookit!" She is proud of her dough rope. "Whoa, whoa, whoa!" she says as she rolls it again. She tosses her head back and laughs. Her feet perform little hops on the chair she is standing on.

Yiayia sings a familiar song as she works: "*Platho koulourakia, me ta thio mou ta herakia, o furnos tatha spisi, to spiti tha me therisi!*" It's a song I've heard her sing many times before, but I've never really paid attention to the words. It translates to something along the lines of "making *koulourakia* with my hands, they'll fill the house with a delicious smell." The song has so much more meaning now, as I listen to her singing it to her granddaughter while they make the *koulourakia* with their hands. I ask her to sing it again.

After a bit, Glykeria turns her head in my direction. "Lookit, Mama," she says as she rolls out more dough ropes. "Y*ou* should pay attention." She says this with a bit of a sharper tone than I usually hear directed my way. I laugh. I know what I'm good at. I know what I'm not. Maybe Penelope will end up being the baker of the family. After I type up the words to the song, I get up and help her roll out some cookie dough, twisting it up, one, two, three times. She praises me as much as she praised Penelope. I eat it up.

Once the cookies are baked, the kids indulge.

"It's not that much sugar," Glykeria says. She knows I try to provide a relatively healthy diet for my kids. "Well, it's four cups, with all that flour I put in there." I just nod and try to push the carbohydrate count out of my mind and focus on enjoying watching my kiddo and her little sister happily munch on the fruits of her labor.

BONUS! YIAYIA'S TWISTY BUTTER COOKIE RECIPE
Koulourakia

<u>You will need:</u>

Butter: 1 lb

Eggs: 12, separated yolks and whites, and both well-beaten.

Sugar: 4 cups

Liquid cooking ammonia: 7 tsp

Whole milk: 1 cup, warm

"And that's the ingredients," Glykeria tells me.

"Um, that's not all of them," I counter.

"And vanilla. Okay."

Vanilla: 1 tbsp

"That's still not all of them," I insist.

"Okay, baking powder. Two tablespoons baking powder."

Baking powder: 2 tbsp

"Not tablespoons! That sounds like too much." Tom doesn't ever make them, but apparently he thinks he knows how to make them.

"That's right!" Glykeria insists. "It's a big recipe!" she yells in his direction before turning her attention back to me. "Why he has to say something? He drive me crazy!" She turns back to Tom and shouts, "I make two hundred out of that, okay?"

"And that's all the ingredients."

"No, it's not! What about flour?" *How can she forget the flour?*

"I'm not there yet!"

Flour: There's really no way to tell until you make them (see directions). Have 3 or 4ish cups handy.

<u>You will do:</u>

1. Combine butter and sugar until well mixed.

2. Add the egg yolks to butter mixture.

3. Add ammonia to warm milk.

4. Add milk to butter mixture.

5. Add flour. "A little bit at a time until you make a soft dough. There's no measurement on the flours. You have to put it on your hands, to make it not stick on your hands. Just make enough dough not to stick on your hands and be able to roll it."

6. Twist dough into the shape you want (Yiayia rolls out a dough rope, folds it in half lengthwise, and twists the two ends of the rope around 3 times).

7. Optional: Beat an egg yolk and brush it over the tops of the cookies. This adds a bit of sheen and color. Yiayia never does this, unless she's making cookies for someone she doesn't know that well. Don't tell yiayia, but I like them better with the brushed egg yolk and a slight sprinkling of sesame seeds on top.

8. Bake at 350 degrees for 18-20 minutes.

These freeze really well after baking. Thaw at room temperature in a Ziploc bag.

FOOD
A full belly

The dishes my mother-in-law cooks are simple, yet always so delicious I want to devour half the pan. Actually, one time, I DID eat half the pan. I think I shocked her with my gluttony.

It was *melizantes*. Eggplant and onions. I usually have some self-control, but that time I just couldn't stop. She is such a remarkable hostess that we don't ever alternate which side of the family we visit for Thanksgiving! We *always* go to her house. Her food is the best. She learned by watching her own parents, and from Tom's mom, Yiayia Athena, who lived with them after they were married.

Even though I greedily devour everything my mother-in-law puts on a platter, the downside to her robust kitchen presence is that she is a total food pusher. It used to give me anxiety, imagining her basically force-feeding my children. I've gotten over it, since we go over there and get free meals several times a month. I have traded any worries about my children learning to shovel food into their faces when they aren't hungry, for homemade *dolmades* (grape leaves) and *horta* (cooked wild greens) and *loukanika* (sausage). I've even gotten to the point where I sometimes brag to my mother-in-law about how much I get my kids to eat so she'll be proud of me. It doesn't always work.

"She ate two eggs today!"

"Hmmm, well that's good she ate. But so many eggs! Too many. All that cholesterol!"

Never mind that after offering my daughter homemade spinach pie and french fries and *koulourakia* and spaghetti and pancakes and sausage she will also offer fast food kid's meals and cheesy crackers and microwave popcorn and those ice cream sandwiches that aren't made from real ice cream and don't even melt in the sun. She will feed them anything to get those grandkids of hers to eat. And eat. And eat. And eat. And eat. And eat. She can't help herself. It's an atavistic instinct.

Her grandchildren MUST SURVIVE.

Glykeria and Tom grew up eating village staples such as beans, *trahana* (a dried oatmeal-type cereal made from flour), in-season fruits and vegetables, *dolmades*, and *plasto*. Their biggest staple was cornbread.

"Cornbread, cornbread, cornbread. That's all we eating." Glykeria tells me they even drank milk that was stuffed with cornbread. "To fill you up more." Everything was cooked in the *gastra*. It took me a while to understand what a *gastra* was, because this is how they initially described one:

"It had the thing, metal thing you put wood on, in our fireplaces. Pan on top with a lid, cover with kindling so it heats up the whole fireplace."

"I have no idea what you're talking about."

"A stove in the fireplace."

After more explanation, I learn that a *gastra* is a large clay pot with a lid that is used for cooking in a wood-fired oven. Apparently these things exist even in modern kitchens, but since my kitchen is just about as foreign to me as the mountaintop my in-laws grew up on is to me, I had no clue.

Starkly different from our own overflowing pantry, it was very seldom that they would have treats or snacks on hand in the house; the rations of sugar and honey were saved for special occasions. Kathy remembers how the women would always figure out a way to make name days—the day of the saint that each person was named after—a special event.

"On name days, make some baklava, so everyone would get a piece."

Whether or not they had ingredients for spinach pie or salads depended on the season. Green beans, zucchini, and *horta* were some of the typical vegetables consumed, when they were available.

There was no produce section, no grocery store, to supplement their food stores during the off-season. There were no bags of frozen vegetables. There were no (gasp) frozen pizzas. I can't imagine not being able to eat vegetables during the winter. I am so spoiled by my fancy year-round market with its fancy coffee bar.

"Fall and winter we had the grains. Dried stuff," Tom tells me. They kept dried goods in "huge storage bins for grain, you know what I mean. Big boxes, in other words, cover up. Yeah. Storage bins. Flour in one, corn in the other, or beans in that one." The storage bins he speaks of were usually wooden barrels.

"We had milk, butter, cheese and eggs most of the year." I think he fears he's making it sound like they had a massive pantry, so he adds, "I mean, we didn't have anything."

BONUS! YIAYIA'S EGGPLANT AND ONION RECIPE
Melinzanes

You will need:

Eggplant: 1 large, thinly sliced, lengthwise.

Cold water with splashes of vinegar and shakes of salt: For soaking eggplant, prior to cooking. About 3 Tbsp each for the vinegar and salt.

Spanish Onions: 3 large, sliced.

Salt, Pepper, Oregano, Parsley: Use fresh, chopped parsley if you've got it. Add fresh or dried basil if you feel like it.

Garlic: Minced. You should know by now that Greeks never use any less than 3 cloves of garlic per recipe. Maybe it's an unorthodox representation of the Mother, the Father, and the Holy Ghost. Garlickiness is close to godliness?

Tomatoes: ½ cup paste, dissolved in water, OR small can of chopped tomatoes.

Parmesan cheese: For sprinkling on top.

You will do:

1. Soak eggplant in water solution for about 5 minutes.

2. Brush eggplant with oil and broil or grill. I've seen Yiayia make this and she makes it look really easy but I've never tried making it myself, so if you figure out the temperature that works best and how long you cook it for, let me know.

3. Sauté onions and garlic for about 5 minutes.

4. Combine spices, parsley and tomatoes.

4. Layer the eggplant and onions similar to the way you would layer lasagna, top with tomato mixture and sprinkle with parmesan.

6. Bake at 350 degrees until it's cooked through, for 1½ hours. Or however long it takes to get done.

Serve with Yiayia's white bread and feta cheese.

FOOD
A long-lost cheese

During one of our interviews, my in-laws talk about *klotsotiri*—a food I have never heard them speak of before—with so much excitement and desire that it appears to border on orgasmic. It makes me slightly uncomfortable and also a little bit hungry.

Glykeria explains how *klotsotiri* was made in the *xorio*, using fresh goat milk (apparently cow or sheep milk do not work, something about the fat content) that was swirled and tossed around in a wooden churn every other day. The continuous agitation beat the milk until the butter rose to the top. The butter was removed, and presumably used for cooking or for slathering on bread, and the remaining milk was heated in a kettle over the fire. When the milk reached the boiling point it curdled, and these curds were collected and placed in a cheesecloth to dry out. After they were sufficiently dry, the curds were salted and could be eaten. Ziploc containers were not something that existed in their community, so the *klotsotiri* and other foodstuffs were stored in bags made of dried goat skin.

Glykeria sums it up: "Saved it, put in big goat skins, stuff all the cheeses in there with salt and it would last the whole year." The *klotsotiri* was stored differently than some of the other dairy products; it was "not in barrels like you put other cheese."

"Farmer's easy way to do it," Tom chimes in. I raise my eyebrows at this claim. If this was the easy way, I'd really hate to see the hard way.

I try to picture what my life would be like if I had to stand barefoot, the bottoms of my feet blackened from standing on a dirt-packed floor, swirling butter in a wooden churn, wearing the same dress I've worn for weeks. Months. That I made by hand. I can't.

I have a picture in my head of a pioneer-type woman churning, and I can't put my own face on her body. I look at my mother-in-law, in her trendy black scoop neck from Kohl's, sipping on a cup of coffee out of a lime green chevron mug. I try to picture her face on the body, agitating goat's milk in a wooden churn. I can't. I know she did it, she was sitting here in front of me telling me *how* she did it, and I still can't picture it. It's like I really can't believe that these stories are true, even though I know that they are. I wonder to myself if that disbelief is some sort of defense mechanism, my brain protecting me from visualizing such hardship, preventing me from experiencing, even vicariously, undue stress.

Or is it just my own ignorance that prevents a picture from forming in my mind? My privileged suburban self doesn't have enough stored images to relate to, to put together a picture in my mind. I'll keep trying. I'll keep reminding myself that it was only luck that resulted in me being born where I was. That I could have been the one churning. That I am not far removed from such a life.

As a female, Glykeria was typically involved with churning and separating the milk, butter and curds, while Tom had more experience with butchering the animals. He adds, "Every time we butchered a goat, we had to be very careful not to punch holes in the skin."

He gives me the rundown on how to prepare a skin so it can be repurposed into useful storage containers: "Put it in hot water, hair comes out. Shave the hair, clean them out, put them in salt and dry them out first." The skin could be cut into sections and tied to create a sack, or various nature-made sacs, such as the bladder, could be used as they were.

Tom closes his eyes and tilts his head back slightly as he describes the *klotsotiri* cheese to me: "Kind of crumbly. Dried up. Mmmm. You make that with bread. I still smell it. I DREAM of it."

Was he salivating?

He describes what used to be his favorite way to eat this dried goat cheese: "Put the butter and melt it, start burning, brown, add scrambled eggs and then put that in. Not feta. I wouldn't care for feta if I had that." Eating scrambled eggs with feta is a staple in our households, so telling me the *klotsotiri* is even better than that makes my stomach yearn for something I've never tasted before.

He is transported back to his time in the village as a young boy: "Boy that was good stuff! Of all the things I miss, that cheese and the eggs!" He shakes his head. He can't believe he misses anything at all about his time living as a poor villager, let alone misses something as simple as scrambled eggs with cheese.

Tom remembers Yiayia Athena, like the other women in the village, making *klotsotiri* regularly for guests.

"Every time somebody stopped by, they had to feed them. That was the quick thing to make. They didn't have anything, like, from the day before, like we have now. What you had you had to finish because it was going to spoil if you didn't eat it. That was the bad thing about summertime, couldn't save anything out unless it was salty. Even our bread. Cornbread, after one day, we'd get this stringy mold." He grimaces and then adds, sounding surprised, "We never got sick! We hated to throw it away because we didn't have any more to bake." He credits eating slightly moldy bread to their overall good health: "Maybe that's why we were so immune."

As I listen to Tom talk, my mind returns to my mother-in-law's food pushing. I think about her continual requests that my children eat. And eat. And eat. I envision her displays of pride when they consume platefuls in her care, and her visible frustration when they don't take a bite. "Finish what is on your plate" makes more sense when you grew up having to throw out what remained, and didn't have anything left once it was gone.

BONUS! YIAYIA'S SCRAMBLED EGGS WITH FETA RECIPE
Avga kai feta - it's not klotsotiri, but it'll do in a pinch

<u>You will need:</u>

Eggs: Beaten. Enough to feed you and your breakfast guests.

Milk: A splash added to the beaten eggs.

Salt and pepper: To taste. Keep in mind, feta adds saltiness.

Feta cheese: Yiayia never buys the dry crumbled feta in the grocery deli department. NEVER EVER. Yiayia ONLY buys block feta that is soaking in brine. You should do the same.

Butter: More than you think is necessary.

Dill: Minced. (Optional.)

<u>You will do:</u>

1. Place a ridiculous amount of butter in pan and heat. Yiayia always goes overboard and this is no exception.

2. Add egg mixture to pan.

3. About halfway through cooking, fold in enough feta to make the eggs creamy and salty, but not so much that the eggs become watery as it cooks down. Add herbs (if desired).

Serve with toasted pita bread.

FOOD
A grown-up pig and a grown-out pinky nail

While cheese and eggs could be eaten year-round, meat was an occasional luxury in the *xorio*. Each year both families would "grow" a pig and every Christmas it would be killed and the meat consumed.

All of our talk about food has transported Tom back to the village. "Melt that fat down, melt and melt, and put it in big tin cans, and we had that lard just about all year long." He licks his lips and pantomimes holding a piece of bread in his hand and lifting it toward his mouth as he speaks about one of his favorite winter snacks.

"Big slice of cornbread, put it on the fire to get a little brown and slap on lard. Geez! We thought we had the best!" He shakes his head, remembering how content they were with next to nothing. Sometimes the more you have the less you realize how good you have it.

As he pantomimes eating, I notice his pinky fingernail, the one on his left hand that he lets grow out long while the rest are cut down short. Lambros sometimes does this too, purposely letting the one small fingernail grow out.

"Why do you do that?" I asked Tom once. It seemed a little weird. He explained that having the one long nail was a sign to others that you were well off. A visual cue that you were someone who didn't need to work with their hands to survive. A goat herder couldn't grow a fingernail out like that; it would break from all of the sustained manual labor.

Without electricity and refrigeration, preserving meat meant it needed to be heavily salted. Sausages could remain edible for three or four months after they were prepared. Preserved meats were usually kept in large wooden barrels, some as large as recliners, that sat on their sides against the walls. Alternatively, water and foodstuffs were kept in sizeable plastic vessels or cans. Meats and cheeses, like the *klotsotiri*, could be stored in dried animal skins, obtained on the rare occasions when any of their animals were butchered. Glykeria notes that food didn't taste the same when stored in plastic bins. "Not good," she says, crinkling up her small nose.

Glykeria's stomach growls during our discussion of preserved meats and cheeses. "Salty. But yummy. Oh, that is yummy." She says hungrily, "I wish I had some right now! Oh, gosh!"

This is probably the only time I've been at their house and didn't leave completely satiated.

FOOD
A loaf of bread

The villagers often had a passionate longing for white bread. Glykeria and her friends Eleni, Euphemia, and Niki, often worked alongside each other, watching the sheep. Each day they would take their animals to pasture and the collective of animals would graze together. The girls would be out all day, sunup to sundown.

Glykeria sighs as she recalls her frustration with the perpetual responsibility. "All day long. I used to cry for that." The girls had to watch the animals closely to make sure they didn't wander and eat crops out of someone else's farm, and to protect them from wolves who might want to scarf them down. "We used to pack our lunch and bring it with us. All we ate was cornbread and feta cheese. That was our lunch. And dinner," Glykeria tells me.

While they were often hungry, Glykeria recounts a day when the girls were particularly ravenous. She explains that Niki's parents had a little bit more money than some of the others in the village, so they were able to occasionally go out and buy wheat flour. On this day, the girls proposed a trade with Niki. They would watch her sheep for her, and she would head home and pick up some bread for all of them to share.

Niki agreed and trotted off, while the other girls watched all of the sheep and eagerly awaited their payoff. Niki was gone all day, and as evening approached she returned to where the sheep were grazing. She returned empty-handed. "We started yelling and fighting. 'What is the excuse that you are not bringing us bread?'" Glykeria recounts. Niki professed that her mother didn't have any bread made at the time. Glykeria narrows her eyes as she spits out, "That didn't stop her from letting us watch her sheep all day long."

Glykeria isn't the only one who reports often being hungry in the *xorio*. Even though Tom's sister Kathy is prone to exaggeration, I believe there must be some truth to her exclamations about hunger. "I was starving all day!"

Kathy remembers one day when she visited the neighbor's house, and they asked what she had eaten that day. Kathy disclosed that she hadn't eaten anything. "The neighbor gave me a slice of white bread. Not cornbread." The white bread was a rare treat bestowed upon her that afternoon. "Cornbread, cornbread, cornbread. We had cornbread all the time." Wheat bread was clearly an oasis in a desert of corn.

Her eyes flutter briefly as she tells me, "I remember that bread was so good and fresh." At supper that night, Kathy didn't eat as much as usual. When Yiayia Athena questioned why she wasn't eating, Kathy told her how the lady next door had given her the bread. Apparently Yiayia Athena wasn't happy to hear this. "She said, 'I will cut your hands off if you go take anything else from the neighbor.'" She knew that her family wasn't as well off as the neighbor's family and Kathy understood her mom's reaction. "She had pride."

I remember being surprised by my mother-in-law's intense strength when she taught me how to make her homemade white bread. Reflecting on it now, it is probably a great source of pride for her, making that white bread for her children. She likely rolls her eyes at the gluten-free trend these days. She makes five loaves of bread at a time, kneading the enormous amount of dough in a metal mixing bowl large enough to house a family of four. I kneaded for a small part of the process and developed tendonitis almost instantly in both forearms.

I am a wimp when it comes to manual labor. Compared to her, my arms and my hands are flabby and feeble. Her strength is ridiculous. You know how ants can carry something like five thousand times their body weight on their backs? She's like that. Only she is stronger than the ant.

BONUS! YIAYIA'S WHITE BREAD RECIPE
Psomi

<u>You will need:</u>

Flour: 5 lbs of it, because you know Yiayia never makes only 1 loaf at a time. She makes 5. If you're not feeding an army, you can freeze the bread and save it for later.

Water: 6 cups of warm water. Make sure it's not cold, or cool, but not too warm or hot.

Fast-acting dry yeast: A full strip (3 packets).

<u>You will do:</u>

1. Add yeast to warm water. Allow it to activate.

2. Pour flour into a large bowl. Dig a well in the middle of the flour and add the water/yeast mixture.

3. Knead dough. If you're not as strong as Yiayia, this will involve the realization that she has muscles in her forearms that are stronger than all of the muscles in your entire body combined. (Don't feel bad, none of us are as strong as Yiayia.)

4. Heat oven to 105 degrees. Turn oven off and place dough into oven, covered with a towel. Let sit for 1 hour.

5. Remove dough from oven and knead again. Try not to let your sweat or tears get into the dough. Give yourself a mental pep talk, telling yourself you can do this.

6. Cover and return to oven for 1 hour and 20 minutes.

7. Mash down the dough again. Divide into 5 oiled loaf pans.

8. Bake at 350 degrees for 1 hour.

FOOD
A cup and a teaspoon

The girls are running in circles around my in-laws' living room, alternating between singing "Ring Around the Rosie" (including falling down on cue) and playing on the floor with pillows they have pulled off the couch. Greek music blares out of the tape player, which they've figured out how to turn on. There's always an old tape in there, so all they need to do is push power, then play. Daphne asks for water, so I get up and grab the first sippy cup I spot: the blue one sitting on the kitchen table.

"Is that hers?" Glykeria asks me, thinking that the one I grabbed might be Penelope's.

"Eh. Doesn't really matter. They both share everything." I let them share cups and eat from the same plate, sometimes even off of the same fork. There's less waste that way and I figure it probably helps build up their immunity. Also, sometimes I'm too lazy to get up and grab another cup.

Tom nods his head and says, "Well. We only had one cup."

I glance up at him, encouraging him to continue. "Metal cup," he adds. We had one glass one that we brought out for guests."

"You had one metal cup for the whole house?" I often repeat what I think they said, or meant, to double-check my initial level of understanding.

"Uh-huh." He nods a confirmation.

"Like, literally only ONE metal cup in your entire house?" Triple-check needed, to verify accuracy.

"Yeah! And one glass one for guests."

I look down at the mug he's holding in his hand. The coffee cup he drinks out of day after day. He never mixes it up and uses another one. He never even puts this mug in the cupboard because it is always in his hand or sitting on the counter where his wife washes it out before she fills it up again with fresh coffee. It's a metal mug with the Ford logo wrapped around the side. I look up at him.

"Is that why your favorite mug is a metal one today?"

He looks down at his mug and snorts. I don't know how to interpret that, so I assume I'm right and he hadn't really thought about the connection until now.

"Before that we had wooden ones too. Cedar. Make the best thermos. Kept it cold. And smelled so good. Always smelled like that, even after years. We used to have one of them that we took out to travel, on the mantle."

"I have it! In the closet somewhere," Glykeria pipes up.

"*Endaxi, yenaka.*" Okay, okay, woman.

He grimaces and rolls his eyes. He lifts his hands in the air and shakes his head and tells her to relax, that she doesn't need to go searching for it right that minute.

She jumps up and goes searching for it right that minute.

She hands me an intricately carved cedar canteen. It is glossy. It is clearly not one they used.

"This one is fancier than the one we used. Got this at one of them tourist traps," Tom says.

Aha.

"In the '60s, we got cups and plates," he says.

Being on the topic of kitchenware reminds my mother-in-law, "Lambros should have a wooden teaspoon. Cedar teaspoon." She turns and looks at him. "Lambros, you have that?"

"No, we don't have that," Lambros tells her.

"What's the cedar teaspoon?" I ask.

"I don't know. *Pontinelos*?" She misunderstands me and tells me the name of it in Greek.

"I mean . . ." I try to think of how to word what I mean. English is my first language and I often feel tongue-tied. I can't imagine having to learn another one. "Why would he have a wooden teaspoon?" I clarify.

"My mom's brother used to make it. And when we went to Greece in 1981, he gave him one," Glykeria tells me.

"I don't remember taking it. I think it's still here," Lambros says.

"I thought we gave it to you when we moved," Glykeria states. "If not, I look and give it to you." She gets up and starts rummaging through her kitchen drawers. She comes back with it in her hand. "I don't know whose this is. Yours or one of the girls'."

I look at it. It's bigger than I imagined, and the handle shoots up at a forty-five-degree angle from the large shallow bowl.

"It's for soup," Lambros says, noticing how I am inspecting its funny shape.

"You want it?" Glykeria asks us.

Don't ask me. I absolve myself of making that decision and possibly stealing one of my sister-in-laws' spoons.

"I never took one," Lambros says.

"Here, take it." She throws it at me and it lands in my lap with a plop.

"My great-uncle," Lambros says, as if we're taking a member of his family home with us, instead of just something he once made.

FOOD
Spoonfed a bite of an unfollowed recipe

Lambros has started creating videos of his mother cooking. They decide on a dish and she brings over her ingredients, and usually her own pots and pans, and he records each step from start to finish. He edits the video, adding music and text overlays. Creating an audiovisual cookbook is a creative outlet for him and a pretty cool way to preserve and pass on her recipes.

Tonight she's making rice pudding. She surprises me by bringing over a Greek recipe book that she bought from the church marketplace. She bought me a copy of the same book for Christmas one year and apparently it is the best Greek cookbook she's ever seen, at least in English. She opens it up and points to the recipe titled "Rice Pudding I" and says, "I use this recipe here. I just double it."

"You do?" I'm surprised. I've never seen her use a recipe when cooking a Greek dish.

"Yeah!" she insists. I pull out my version of the cookbook and she compares my version of "Rice Pudding I" to hers to make sure there aren't any differences between her edition of the book and mine (there are not).

She leaves her book open on the counter and my husband starts recording her.

Usually I write down the ingredients and scribble down each and every step she makes. This time, though, I let it go. The directions were right there on the counter, after all.

"I thought you were writing things down." Lambros notices I'm not really paying attention to what she's doing.

"It's fine, she uses that recipe," I tell him.

"She already did something not written," he tells me.

I look at what she's doing and notice she brought the rice to a boil and then let it simmer, instead of just simmering it the whole time. *Not a big deal*, I think. I write it down and then head out of the room to check on the girls.

By the time the rice pudding is done, I'm upstairs reading a bedtime story to the girls. Glykeria comes up with a container of the warm dessert. She holds a spoon in her hand and asks her granddaughters, "You want to try some?" She dips the spoon into the pudding and blows on it to cool it off before spooning a bite into Daphne's mouth.

"Mmmmm!" Daphne says.

"I want some!" Penelope pipes up. She needn't have asked, since Glykeria already had her spoonful ready.

She probably would have offered me the spoon, but I'm sitting on Daphne's bed with my right arm around Daphne and my left around Penelope. My hands are full. So, my mother-in-law dips the spoon into the container a third time and offers it to me. I grin and let her feed me. The rice pudding is deliciously sweet and creamy. I giggle at the absurdity of me—supposedly a grown woman—being fed like a child.

I thank her.

Later that night, Lambros and I begin editing the video. He asks me to list the ingredients so he can type them in. I start listing but get stopped at the second ingredient.

"One-half cup of rice."

"That can't be right."

"The original recipe had a quarter cup, so doubled would be half." I don't know what made me think I was correct, based on this information alone. I hadn't actually seen her put the rice in the pot.

"She put WAY more rice in there." Lambros is sure.

"Let's check the video."

We watch Glykeria on the computer monitor. She puts in two cups of rice.

"That's not double!" It sort of feels like she lied to me.

"I told you, you needed to write things down."

"She said she doubled everything!"

He shakes his head.

"She brought a recipe book!" I yell.

"Yeah, but she didn't look at it."

"Damn it. You're right." I concede.

We watch each video clip and edit the quantities for each ingredient on the list. She quadrupled the rice. Doubled the sugar. Quadrupled the butter.

She used one-and-a-half times the amount of eggs given in the original recipe. The corn starch she didn't adjust at all from what was listed in the book.

As my sister-in-law Voula tells me, "The recipe is just a suggestion." Clearly I'll have to pay closer attention to the next recipe she makes. She can't spoon-feed me everything.

BONUS! YIAYIA'S RICE PUDDING RECIPE
Rizogalo

<u>You will need:</u>

White Rice: 2 cups, rinsed.   **Eggs:** 6, beaten.

Milk: Vitamin D. 8 cups.   **Water:** 4 cups.

Butter: 4 tbsp.   **Cornstarch:** 1 tsp.

Salt: A dash.   **Vanilla**: 2 tsp.

Sugar: 2 cups   **Cinnamon**: to taste

<u>You will do:</u>

1. Combine water, rice and salt in a large pot. Cover and bring to a boil.

2. Remove lid once water boils. Stir frequently to prevent rice from sticking to bottom of pot.

3. Add milk, butter, and sugar to rice mixture. Continue stirring frequently.

4. In a separate bowl, dissolve cornstarch in some milk. Slowly combine cornstarch slurry to eggs while continuously beating egg mixture.

5. Once rice is soft, slowly add egg mixture to rice mixture. How long until it gets soft? "Until it's done," says Yiayia. Stir continuously.

6. Let rice thicken for a few minutes, then add vanilla.

7. Remove from heat and add cinnamon.

GREEK CIVIL WAR
A war, an execution, a life saved, and a finger lost

The Greek Civil War occurred in the mid-1940s, directly following World War II, between the Greek government and the Greek communists. I never heard much about the war until I started needling my in-laws for details about their life, maybe because their memories from this time are unpleasant and fuzzy. They were quite young when their village found itself in the middle of the mayhem.

We're at my inlaws', but it's quieter than usual because Glykeria is out of town. It doesn't happen often, but every now and again she'll go to Greece or somewhere with one of her kids without Tom. He seems to have decided that his traveling days are over.

I put the chickpea salad I brought over for him in the refrigerator and pry open my laptop. He's sipping on his gas station coffee and he gives me some background. "Different groups trying to take over: communists, right-wingers, people in the middle. We were right in the middle of it." Tom explains that everyone was recruiting members to fight for their cause. According to him, the communist party "would promise you everything, give you bread and made communism sound so good. 'Mother Russia, they have everything there!'"

He shakes his head as he tells me how children were recruited and trained from a young age. "You know they were picking up people then, they were picking them up for training, picking up the kids, seven or eight years old, to brainwash them. Promise you everything. Take the kids, promise the parents everything. A lot of the parents were fooled into it and a lot of Greeks were communists, so they would send their kids willingly."

Even if they weren't sent willingly, kids were often taken. Tens of thousands of children were taken to Albania, Czechoslovakia and Russia and raised to become communists. Within the boundaries of the village, there was no escaping the conflict.

"Everyone had a gun and you would just join any group you wanted. Run into a group of people, they would ask you who are you . . ." Tom says, meaning they wanted to know which group you were affiliated with. "But you don't know who they are." He raises his eyebrows and looks at me out of the side of his eye. It was impossible to tell just by looking which side someone was on, which was dangerous. It wasn't just a matter of agreeing to disagree; admitting to having the wrong political affiliations could mean life or death. "If you say the opposite, they would chop you down. It was like everyone had to join one side or the other. Or the third side. It was bad, it was bad."

The Skoutelas family, like the rest of their village, were worried about being caught by one of the military groups and forced to join as involuntary recruits. Or, even worse, they could be killed by one of the groups for refusing to sign up voluntarily or admit affiliation with the wrong political party.

Their concerns were legitimate. The guerillas had captured Tom's would-be godfather, Athanasios, a good friend of Papou Lambros. From what Tom was told, Papou Lambros had tried to warn Athanasios not to head into the village, since the area was littered with guerrillas, but Athanasios was a young guy who thought he was invincible.

He was lured by the scent of fresh-roasted lamb. "He didn't have no business," Tom says, indicating that he didn't need to go there in the first place. "He heard they butchered something. A lamb. He was kinda . . ." He isn't sure how to describe him. "He liked food, in other words."

"Did they do that a lot? Have lamb roasts that people would gather at?"

"Yeah, sometime. Yes."

As Papou Lambros feared, guerillas were surrounding the lamb roast and Athanasios was snatched up. "They grabbed him. They took two or three people together. Took him on a two, three-day walk." A few days later he was executed. "They let the other ones go."

"Why did they execute him?" I ask.

"Who knows. Maybe something personal. I don't know. There were different groups, ideologies, there were two, three different groups. I don't know which side that was. I don't think his family was active in any particular group. He was in the wrong spot, I guess." Tom shrugs and takes a deep swig, sucking the coffee in through the sides of his mouth so he doesn't burn his tongue.

Long-established Greek custom dictates that the godparent is the person who names a child. Infants are called *moro*, baby, until baptism, when they receive their official name. While the godparent technically gets to choose the name, per tradition they typically name the firstborn son after the new father's father, and the firstborn daughter after the new father's mother. So, there's not very much pressure, as one might initially imagine, when it comes to naming the child. This is why so many cousins in Greek families have the same name—they are all named after their grandparents. Athanasios's mother ended up baptizing Tom, in lieu of her son. Instead of naming him Andreas, which was Tom's grandfather's name, "she baptized me in honor of her son," so he was named Athanasios. Tom, for short.

Sometime after Athanasios's execution, the guerilla army won a particularly big battle nearby. As a result, they occupied an area which included the village. During this period of the occupation, Papou Lambros was captured by the guerillas and taken captive. "They took the prisoners, who were all members of the regular army before, and they paraded them through town to show others what they do. It was like they were prisoners of war."

He made it out alive, but not without injury. "He got shot in the leg. He got shot, crawled into a church, hiding," Tom says. At the time, Glykeria's dad, Dimitri, was also a prisoner and he came across Papou Lambros in the church. "He took him to get washed up and moved him so they wouldn't kill him," Tom says, nodding in appreciation. "Helped him out, took care of him for a little while."

"He saved your dad's life." A statement and a question.

"Probably, yes," Tom nods.

"Wow. You guys had a pretty big connection even before you met. Did your dads know each other before this?" I ask.

"*Neh*." Yes. "Knew who each other were from the village."

Tom tells me about a time when a couple supporting the communist party came to their house. "They were dressed in army fatigues with rifles and bandoliers. They came up with guns drawn." Two of his older sisters, Eftihiea and Chysanthe, who were teenagers at the time, hid out in the woods while the "recruiters" came to the door and let themselves in.

Tom explains why they needed to hide: "They would take anyone, boys or girls." While the men were taken for fighting, the women were taken to carry supplies, cook, and look after the men. Tom says they "took all the women. Since they didn't have mules, load up the food stuff, carry ammunition and so on. A lot of women did that. Whether you wanted to go or not, they would take you."

One night my husband and I watch a film about the Greek civil war with his parents. The movie depicts a story of a young mother's struggle to keep her children safe during this time when many were dying, starving, or being taken from their families. People were killed trying to keep their families safe. "It was just like that, Christine," my mother-in-law tells me. "My mother tell me one of her cousins. Not first cousin, but second, third, something like that—they chop him up and line him up through his house. They tell him to do something, and he didn't do it, they lay him down inside the house and poof!—with the axe—and cut his head off."

"That's horrible."

"That's right."

Watching the movie sparks further conversation and it comes up that Tom's Uncle Gregory, who I have heard was a priest who loved beekeeping, left Greece and came to the States in order to escape from the communists.

"Really? How could I not have known this? I thought he just came here because he wanted to, and he was able to because he was a priest!" I stare at Tom, accusingly.

"Oh yeah, he was a priest and a teacher. He *had* to leave." The communists targeted those who were most educated. Those who spread messages other than theirs.

Apparently up until he left Greece, Uncle Gregory would hide people in his church during this time period. He requested to be transferred in order to escape the horrors he'd witnessed in his village. He is the one who opened the door to other members of the Skoutelas family to make their way to America.

"I knew he came to the States because he was a priest, but I didn't realize it was to escape the civil war."

"I'm sure I told you that, how could I forget that?"

"Oh yeah, he told you," Glykeria takes his side.

"He must've told you," Lambros chimes in.

"I see what you guys are doing here." I'm ganged up on, so I just shake my head.

The ultimate goal of the guerillas? "They wanted to take over the country so communism could take over." When the communist couple entered the house, causing Tom's sisters to hide, they didn't see any people suited to their needs. "It was just my mom and I, I think. They didn't want the small kids. They didn't want to babysit." Tom remembers seeing them walking around inside his humble home, that they, "walked around like they owned the place. They did anything they wanted to." Apparently the Skoutelas family didn't have much to offer them, in terms of people or supplies. "They left, because they didn't find anything." Tom remembers the feeling of being violated, of not being in control. Unfortunately, it wouldn't be the last time he felt this way during the war.

GREEK CIVIL WAR
An unwelcome guest

In 1949, a member of the guerrillas demanded to be put up in the Skoutelas household so he could use it as a lookout. Being on the peak of the mountain, their house provided the best visual of the land below, making it easy for him to see if the Greek army was coming their way. "His name was *Agelada*. Last name like the cow."

Of course it was. The animal my father-in-law has always disliked.

"He was there for a few weeks, maybe a month, before moving on to his next location," Tom says. To the family it seemed like much longer. "It was annoying to have him there all day long, over your shoulder. He was worried more about his life than ours. But he had the gun, he kind of ordered you around." Tom waves a toothpick he's been chewing on around while he tells me this. His wife is out of town, so he stopped over after babysitting his grandsons for Lambros's sister Voula. I offer him a beer or a glass of wine but he refuses. He's content for now to gnaw on the thin piece of wood.

Agelada expected Yiayia Athena to cook for him and threatened to take the family's precious goats and sheep away if she refused. This was a serious threat. Those animals were their livelihood. They provided wool for clothing, milk for drinking and were used to make cheeses. They provided meat on occasion and served as something of value to trade for supplies, or to use as part of a dowry. Agelada exploited his position of power, greedily eating every last egg produced by the family's chickens while the rest of them went without consuming a single one.

In the end, even though Yiayia Athena followed his orders, Agelada took some of their goats and sheep anyway. Tom's resentment is evident as he puts the toothpick back in his mouth and bites down on it, hard. "I hated that guy," he spits. He changes his mind and takes me up on the offer of wine.

He sips on a small glass of cabernet and shares a memory: one full of spiteful amusement, at the expense of Agelada. "A fire was burning in the fireplace and there were cedar logs fueling the fire. Cedar tends to pop quite a bit while burning. One morning my mom was making breakfast for him and the cedar logs popped loudly, making a loud PABOOM!" Everyone was used to the sounds of gunshots, but apparently this noise startled the resident guerrilla.

"Agelada jumped all the way across the room!" Tom laughs gleefully as he tells me this. Once he stops laughing, he takes another sip of his wine. "You know," he says, "my mom saw him once, when she went back." In an odd coincidence, when Yiayia Athena went home for vacation to Greece in the 1990s she actually ran into Agelada in the small town that borders the village. By that time he was an old man.

I ask about her reaction to seeing him again, after all those years. Tom tells me, "She told him who she was and she said she was ready to kill him." Agelada downplayed their history, brushing off his behaviors with an excuse about back then being "different times" and tried to give her the impression that he hadn't wanted to act the way he did, but he had no choice. "Like he didn't want to do it, but he had to."

Tom has a brief moment of understanding for the position the man was in: "But, he probably did too. I don't know." Tom sits silently for a few moments, quietly reflecting on what he has shared with me about his village being taken over, at the expense of his family. Stories that have been buried inside him all of these years.

He shakes his head, looks at me and says, "You know, I'm still getting mad at them." After a moment he drains his wine, pushes back his chair and heads outside to have a smoke.

GREEK CIVIL WAR
A retreat into the woods

Tom says his family was afraid of the communists. "We were right-wing. We never joined the communist party in any way. They were after priests, school teachers, policemen, anyone with a little education. They didn't want them around. First chance they got, they chopped their heads off."

But, Tom points out, "It wasn't just left and right. There were so many different groups going through." Any time a group of activists came to the village, you were forced to "declare which side you were on, and you didn't know what side *they* were on, so you tried to avoid them." The Skoutelas family was forced to move twice, as different groups swept through the area.

The first move was prompted by a group of guerrillas taking over the *xorio*. Tom's parents were forced to move him, his siblings and his cousins—all of the women and children—in order to protect them. His dad had to hide to avoid capture. He had served in the Greek army before the civil war began, fighting in World War II. After the war ended, the Germans left and army members started returning to their homes. The guerillas specifically targeted Greek army members when the civil war began.

Tom's dad helped his family cross the river so they could get to safety, then went into hiding. He didn't want to get captured again.

"Where did your dad go to hide?"

"I don't know where he went. I just know he came back and helped us move, him and my grandpa and some other people, and then he disappeared. Even if they told me, I wouldn't know what they meant." He was so young.

Kathy remembers more of this time, since she is a few years older than Tom. She was seven when the guerillas took over the village. I make a point to bring my computer when I go visit her one afternoon so I can fill in the gaps in Tom's memory. "They told us we had to leave the village to go far and far away," she starts. "We had to go where it was more safe because the civil war was going on and the opposite side was going to try to kill us."

She says this nonchalantly, as she brings me a cup of coffee and a small, white, china plate piled with homemade *baklava*. Her tone is the same one she would use to respond to a waitress at a restaurant that told her they were out of the type of toast she ordered. *No biggie. Get the wheat instead of the rye.* "Okay, we pick up whatever we can lift."

In addition to carrying any possessions needed for survival, Yiayia Athena had her children to bring with her. Some of the older children had to carry the little ones. Tom was about two and a half at this point, and Andy wasn't born yet. Oh yeah, did I forget to mention that Yiayia Athena was pregnant and carrying Andy in her belly during this time? *Yeah, that.*

"My two older sisters, and mother, and neighbors, and grandparents—we left. We passed the water. I remember just like yesterday. My mom carried Tom across and my mom's friend carried me across," Kathy says.

Tom remembers crossing the river a bit differently. He tells me, "We had to evacuate the house, so we loaded the bull with all of our household stuff, pots and pans and stuff, and we went to cross the river to the other side," Tom says.

"I could hardly walk, I was like two years old, and my mom tied a horseshoe on a string and said, 'Pull this.'" The bull was the one they had acquired via the Marshall Plan. The behemoth. They kept the bull while in exile, but once they returned to their home they couldn't afford to keep it. He was too expensive to feed.

After wading across the river, the Skoutelas family walked for a while before stopping at the home of a family friend. The woman kindly agreed to feed the children and let them warm up for a bit before they continued traveling. She made them spaghetti. Whether it was due to the rigorous trek or the woman's natural talent for cooking, Kathy was impressed with the meal. "Oh my God, that was gourmet. For real. So grandfather and I started to eat and Tom was waiting, and the lady said, 'The boy, he no eat. Why?' And Tom goes, "You didn't bring me a knife.' 'We don't have no knives,' the lady said."

When Kathy laughs, her laughter sounds just like it is spelled. Hah-HAH! She titters loudly, remembering how Tom attempted to be so proper and civilized, particularly at this point, having left most of their belongings behind, their house abandoned, with no real refuge in sight. "He wants a knife!" she shrieks.

After being warmed by the fire, bellies full of *macaronia*, the family continued on their journey until they reached their destination.

"We put some pine tree branches around and made a shack and that is where we lived all winter. We lived there for a year and a half. In the summertime we had a beautiful time. We didn't know any better. But winter was horrible."

Ummmm, I couldn't have heard her right.

Is it possible that Kathy just spent five minutes telling me the story of Tom wanting a knife, and thirty seconds on the story about living under pine tree branches for a year and a half?

No way.

"Wait, what?" I blurt out. "You lived under PINE TREES?"

"Oh yeah! For a long time, too!" Kathy replies.

". . ."

I look around at her kitchen, at the freshly painted cabinets, the newly refinished hardwood floors, the neatly lined bottles of ouzo and wine on the shelf next to the sink.

"WHAT?!"

I'm incapable of saying anything else. I'm having a hard time digesting this.

Tom confirms that I wasn't hearing things and that his sister hadn't lost her marbles. They actually left their house and, with no shelter available, were forced to live in the wilderness.

"I don't know how this could never have come up before!" I shout at him in his own kitchen. I'm feeling a little hurt, actually. I thought I knew them so well and this is a pretty big thing not to know.

He shrugs.

"How did this never come up before?" I demand.

He shrugs again.

I'm starting to have serious doubts about being able to document the full scope of their time in the *xorio* in any self-respecting manner.

"Well, what do you remember about it?" I'm not ready to quit trying yet.

"I remember walking down and my dad crossed the river and we lived under the pine trees, and we made a little cover out of ferns so we could stay underneath there." Many of the displaced members of the village had gathered together in this location. Kathy provides more detail: "Everyone was there, twenty to thirty families. We created a little nest with the pine tree branches. We were all pretty much near each other."

Most people had brought as many of their animals with them as they could. Goats, sheep, and pigs were penned in one area. "We mixed all the animals together," Kathy says. The villagers literally lived off the land. Tom points out that they "didn't have a tent or anything" but, despite having no formal housing, the families attempted to set up the area to create as normal an environment as possible. One of the features Tom remembers was "a little kiosk: four posts with ferns on top for a roof, no sides, selling ouzo and some roasted garbanzo beans." He remembers the kiosk as an oasis in the area and speaks of it fondly. He tries to remember the name of the man selling the goods, but he can't come up with it. "I forgot that guy's name. Geez, I forget everything now," he admonishes himself.

"Yeah, Tom," I say. "How could you forget the name of the guy who sold you garbanzo beans when you were a toddler?" I ask him sarcastically.

"Ah . . . what was his name?!" My teasing doesn't lighten his mood. He isn't used to forgetting things, like I am. I'm the kind of person who forgets why I went into a room the moment I walk through the doorway.

Yiayia Athena's father, Elias, was one of the few men who was living outdoors with the women and children, since "he was old, so nobody bothered him anymore. He was an old schoolteacher." Elias treated his grandchildren from time to time.

"My grandpa used to buy us chickpeas. He bought us those or raisins." I know Tom enjoys chickpea dishes quite a lot. Maybe his love for the beans stems from this "luxury" he was indulged with periodically as a young child. "They were kind of nice, I miss them!" He laughs, knowing how absurd it sounds to miss the village food of the dispossessed poor.

Though they were living in a forested area, the group was relatively close to a small village nearby.

"Why couldn't you stay with people in that village," I ask. It might have been a burden, but considering they were living like refugees, I don't think it would have been all that unreasonable.

Then again, as we saw with the Syrian crisis, when it comes to refugee needs, people in the U.S. can become pretty damn unreasonable.

"There was nowhere to stay in the village. Everyone was in tiny houses," Kathy tells me. Even though they were still in their homes, the people in the nearby village were needy themselves. Still, they helped out any way they could. "They don't have much either, you know. But most of them have potatoes in that area. Every once in a while we'd go to their village, they would give us potatoes or bread." As the seasons changed, the warmer weather brought with it some relief. Not only did the improved climate provide some comfort, but the animals the group had brought with them began to pay off, producing milk that could be drunk or made into cheese and butter. This made the group feel better about taking bread, potatoes or macaroni from the villagers nearby, as they were able to trade for them with their dairy products.

The warmer weather also brought a baby, born under the pines. Kathy states, matter-of-factly, "And then comes May. Andy was born under the pine tree. May 29. No doctor, no food, no nothing. We have milk by then, that's all we had." I shake my head as she tells me this.

Theio Andy was born underneath pine trees. He was born underneath pine trees because *that's where the family was living.* It's unfathomable to even think about. It's like trying to understand the vastness of the universe. You might watch a show or read about it, but actually comprehending the scale is just impossible. Our brains can't fully grasp it.

In the fall after Andy was born, about a year after the Skoutelas family had fled their home, they were hit with another blow. "My mom's sister Eleftheria got sick. Cancer." It took an extreme circumstance for them to seek out a physician and this was one that qualified. "They took them to far, far away, to the capital, and then there was a doctor there." The trip was for naught. "The doctor said the aunt has breast cancer and there is no cure for her." The doctors told the family that she should be taken back to her home so she could die as comfortably as possible. "But we cannot go back to the village. If we go back, we'd get killed."

They couldn't risk heading back to their home, as they hadn't yet received word that it was safe to return to the village. Even if the guerrillas had left the area, there was no guarantee that their home was even still standing. "A lot of houses got burned over there."

So they returned to their outdoor den. Kathy's tone turns somber and she shows me a side of herself that she generally keeps well-guarded behind her sarcastic humor. Her typically buoyant affect is weighed down by the sadness of the memory. "My aunt died in the pine trees. We buried her. I remember that, that is never going to go away. I am terrified from that. Five or six of us relatives and we buried her in the field." Their aunt was only twenty-nine years old.

When I heard these stories for the first time, I was pregnant with our second child, Daphne. I felt weary and exhausted from working fifty hours per week, keeping up with my one-and-a-half-year-old, and being in full-on nesting mode, obsessively scrubbing every square inch of wall in our home. I went for a walk around the block one afternoon and ended up coming home in tears because I felt so tired after a short turn around the neighborhood.

But even then I didn't have a clue what true weariness and exhaustion feel like. Sure, I was a little tired, a little run down, but I didn't have six other children, I wasn't tending to the herds or fields, or making my own clothing, bedding, and *housing*. I wasn't running for my life from political fanatics. I cannot imagine these circumstances, because I haven't had to.

Good God, I hope I never come close to that level of understanding.

Yiayia Athena had no doctors, no hospital, no time to rest (before or after giving birth); she indeed had "no nothing," as Kathy put it. Maybe that's not entirely accurate. She had guts. And stamina. And will. And a whole lot of fight in her. That woman was tough. She had no choice but to be.

Sometimes we give superhero-like attributes to people who are able to withstand tough times or circumstances. We say things like, "I couldn't do it!" or "I don't know how she does it!" I think it might make us feel better, to think that they have some special powers that allow them to survive through unimaginable circumstances because, by believing this, it gets us off the hook when we grumble about our own, often trivial, complaints. We give ourselves the excuse of being so much weaker than these everyday superheroes and, in turn, give ourselves permission to embellish the severity of our own struggles.

After about a year of living under the pines, the "head of the town told us we had to leave." The whole village was evacuated, not just the pine-tree dwellers, because there was word that the guerillas were headed that way. "They said 'They are coming here.' It was a horrible time."

The *xorio* residents again picked up what they could carry and walked for a few days until they reached their new destination: another outdoor venue, several miles south of the pines. Kathy speaks of this location with distaste: "We went there and it was horrible. It was like no forests, there was only trees, like maple, but not maple, but full of allergens." I don't have to understand what she means to know it sucked.

"After a year of living outside in the woods, you were worried about allergens?" I ask.

"This place was worse," she says. "We had nothing to build little shacks out of, so people had to search far and far to find branches. Had to go far away to get water, no good for the animals we have. No good place at all." Not only were the conditions less than satisfactory, there were now many more people. "The people was maybe two hundred families in a distance like my property, maybe a little more." When she tells me this, I look up and scan her property line. Kathy's plot is a little more than an acre in size. "Crowded. A lot of fights. People were so frustrated. Kids fought. Older people fought. One person had a little more and people would steal from you." She doesn't have anything good to say about this place. "We stayed there about six months. I never will forget that. The place further south was horrible."

In May of 1949, after six months of living in the second outdoor space, and about eighteen months of living away from their village, the Skoutelas family was told they could return to their home. "We came back and I remember the first thing I saw when we go back after close to two years. The first thing—the cat. Waited at the doorstep." Kathy shuts her eyes and smiles, telling me, "He was a beautiful cat. He was black and white."

Their house was thoroughly covered in weeds after being empty for so long. "And thank to God nobody burned our house. When we left my papou said, "'Leave your house wide open, don't lock it.'" Their papou Elias knew that the guerillas would likely be entering the houses, using them for shelter or nosing around for supplies. "He said if you locked it they would bust the doors and burned your house." Apparently he had good foresight.

"All of our neighbors' houses got burned."

Evidence of the burnings linger today. The village offices that kept official documents were destroyed. "Birth certificates, they have them in the office. They have a little office, everybody's from the village, that's where they keep all the papers." Somehow, when new papers were issued, my mother-in-law's birth year got changed.

"How did the date get changed?" I ask.

"I don't know what happened to that," she says. "They don't tell me either why they put me that." She's not sure why they wrote the incorrect date. "They burned the papers and everybody's guessing when everyone was born, I guess," she tells me.

There weren't enough people to recreate and file the papers, so it was an ugly scramble getting documents back in order. "Even if my dad told them, they never remember and guess and put the date down, and no one went back to check." It sounds to me like whoever filled out the forms basically tried remembering birth dates from memory.

"The same thing happened with Tom's birth date?" His birth date got screwed up too. Wrong month and day.

"Yes!"

"Were they in the same place, both of your papers?"

"No. His were in the village next to mine," she tells me.

"So his office place burned down too?"

"Yes, everybody."

"They burned all the government offices?" I ask to clarify.

"Yes, everything." Glykeria is being incredibly patient with my questioning. "Offices, houses, people burning and did everything."

"This was all during the civil war?" I ask this because up until now the only thing I had heard about this was that their birth certificates had burned in a fire. For some reason I had assumed they were kept in the church and the fire was random. I also thought the dates on their IDs got screwed up when they came to the States; I didn't realize it had happened in Greece, so much earlier.

"Mmm hmmm."

"But both your houses were alright?"

"NO! My house burned down two times. Before I born, my dad was in the fighting and my mom send them in a different place because the army was coming there and they burned my house there. They burn it down, not the whole thing, they put fire and damage the house," she says. "Oh yeah." She nods her head.

Eight-year-old Kathy was ecstatic to be home, and to find her house intact. "Everything looked so beautiful!" Unfortunately, her joy was short lived. "We stayed there maybe two, three weeks, they told us to leave again."

"No way." This story just keeps getting worse.

She nods silently.

The Skoutelas family was displaced for a final time when the Greek army informed the people that it would be dangerous to stay, due to guerillas traveling through the area. The group moved to a slightly bigger town of which their own village was a "suburb." The town had been largely untouched by the war, and while they were by no means a well-off bunch, they at least had enough for the mayor to tell them to stay in their homes. Kathy got the impression that the people living there were not very receptive to the idea of housing refugees.

"They see us as strangers, like, 'What are you doing in my area?'" The couple they stayed with had nine kids, and there were now another six of them cramming into the small villa. "The husband was a sweetheart, but the lady, UGH!" Kathy complains. The family resented being burdened by the war, and by the strangers they felt forced to house and feed. I think about our current situation with the Syrian refugees. So many are, at best, hesitant to help, and at worst, adamantly opposed to helping.

"Every chance she has to take it out on us, she would," Kathy says. "'You aren't supposed to do that. You are supposed to do this! You took this away from me!'" she mimics her with a shrieky voice. "This lady, she hated us so bad. She didn't have no choice, they put us in her house because they told her to."

As if to prove her point about what a witch she was, Kathy tells me, "Every morning, she would grab big buckets of water and she'd throw it down and wash the floors, hardwood floors, and the water would drip down onto the poor animals underneath. Mom said, 'Don't do that! You're going to kill them!' She said, 'I don't care.'" Apparently this epitomized her demeanor, and she showed disregard for every living being in her house.

"We stayed there a few days, my mom says, 'I've had it.' She said, 'I'm taking my kids and going back to my house and I don't care if they kill me, I'd rather be killed than take this abuse.'" The mayor convinced Yiayia Athena that going back was too dangerous.

Tom's memories from this time differ from his sister's. He was much younger and he doesn't recall feeling the animosity from the families whose homes they stayed in. In fact, he hardly remembers the families at all, but he does remember the soldiers. He said that they looked out for him, were nice to him. "They gave me food, rice and raisins, and they were giving me other stuff. I remember one of the soldier's was named Makki."

Kathy tells me that Tom always wanted his mother's attention and he didn't want to be changed, clothed, or bathed by anyone else. Kathy says, he "always wants to go with the mom, and that guy, Makki, calling him, giving him raisins, peanuts, cookies." Makki distracted Tom and allowed Yiayia Athena to get work done around the house.

It didn't always work out that way. One time, "Tom, he no take it, he wants to go after my mother someplace." While he usually accepted the gifts from the soldiers and got along particularly well with Sergeant Makki, he tells me about a day when he wasn't so gracious. Tom prefaces the story by saying, "I was a little spoiled probably. Well, I WAS spoiled."

Makki came out of the house and said "here," holding his hand out and motioning to a little metal box a couple of inches long, containing some raisins. Tom said "No!" He says he was mad about something at the time, but he can't remember what. Based on what Kathy has told me, I'm guessing he wanted his mom. Makki said to him, "If you don't take it, I am going to throw it away." Tom still refused and after coaxing him several times to no avail, the sergeant threw the metal tin across the porch. On impact, the tin popped open and raisins exploded everywhere across the stone. Tom admits with a chuckle, "Later I picked up the raisins off of the porch and ate them."

The Skoutelas family stayed on as unwelcome guests for six months. In November, about two full years since they were originally displaced, Yiayia Athena had truly had enough. "My mom says, 'I'm going home. I don't care what happens.'" The family packed up the few belongings they had carried with them and headed back to their home. Not too long after, Papou Lambros came out of hiding and joined them. Kathy remembers he returned with long, shaggy hair, ripped clothing, and a scar from a bullet that had gone through his left arm. He had aged immensely. "I remember he came back as an old man."

I turn my head away from my computer when I'm editing this section and look at my husband. "It's really too bad we didn't start getting these stories before Yiayia died. Can you imagine all of the stories she could have told?!" I spit out a laugh, a rough bark that resonates with regret. That vocalization still echoes through the empty voids, reverberates through all the gaping holes of information that this woman could have filled if we had thought to ask her about her life when she was still alive.

For the millionth time, I think to myself that this compilation of stories won't be good enough. That it might not be worth doing at all, with so many missing moments embedded between each sentence I string together. I take a deep breath. "Well, I guess that is why we're getting the stories from your parents now." I continue typing.

GREEK CIVIL WAR
A 70th birthday. Maybe.

We're over at my in-laws' house. It is my father-in-law's 70th birthday. Maybe.

"I don't know, we didn't have records. Just my mom saying the date. You think she could remember?"

"I'm pretty sure your mom would remember the day you were born, Tom."

"I think I'm older."

"You really think you're older than 70 years old?"

He nods his head in affirmation. "How could I remember some of that stuff from when I was two? I mean, I really remember it! I remember crossing the river on my dad's shoulders. We used to say to the mules, 'Whoosh!' to make them go faster. I said to my dad, 'Whoosh!' and he almost threw me in the river," he chuckles.

"You know, they used to wait to register the boys. Wait a few years so they wouldn't be in the war. Would be a few years older before they had to join the army," he tells me. "I'm probably . . ." he shrugs his shoulders, ". . . 75 maybe?" he says. "Who knows?"

In my head, I tell myself that I really need to finish these stories as quickly as I can.

GREEK CIVIL WAR
In exile

Glykeria doesn't have as many memories of the civil war to share.

"I don't remember anything because I wasn't born yet, but my parents said they were roasting a pig and burned the house down," she says, talking about the guerillas. The guerillas captured her dad and he was missing for six months. Eventually he escaped.

"From Athens to the village, he walked. Seventeen days to *xorio*," Glykeria says. When he got close to the house, he found it was guarded by guerillas. He went to a friend's house, explained that there were guerillas everywhere and asked if they would hide him. "Stayed there for three, four days and one night they took my dad to our house," Glykeria tells me. "My dad showed up and his dad passed out. Didn't expect to see him again," Glykeria states.

"What was your grandpa's name?"

"Giorgos," she says. Her brother's name, too. I should figured that out, since the first born male is always named after the dad's father.

"My grandpa was so excited and was so sad because he thought the guerillas were going to come after them and kill everyone."

Yeah. That would cause some anxiety, I imagine.

"He saw the kids, my sister and my brother, and he wanted to kiss them and the kids said, 'There's Dad!' so my mom had to cover their mouths so no one would hear them. Then my dad went to live in a cave and hide."

Which is worse, the forest or the cave?

Glykeria's grandfather ferried him to the cave and periodically brought him food and supplies. "He stayed for three, four months," she tells me. "One night he was out, helicopters were around and they saw him, so they knew where he was hiding and he had to move away from the cave and went to a different place to hide." In a situation strikingly similar to Yiayia Athena encountering Agelada, "In the '80s, one of those guerila guys met my dad, they just happened to meet, and the guy said, 'I wish we were somewhere else right now. I'd still kill you.'"

It took a while, but life eventually got back to normal once the war ended. While people moved on, many felt compelled to do something to actively protect their country. Tom nods proudly as he tells me, "Glykeria's dad did. He stayed as a national guardsman after the war ended. Anyone who wanted to join, you went in once a month or something. Reserves."

Getting these wartime stories is particularly difficult. Some of what Tom and his siblings remember is based on the family rehashing the stories after the war was over. Any memories that are their own can't fully be trusted, since they were so young at the time.

"I don't know if I got it right, Tom," I tell him at one point, seriously concerned that what I'm writing down isn't totally correct.

"I don't know myself!" he responds.

Tom shrugs off the wartime experiences, at least on the outside, dismissing the significant turmoil and upheaval he and his family experienced. I suppose he's been that way his whole life. In his laid-back tone he tells me, as if it explains why these stories had never been brought up in my presence, "During peace times though, we were nice. We were happy."

SCHOOL
A classroom by the creek

I call Glykeria. "Want to come over tomorrow morning? I have physical therapy in the afternoon, so if you want, come early."

"How early?"

"Whenever." My in-laws get up at the crack of dawn. My kids get up slightly after that. "I'm going to make the kids breakfast and then take them to daycare. Come over for eggs, bacon and pancakes if you want."

"No no, we don't eat breakfast."

I'll have regular coffee too," I say, trying to lure them in. They don't like French press. They don't like flavored. They only drink Maxwell House. I do not have Maxwell House, but I have a breakfast blend from a local coffee shop, so I figure they might not hate that. I mean, probably they will hate it. But maybe not.

"Do you want me to make something? Make breakfast?"

"No, no, no, I'm just telling you our plans." I honestly don't know if she wants me to tell her to cook, so she has something to do when she comes over, or if she just thinks I suck so much at it that I'm reaching out for help. Both seem equally plausible.

I can hear Tom in the background, asking her what I'm saying.

"She's asking if we can come over tomorrow. To ask us some questions," she replies.

"Eggghhhhh," I hear Tom grunt. I can't see him but I'm guessing he rolls his eyes and pushes away air with his hand, dismissing me over the phone lines.

"Well, I'll probably come over Christine, even if he doesn't," she tells me.

"Tell him the guy is coming to start demoing our kitchen," I say. We have a guy knocking down the wall between our family room and kitchen. "He might want to see that." Half the time my father-in-law comes over, he and my husband end up repairing leaky plumbing, patching some drywall, or doing some other project. This time we've hired someone, which doesn't happen often.

"We'll see."

They can never make plans. Never until the day of an event. It's cool. They usually come when we invite them.

The girls get up late the next morning, so I am still making breakfast when Tom and Glykeria ring the doorbell. They walk in just in time to hear Penelope say, "Mom. Don't make the pancakes like you did that one time." I tried making some healthy pancakes from scratch once and they were horrible. We each took a bite and then I threw them straight into the trash. She reminds me of this every time I make her pancakes now, even though I succumbed to the box mix a long time ago. I run outside for a minute and Glykeria mans the griddle. She flips the pancakes over and each one of hers turns out a perfect golden brown. They do not match my mottled ones when she scoops them onto the serving platter.

"Do you want some coffee, Tom?"

"Well, I was going to run to the gas station to get some in a minute."

"There's coffee in the pot, already made."

"Well, I like the other one better," he says. "Ah, okay, I'll take a cup. Why not?"

He's living on the edge today.

When the kids finish eating, I say, "Let's go! Time to go to daycare!"

"What am I going to do here with the kids gone?" Tom says loudly, making sure the girls can hear him.

"Don't leave! Don't leave, Tom." I try to sound fierce. It's summer, the time of year when I can buckle down and work on the stories. Time is precious.

I drop my kids off at daycare and I come back home to find that my mother-in-law has washed all of my dishes and cleaned up the breakfast plates. I thank her and she responds, "No problem, you want me to do anything else?"

A litany of tasks I should do around the house scrolls through my mind. Anything I want help with, all I have to do is ask. The temptation is there, but that's not why I asked them to come over. I need to interview them, so I tell her to sit down.

"Tell me about what school was like for you guys."

"School?" she asks me. Her tone indicates that I'm asking a ridiculous question and her time is probably better spent doing my laundry or something. "School!" She repeats the same word but this time her tone says, *It's just school, Christine. What more do you want to know?* My mother-in-law's limited English vocabulary has never impeded our conversations. So much can be said with inflection alone. Even so, I've often wondered how different she would sound to me if I could understand her when she speaks in her native language.

Without any more prodding from me, she starts talking: "Going to school with sixty-two kids in one school. In one room, all of it. They used to put you in orders, you know. First, then second, then third, all the way to sixth grade." She uses her hands to indicate that the students sat in rows by grade level. It wasn't unusual for a school to have so many children at once. "Some others were more kids," Glykeria adds.

"When I started, 1953, they didn't have a teacher in our school," Tom says. "Well, actually, we didn't have a school," he says.

Little difference there.

"I had to go someplace else, down in the village." It was crowded, "A hundred and fifty. One teacher. A school room full of kids."

"That's way too many kids."

"They didn't even know you were there," he agrees with me. "I went there two months."

After a couple of months, his village started holding school nearby, but it was a few years until they had a teacher stick around for the long term. Tom speaks fondly of the teacher who finally stayed: "An army guy. That teacher was a good guy. He wanted to teach you everything. Dedicated." Until he arrived, new teachers rotated through every couple of months. The kids studied in various locations, first at the church and then in a few different homes in the village, until a schoolhouse was built. About thirty or forty kids attended the new school. A much more reasonable number.

"We had an earthquake. 1965, I think," Tom tells me. "Biggest one we ever seen. We didn't have school yet, we were holding school in a house. Empty house. They had moved out, so we used the room as a school. The little ones were in the front by the door. I was one of them. As soon the earthquake, teacher says, 'We gonna get out.' We piled up. One door, that was it."

They were all holding on to the doorframe, but there wasn't enough room for everyone.

"The big kids in the back couldn't get to us. This guy jumps out of the window, takes off," Tom says. His teacher was dedicated, but not at all comfortable with earthquakes. "After that, we didn't hold school in the house anymore. Picked up our desks," he points his hand away from his body, his arm in a straight line, "out, found a little flat spot, setback of a creek. And that's where we finished school that year."

The setback of a creek. I shake my head.

I ask Tom what kind of lessons they had and he tells me, "Reading, math, grammar, history, religious history. Tests we had just about every other day, just about the previous lesson. Reading and grammar every day. Then every once a week, religious education. Sometimes a priest was coming in, or we had the textbook."

"Did you use paper? Or like, slates?" I'm about seventy-five percent sure he's going to tell me they used slates.

"Paper, paper," he says with his mouth. His tone tells me he thinks I'm a little ridiculous.

"You ready, Tom?" Glykeria asks.

She's been hearing him prattle on about school for a while now—a topic she doesn't have a whole lot to contribute to. She's not talking, cooking, cleaning, or taking care of the kids, so she's bored. Maybe I should have asked her to clean my windowsills. Tom's not quite ready to leave, but I know I'm working on borrowed time.

Tom was an academic all-star. As a sixth grader, the teacher would have him teach the religion and history lessons to the third graders. He would read aloud from the book and then lead question and answer sessions with the younger kids. He was voted school president for three years in a row.

Tom has always been a natural academic. Even before starting school, he enjoyed writing the alphabet. As he got older, he'd read anything he could get his hands on, from the magazines and newspapers his dad brought home after completing a stint of work, to the old newspapers that were used to wrap goods sold at the market. He devoured the words, consuming the ones he didn't recognize with the same insatiable appetite as the ones he did. He'd rewrite sections of the text for fun. "I used to fill a whole notebook. I copied just about everything."

He pauses, looks down, and shakes his head. I can see him reliving a memory before he speaks. "I filled the whole notebook, then I start erasing!" he barks, looking at me again while he chokes on his laughter. "One notebook for the whole year. That's all you got!" It was the one material possession he craved. "Man, I wish I had the books and the paper. I could read, write. I could do that all day long." No piece of paper he encountered was safe from his grasp: "Every scrap of magazine that came along, I stuck in my pocket. Wrote until it wore out."

I guess that explains why he traded the stolen pocket knife for a notebook. Paper was more precious than gold.

Tom remembers when his uncle, Father Gregory, came to visit after moving to the States. He pulled two large brochures from his suitcase and handed them to Tom. Tom pored over those magazines, enthralled by the images.

"I remember it showed pictures of the redwoods in California. Huge pictures that showed the guys chopping them down so you could see the comparison. We didn't have anything like that, and that stuck in my mind; the trees looked huge."

The other brochure showed images of jet airplanes. Tom remembers trying to decipher the text. "I was trying to figure out the words, but I couldn't read it." He specifically remembers seeing the word "people" and pronouncing it "pey-oh-pley" and not understanding what it meant. "I kept those books. I hung on to those two brochures for a long time, I wanted so bad to read." He adds further, "Ever since I saw those brochures, I wanted to go to America."

In regards to his desire for paper and reading, Tom most certainly has achieved his American Dream. He can almost always be found sitting in his blue recliner filling out a crossword puzzle or reading a book on his Kindle. Even when he's outside smoking in the garage, he's got the Kindle in one hand, the cigarette in the other. I once saw him shoveling the snow like that, the shovel in his left hand, the Kindle in his right.

"Stop buying him Amazon cards," Glykeria told me once. She meant it, too.

"What else would we get him?" It was a serious question. He uses the Amazon cards solely to purchase books for his e-reader. His Kindle is a black hole that swallows books from the internet's massive virtual bookshelf. Every book nearby gets sucked in. The only other thing we can ever think to get him for his birthday or on holidays is a gift card to Speedway, the gas station where he buys coffee once or twice a day. Books and coffee, coffee and books. He doesn't want anything else, other than Winstons, which we let him buy on his own.

"I'm serious. All he does is read, read, read. Nothing but sitting the couch," she told me. "Never moves."

I wouldn't help but snicker. A lot of women complain about things their spouses do, but reading isn't usually at the top of that list. Nothing is going to get that man to read any less, especially not nagging from his wife. In my opinion, you can't just give someone a gift card to a gas station and call it good, so I know damn well that an Amazon gift card is exactly what we will get him.

"I mean, I know the books is good, too, but that's too much," she sighed.

SCHOOL
A custodian, a haircut, and possible dyslexia

Glykeria wasn't class president, but she was one of the students who helped take care of the school. "They call me a *militria*, to clean the school and everything."

"Custodian," Tom translates. "Like a custodian."

She, along with her friends Christina and Kiki, worked every day to maintain the place. They lit the wood stove in the morning and cleaned the erasers in the afternoon. During recess they would line up the desks and clean them. This is the one aspect of school she enjoyed and is one of the few things I can almost picture. At home she is constantly cooking, cleaning, and tidying up. She comes to our house and washes and scrubs and asks if there is anything to fold. If she has nothing to do and we're sitting on the couch just relaxing, it won't take long before she'll get antsy and leave. If we're outside pulling out fifteen overgrown raspberry bushes that line our fence, she'll stay all day, ripping out shrubbery with her bare hands for hours, outworking us all.

Tom was in charge of a few odd jobs at the school as well. "I was the barber. Hair has to be short. So he gave me, our teacher, he bought a hand-operated, because no electricity, like the clippers." He starts making a scissoring motion with his fingers while he says, "Ch ch ch ch ch."

"Oh my God, how did those things cut?"

"Easy! Beautiful!"

"Really?" I'm surprised.

"Oh yeah!"

"What other weird things did you have to do?"

"Every day we check the ears, hands, nails. They had to be all clean. Everything. Check the bottoms of feet," Tom lists. I think about the desks set up in the setback of the creek. I imagine they skipped checking the bottoms of feet when they were educated in that classroom.

"Checking for lice, for all those bugs and everything. Those people didn't have soaps and stuff, and they just yucky dirty," Glykeria adds. I find it ironic that, because of her broken English, she makes it sound like she wasn't one of "those" people.

"We didn't have anything!" Tom's decibel level shoots up. "Couldn't change clothes. Once in a while you change it. Just wash it and put it back on."

In terms of academics, Glykeria doesn't have any fond memories. "I was not very good," she tells me.

"You didn't like school?"

"No." It's a firm no. "It was hard and not easy for me."

Tom chimes in, "I think she might have, ahh, whatcha call it. Dyslexic. Sometimes she switches the *b* and the *d*, you know?" He moves his pointer and middle finger back and forth, back and forth, illustrating the switching. "The thing is, at school either you got it or nobody cared."

"I can't remember things, Christine. Five minutes after I learn them, poof! Gone," she tells me.

SCHOOL
A falsified document

"Like the Chinese kids, we were! Child labor!" Tom yells.

"In third or fourth grade they didn't send me to school so I could watch the farm," Glykeria adds.

In the village, going to school was viewed more as an option than a requirement. This was particularly true for girls. "All the girls out with the animals. Couldn't go to school because no one to watch the goats or sheep." Tom explains.

There were no compulsory attendance requirements when they were young, but eventually the laws began to change and participation in formal education was mandated for all children.

"What did they mandate?" I ask. "K-12?"

Glykeria shakes her head. *No.*

"K-6?" I guess again.

"Yeah," she says. But no K. Started first grade."

Tom and Glykeria grew up right in the middle of this shift. "Tried in the '50s to start that, with Kathy." Tom talks about how it might have sounded good, but in reality it was difficult for older children to start school at square one. He shakes his head and says, "Fifteen or sixteen, trying to go to first grade. I was going first grade and there was fifteen-year-olds. But after that it settled down, we were kind of the last part of it."

There was not a high school in the village; the closest high school was located about twenty-five miles away. Since there were no cars or busses, my in-laws would have had to move there to attend. Instead, both attended through the sixth grade. After Tom and Glykeria had moved away, a school for seventh through ninth grade was opened in the village, but it wasn't open long. Village residents also had access to night classes to continue their education and complete their high school credits.

Changes in laws eventually made it difficult to get a job without having a diploma. Becoming certified or licensed was the new norm for all kinds of professions, not just the elite ones. In addition to many kids not attending school because they had to tend to the animals or because there wasn't a high school nearby, "no kids went to school for about ten years around civil war," Tom adds. As a result, "Kids needed a favor to get a driver's license, or to get a job or something, taxi license, whatever, need to prove that you attended school."

Tom's grandfather Elias aided and abetted those in need. He was a retired school teacher and he still had his hands on an official stamp from the school system. "He would stamp the certificates even though no one had went to school for years," Tom says. "He would help these people out." He nods in approval. "Free of charge!" he adds.

SCHOOL
A ridiculous amount of fun

"I was one of those guys that didn't want to go home. Stopped someplace, playing. I always in trouble with my mom and my dad. 'You gotta come home right after school,'" Tom says, imitating his mom yelling at him for the millionth time.

"Andy? Andy was the first one." Tom rolls his eyes at the memory of his younger brother following the rules. He sighs in disgust. "School got out, he took off, go home," he tells me, sounding like the annoyed older brother that he was, angry that his sibling was making him look bad in comparison. "I said, 'Why you do that?!' Gah!" His fists are clenched and he throws out a few air punches.

"So, what did you do after school then? What did you do for fun?" I've wondered about that. Between herding, plowing, planting, sowing, reaping, washing, butchering, cooking, knitting, crocheting, sewing, carving, building . . . did they ever have any fun?

"Made our own toys," Tom answers. "With a folding knife." He raises his eyebrows, telling me with his eyes that not only were they forced to make their own toys, they had the worst tools to make them with.

"It wasn't even sharp," Glykeria adds wryly.

"Sharp?! It was soft metal! Cheapest things you get, I guess," Tom scoffs. "Yeah, we used to make our own knives if we ever found a saw blade. Boy, that was the best one for knives," Tom tells me. "And toys we made out of wood. And what we made? The things we knew. Plows or sandals, you know."

"Sandals?" I ask, confused.

"You put on the mules?" Tom explains, in that way he has where it sounds like he's asking a question.

Ah, they carved plows and saddles to play with. Things they were familiar with.

"A saddle?"

"Not like they have here, they're different," he says, totally missing that I misunderstood him for a minute there. He keeps listing things they made out of wood: "The things the women used. The *rokas*, the *drakthas*." Spinning paraphernalia. "You used to make that out of cedar. That was soft wood, but last forever. Never wore out. Never rot. Eh! Ax handles. Stuff like that. We used to make everything by hand," he says.

"What else did you do besides carve toys?" I ask them.

"Play games. Chasing each other," Glykeria tells me.

"So many things we invented," Tom says.

"What you call those things, Christine? The square?" Glykeria asks me.

"Hopscotch?"

"Hopscotch, yes. Leapfrog. Get together place for an hour, two hours. We play like the hockey, we pile up the rocks and hit them with a stick," she says.

"You throw the rock, knock them down and run. He had to pile them up and grab you, in other words," Tom says, describing another made-up game they used to play. "Things like that."

I'm sitting at their kitchen table and the two of them are standing. They're becoming more animated as they talk about their childhood games and are slowly getting closer and closer to me, their voices becoming louder and louder. They're really amped up today.

"And then we have a stick, sharpen them like this make them flat on this side, just say, thirty-five degree. Beveled, jumps up and then you have to swat the thing." Tom shows me how they'd bang the end of the little stick, making it fly into the air, similar to throwing up a pitch to themselves. "We hit them like this." He swings an imaginary stick like a baseball bat. "Hit it as far as you can and whose goes farther, wins."

"Every time snows out, outside, what they do? They put a string, long one—my mom used to make the string, how you braid the hair, from the sheep hair?" She looks at me to make sure I know what she's talking about. I nod. "And we make a string. Looooong one, and they get us a little wood like this," she raises and lowers her hand, showing me how they set the stick vertically into the ground, "and get the pan of the pita and put it on top, just like that." She says this while moving her hand diagonally, showing me how the pan sat perched on the stick. "Tie the string in here, and then the pan was up there, and they put food under for the birds. They put food under and the birds go under there and they pull the string and catch the birds."

"What did they do with the birds?" I'm a little afraid to hear the answer.

"Sometimes they eat 'em sometimes they let them go," she says.
Could be worse.

"Christmas every year, had the pig, clean the urethra of the pig, dry it out, blow it up, tie it with a string, add salt, and make a ball," Glykeria says.

I choke on my coffee. It takes me a minute to be able to breathe again. "That's disgusting." The idea of the bladder ball is equally riveting and repugnant. "Tell me more."

"Had to wait for Christmas," she tells me. The only time they could afford to eat pork. "Makes a niiiiice ball! A nice white one! Put them in a safe place from the cats. The cats loved them," she says with a grin.

I shake my head. Just when I think I've heard everything, they bring up something bizarre like this. A piggy pee-pee present.

"That's absolutely ridiculous," I tell her.

"That's all we had, Christine!" Glykeria laughs at the expression on my face.

"Our favorite toy?" Tom says, his speech slowing down a bit as he settles back into his chair. "Slingshots. Every time we got ahold of a rubber. Then they started selling them at the stores. We just didn't have money to buy them," Tom tells me. "What did we play?" He looks at me wryly as he asks his rhetorical question. "War," he answers himself. Looking back, the game held some significance, being played on the tail end of the actual civil war.

"One of my cousins, he lost his eye."

"No, he did not!" I insist. "That sounds like a tale out of a movie."

"No it's not." Tom looks at me as if he's confused. "It's the only thing we had," he says, repeating what his wife said about the pig bladder ball. "He was younger than me. He's my first cousin."

"Who got him in the eye?"
Prove it, Tom.
"One of the other kids."
"So, you're not going to snitch?"

"Oh, they knew, they were there."

Still skeptical.

"Maybe someday you meet him when we go to Windsor? At a wedding reception or something?" he asks me, thinking I'll believe him if I can picture his cousin in my mind.

He swears this is a true story.

We've deviated from the educational topics. I guess recess is usually everyone's favorite subject.

CHURCH FESTIVALS
A graceful dance and a greasy apron

"You want some coffee, Christine?" my mother-in-law asks.

"Sure, I'll drink some."

"Good, we make more," she says. Sometimes drinking coffee is like drinking beer. You don't feel so bad about having another one if someone has one with you.

She just got done making the kids breakfast. Eggs, pancakes and sausage links. I'm supposedly an adult, one who didn't come over expecting to be fed, so I tell her I'm not that hungry and wait until the kids are done eating to make my way up to the counter and pluck a few sausages from the platter.

"Get a plate!" she tells me.

"No, no. Don't dirty one," I tell her as I shove a couple more sausages into my mouth.

The kids leave the table and start running around the living room. Penelope approaches the tape deck and pushes a couple of buttons. Greek folk music blares from the old machine, the warped tapes going in and out of tune. Even though the kids aren't currently near the tape deck, I have anxiety that they will open it up and pull out the tape from the cassette. Finding those old songs again might be difficult. Figuring out a way to put them onto cassette tapes might be even more difficult.

"Opa!" Daphne says as she hops around in circles and tries to snap her fingers.

"Let's dance, girls. *Ella.*" Glykeria holds out her hands and soon she is holding a small palm in each of hers. She shows them the steps. One, two, three steps to the right. Kick. One step to the left. Kick. The kids dance in a slow circle with their *yiayia*, kicking their feet. They get bored, being directed to move so slowly, and they release their hands and start spinning and jumping erratically to the music.

The kids are used to the rhythms. At home we listen to Greek folk music, though it is in digital format instead of tapes. My husband holds the girls, like I imagine his parents once held him, their little legs wrap around his waist while he circles the kitchen. He leads with his right arm raised high in the air, fingers snapping to the beat.

He's been dancing to these songs since he was born. Probably danced to them in the womb, even. When they were toddlers, he and his sisters starting taking Greek dance lessons at the church, each week after the Sunday service. The Greek church isn't just a place where the Greeks go to find God. It is also a place to go to find friends among the pews, donuts and a cuppa at coffee hour afterwards, and once a year it hosts the annual *panayieri*—a festival celebrating the church's patron saint. These festivals include an abundance of music and dancing, baklava and gyros, plastic cups full of beer and small shots of chilled ouzo.

The church *panayieri* at our church has been held every June since the year my husband was born. He and his family all work at the festival each year, each contributing in some way. Lambros, along with his sisters, cousins and friends, perform their recital on stage in front of the audience. Even the toddlers dress in the traditional garb. The boys wear *foustinellas*, *gelleko*, and *sourakia*: thick white skirts that are folded over so many times they stick out from their bodies, navy or black vests embroidered with designs, and black shoes topped at the toes with large red balls made of yarn.

The girls don *karagouna* and *mandili*: long dresses of emerald green or ruby red, and off-white kerchiefs that cloak their heads. Everyone wears thick white tights and black dress shoes. For the children, dancing and dressing in the traditional garb is their contribution to the *panayieri*. When they get older, the kids continue to dance and began to also man the food stations. The roles have not changed much over the past few decades. The boys work the *saganaki* booth, serving flaming cheese, while the girls work the *loukoumades* station, making orbs of fried dough drizzled with honey and cinnamon.

When I envision my husband as a young child, my brain brings up images of photographs I've seen when we've gone through the box of photos in his mom's closet. I see him wearing his tiny Greek dancer costume, the one with the small black vest with gold embroidery and the white skirt with thousands of folds. I see him wearing a white apron, folded up so it doesn't drag on the floor, wielding a blowtorch. A scrawny eight-year-old ready to light the *saganaki* on fire.

Even now, he and his siblings dance. Not every year anymore, but on occasion. They circle the stage with elegant and graceful steps, with kicks and hops that embody strength and softness at the same time. All of the dancers are good, but the Skoutelas siblings are outstanding. I swear, I could pick out my husband and his sisters from among all the Greek dancers just by looking at their feet. They are more graceful than the rest. They have an energy, a spirit about them that is hard to explain but is easy to spot. While many of the other feet fall flat in between steps, or lack much bounce or hop, their heels hardly ever strike the ground. Their ankles always swivel at just the right moment. When they pick up their feet, their ankles circle and arc and bend, always synchronized and graceful. I suppose I could say the same thing about their wrists or their hips, but it's their feet that my eyes always get drawn back to. Coming from someone who can't walk in a straight line, who constantly runs into the edges of door frames, their grace is something to be envied. Every time I watch Lambros dance, I am in awe. I love watching him.

The first few years I attended the Greek festival, I enjoyed watching the dancers as I sat, ate a gyro and washed it down with a cold beer. Before I knew it, though, I was no longer a guest, I was a part of the family. So they put me to work.

Wait, wait, wait, wait, wait, I have to work . . . the whole time? Seriously?

Since I'm female, I am assigned to *loukoumades*. What the white folk call the Honey Puff station. The old Greek ladies who sell the *loukoumades* to the customers come to the back of the tent, where us youngins mix and fry up the dough, to provide guidance and to ensure that our supply aligns with their demand. They say super helpful things like, "There's too many! Too many, slow down!"

A few minutes later they rush in and complain, "Hurry up! Hurry up, people are waiting!"

Even if the quantity is on point, the quality usually isn't.

"They're too doughy!"

"They're so dark!"

"They're too crispy!"

"They're too soft!"

"Look at these, they're weird shapes! What you do?"

They help us figure out why we're screwing things up so badly.

"The fryer is too hot!" they shout, and turn it down.

"The oil is old," they insist, and pour in more.

"The fryer is too cold," they complain, when the next batch looks different.

There is no point explaining to them that the variation is inevitable, with all of the factors involved. All you get is the evil eye. Let's hope you're wearing your *mati* to ward off their curses. At some point, one of us inevitably decides to take a break to go buy an insulated bag and fill it with ice and wine coolers. In that moment, the beverages are more beautiful than the dancing.

BONUS! YIAYIA'S HONEY PUFF RECIPE
Loukoumades

You will need:

Flour: 16 cups

Water: 12 cups, warm

Butter: 1 stick

Yeast: 2 tbsp. You don't actually measure this, you just use a random spoon, heap it up and call it good.

Baking powder: 3 tbsp. Same measurement tips as above.

Salt: 1 tsp

Frying oil: Yiayia uses peanut oil.

You will do:

1. Mix all ingredients except flour. Let sit to allow yeast to activate for several minutes. Add flour and combine.

2. If you're making this large of a batch, you're also using an industrial fryer. If you're figuring out how to reduce this batch, grab some dough with your hand, squeeze some between your thumb and pointer finger, and use a tablespoon to cut off a dollop.

3. Fry until golden brown.

4. Top with drizzled honey and cinnamon.

CHURCH FESTIVALS
A cheap souvenir, exploding sheep, and utter patriarchy

"Hey, what are you doing?" I ask my mother-in-law over the phone.

"Not much, why?" she asks.

"Well, I'm going to make chicken and potatoes, but Lambros bought a whole chicken and I don't know how to clean it. Can you help?"

"Sure, I'll come over now."

"Well, I need a few minutes. I was going to head to the store real quick. I realized I don't have a lemon."

"I have lemon, I bring you one."

"Well, I also need chicken base. I thought I had that, but I don't."

"I have the one I use. Want me to bring it over?"

"Sure. Thanks!"

"No problem, Christine. See you in a few minutes."

That saves me a little time, so I am able to mop my kitchen floor before she gets there, using the steam mop she got me for Christmas.

Tom comes over with her, and the men work on installing recessed lights over the new eating area between the kitchen and family room while Glykeria and I work on dinner. Once the chicken and potatoes are prepped, I sit down on the couch with Glykeria and start asking some questions.

"Tell me abou the pan-ah-yeedi," I say, trying to pronounce it correctly.

"*Ayieda trienta*," Glykeria says. She's looking at me like she expects me to know what she is saying.

". . ."

"*Ayieda trienta, sto panayieri*," she says. She doubled the number of foreign words, which doesn't clear anything up for me.

"You're talking in Greek. I don't know what you're saying." *Maybe she didn't realize.* Sometimes that happens.

"I tell you the name of the *panayieri* you said," she tells me. *Ah.* She thought I asked her what the name was of their church in the village. *Their panayieri.*

"Oh, that's the name of the church? The Holy Trinity?" I confirm.

"Yes, that's the name you said," she says, making sure I know the miscommunication was my fault.

"Goddamnit!" my husband shouts, startling us both. We turn and look at him. "I gave them the lights and they said they'd give me a little extra room and the lights don't fit." The construction workers built a soffit that apparently isn't quite big enough. He looks at the directions for installing the lights again, while his dad wiggles the metal on the fixture itself. Lambros picks up his Dremel and starts drilling out some wood from the hole that the fixture needs to fit into. "Errrrhhh." He puffs out his cheeks and then exhales loudly.

He acts like he's pissed, but this is him enjoying himself.

After a few more minutes of finagling, the two of them get the fixture all the way in.

"Smart mans, huh?" Glykeria says to me. We're talking a little, but watching them more.

"It won't lock," my husband says, having found another challenge.

"Twist it, Lambros," my mother-in-law says. "A little bit."

"They don't twist!" he shouts back at her.

"Shhh, shhhhhh," Tom says.

"It always takes longer than you think," I say to her as we watch them work.

"Take forever, I know," she replies. "Come on. Don't be stubborn, little light!" she says in a sing-songy falsetto.

The two continue working, complaining, discussing, tweaking. I hear bits and pieces of their conversation, which start in English and end in Greek, while my mother-in-law and I get back to our discussion about the church festivals.

"See how we do the festivals in here, every community? Every church, the name day, we have the *panayieri* there."

"How many churches were relatively close to your house?" I ask her.

"Ours, one, two, three, four," she closes her eyes and she counts, "five, six . . . seven. There's more churches, but those are the most that do the *panayieri*," she tells me.

In Greece, just like here, church festivals were festive occasions that brought together villagers. Even if the church was far from home, many people would travel on the church's name day to celebrate. Some had extensive festivals, with music (always a band that played the classic clarinet music) and merchants, while others had only a simple church service. The church Glykeria attended had a festival that lasted all day, beginning with a three-hour service that started at seven a.m., and continuing with food and dancing all afternoon and evening.

"What kind of stuff did the merchants sell?" I ask.

"Cheap stuff, hanging there," Tom answers as he hands my husband a screwdriver. "Sell fruits, coffee, little handkerchiefs, hats, little shirts, belts, bracelets."

"Bras," he adds, raising his eyebrows. "Some of the girls embarrassed to go buy the bras," he chuckles as he shakes his head. "One time, dad and son, they had a store in the village and then during the festival he brought them up to the festivals to sell," Tom starts. "He talked really nasally and he said to the son, "Take everything out, so the girls can see if they like it." Tom's beginning to laugh. "He meant the merchandise, not take everything out, like the boobs!'" Tom's cracking himself up. I've never heard him say "boobs," so I laugh at that. "Everyone started making fun of it, but the way he said it, 'Take everything out so the girls can see it.' It was funny. We still make fun of him years later."

"There's a gap here," Lambros says, interrupting my train of thought. "There shouldn't be a gap. I can't get these two clips to lock." He's getting frustrated. "How bad does it look? Terrible," he answers his own question. "Whatever. That's as good as it's going to get."

"Oh, it's fine. If it works, it's fine, it's not that bad," Tom tells him. A second later he says, "No. It's got to go in, we just don't know how. Just pull it on this one?" Tom gets on the stepladder and starts tugging on the light.

"He told the guy to build a ten-inch soffit. He built a five-and-a-half-inch soffit," Lambros complains.

"Okay, just cut them a little more and get them over with," Tom tells him.

"Tell him when he comes back," Glykeria says, meaning to tell the construction worker that what he did wasn't right.

"FOR WHAT? HE GONNA REDO IT? NO. SO, WHAT'S THE POINT?" Tom yells, his temper coming out. My children come from a long line of yellers on both sides of the family.

Even though the churches had festivals on a regular basis, someone had to stay behind to take care of things. Effie remembers, "We, the younger ones, didn't get to go to that many. The older ones went more than we did." The girls usually couldn't go because they had to tend to the sheep.

"You couldn't go to a lot of festivals, right?" I ask Glykeria. "You had to watch the animals, didn't you?"

"You don't know what to do with those, can't leave them in the shed all day. They have to go eat, you have to feed them. So you have to go take care of them," she tells me.

"And I remember one time," Glykeria begins, "we used to have the sheeps, you know, the *proveta* we call them, you know the sheeps? Through the summertime we get them out in the morning and the afternoon they sleeping through the shades in the trees. Five o'clock we used to get them something to eat. My cousin, she took them somewhere to eat, to *hourafi. Trifi.* How you say *trifi?*" she asks herself. "Like the clover, it is. She took them there and they got soooo too much gas, they see their tummy puff. The sheeps die of that."

"They died from eating the clover?"

"They give you gas, that's it, and they pop! Six, seven of them," she nods in confirmation.

The corners of my mouth turn down, involuntarily.

"They took the needles and they poking them, but they couldn't save it. My dad, her dad, tried to save them with cold water, but they couldn't save it," she says. She tells me that they tried to avoid that specific type of clover from being eaten: "We used to be extra careful about that."

"What did they try poking??" It sounds horrific.

"Just a little needle, you knit," she says, making sure I can envision a knitting needle, "and try to poke its tummy. You know, they blow up the tummy." She takes her hands and presses them on her stomach and then pushes them slowly away from her, hands splayed to demonstrate a distending stomach.

"That sounds horrible." I do not want to know any more details about poking the sheep.

"My cousin was crying. She was losing her sheep, crying."

After this experience, Glykeria was even more careful of that particular clover. A few years after this, she and some of her friends asked if they could send the sheep up into the mountains and leave them unaccompanied while they attended another festival. They promised to retrieve them later in the evening, after the festivities were over. The girls weren't expecting to be able to go, but surprisingly, this time, they got the okay. "We walked WAY up into the mountains to drop them off. We got all dressed up and went to church," Glykeria tells me.

The girls were only at the church festival for what seemed like a matter of minutes, when a neighbor from across the village ran over to them and breathlessly announced, "Your sheep is in someone's farm and eating the hay!" It turned out that this was more than just an inconvenience, "It was the type of hay that if they ate too much they would blow up and die. So my dad said, "RUN!"

Glykeria ran.

"I was running and running and in the middle of the run I thought I would collapse." She managed to get to the sheep before they consumed too much of the dangerous leaves. "So I missed the *panayieri*." She resigned herself to the fact that she would just have to miss out on most social events, since she had to look after the animals: "After that I never used to go anywhere."

Typically, Glykeria was able to control her temptation to ditch work, as she knew it needed to be done, but she recounts one time when her temper boiled over. It was around the Easter holiday and her mom and sister were supposed to attend a *panayieri* function at their church. Her mother woke her up so that she could go tend the sheep, but she was upset because she really wanted to attend the church event. Her mother had made some homemade yogurt, which she really liked. Glykeria, feeling slighted, said that she wanted some of the yogurt or she wasn't going to go out with the herd. "I'm not going to tend to the animals," she said in an attempt to get some yogurt.

Apparently, her mom was expecting guests to come over and she had made the yogurt especially for them. Even though she was crying and crying, her mom wouldn't give in. In a typical teenage display, when she didn't feel in control of much, Glykeria chose to take charge over anything she could. "I refused to take any lunch with me when I went out to tend the sheep. I didn't bring any food for the whole day." Her mom felt awful and came after her, begging her to take her lunch. While she might have felt badly, Glykeria raises her eyebrows and adds pointedly, "She didn't ever give me the yogurt, either."

Tom holds the Shop-Vac up and collects dust, while Lambros uses the Dremel to cut out a bit more space for the second light.
"You remember anything else from the festivals?"

"I don't know what else to say. You think I remember?" Glykeria responds.

"Nothing different than here," Tom chimes in while he works. "You just go there, go to church. Some had food, some didn't," he says. "Some just fed some other people that came from other villages. I cooked the lamb, I split it with the outsiders. The long way friends. Not the next door neighbor." He explains why it wasn't necessary to provide food for the people who lived there: "He had his own, you know what I mean. First they treated those who walked for a day or two."

"*Xenos*, Christine. *Xenos*," Glykeria says.

"Foreigners," Tom translates. "You didn't know them—you fed them."

"Have stuff for the kids. We didn't have money but something was available little toys like things or candy or . . ." His voice trails off as he turns his attention back to the lights.

"What else do you remember?" I ask them both.

"I remember one time," Glykeria answers, "at that one, the *panayieri*, I went with my parents I guess, so you know, how they have the tradition, they cook food, roast a lamb and put it on the ground and everybody sit down and eating," she says.

"Oh, I didn't realize you sat on the ground to eat," I say.

"But they have to tell you where to sit, families and friends and relatives. I was standing up and nobody told me where to sit. I was the only one standing up, no one told me where to sit!" She still sounds mad about this. "And my mom came and took me." She remembers asking her, "How come no one told me where to sit?"

"Not very smart, can't sit down without someone telling her where to sit," Tom laughs at her expense.

"I didn't know where my mom was!" Glykeria defends herself.

"First the men," he said. "Never eat together!" he tells me.

"Tradition is first the man, and then the woman and the kids," Glykeria confirms. "The men on one side, the women on the other. Still, to this day, it's like that. Always the same side. I mean, sides. Men was on the right."

"Those are old Eastern customs, Christine. The man always first. On top. Whatever happen," Tom tells me. "But the worst thing," he nods his head towards me, "the men on top of the mule, the woman loaded with whatever she was carrying, that stuff." He uses his hands to demonstrate how the woman would walk carrying goods on her back, while the man rode the mule next to her. Tom doesn't think it was right, and never did. "That's where I was a little way ahead of that time. That was a shame!"

"No one say it's a shame before," she says under her breath.

"She didn't get what I meant," Tom says to me, as if she isn't in the room.

"Nobody said that was a shame when they go on the horse and do all that," Glykeria says more loudly, remembering being the one who had to carry things, at times.

"That's what I'm saying!" Tom says. "They did treat the woman as second, or third class, or slaves actually."

"No respect for the women, in other words," Glykeria adds.

"Bend it open," Tom says to his son, turning his attention back to the lights. "Is that what you did?"

"Yeah," Lambros says, finally getting the light in place. "There!"

"Did you get it?" Tom asks him.

"Yeah," Lambros says.

"See? We solved one problem. We can do it on the rest, too." Tom is satisfied.

"That's why I said, 'Let me give you the lights before you build it.' Five-and-a-half inches for a 6-inch light," Lambros continues to complain.

"Okay, Lambros. A thousand times." Glykeria sounds annoyed.

"Turn the light on." He wants to test it and make sure it works.

The lights work. They are done.

"Okay!" Glykeria says gleefully. "Done and over with!"

"Alright Christine, you want to help me clean up over here?" my husband asks me.

I get up to help and my mother-in-law comes with me. She grabs the extension cord connected to the Shop-Vac, trying to get it out of the way.

"Mom! Stop! Don't pull it!" There is the temper he inherited from his father.

"I'm not pulling it!" she protests, right before she pulls the plug out of the wall.

"You didn't pull it?" he scoffs.

She plugs it back in and then, when he's done using the vacuum, she unplugs the extension cord again and wraps it up neatly, folding the cord around and then into itself.

"That's what I used to do with my *trihah*. My rope." She lifts it up to show me and smiles proudly.

I put the cord away, the one she just tied up like she used to tie up the rope she led her donkey with, and then go into the bathroom. When I come back out, she's vacuuming the floor.

"Why are you making my mom do everything?" my husband accuses me.

I give him a look that says, *Like I could ever stop her from doing everything.*

He lets it go.

Yiayia and Papou   225

BONUS! YIAYIA'S GREEK MAC AND CHEESE RECIPE
Makaronopita

<u>You will need:</u>

Ditalini: 1 package, uncooked. Ditalini looks like a small penne pasta that has been cut up into tiny pieces. You might not have heard of it, even though I guarantee you've passed by it on the shelf. It's right next to the angel hair and the linguine.

Eggs: 6, beaten.

Water: 2 cups

Whole Milk: 2 cups

Parmesan: You need enough to cover the top of a 9 x 13 pan. Any kind of parmesan or parmesan blend will work. A little too much or a little too little won't make or break this dish.

Feta cheese: Enough to cover the top of your 9 x 13 pan. Don't neglect the corners.

Butter: 1 stick

<u>You will do:</u>

1. Melt butter and pour into bottom of 9 x 13 pan. Coat all edges.

2. Pour ditalini in pan. Cover with water and milk.

3. Add crumbled feta cheese, spreading evenly throughout.

4. Add parmesan, following same directions above.

5. Cover layers with beaten eggs, using a fork if needed to spread around so they cover entire top.

6. Bake at 350 degrees until the top is golden brown—1-1½ hours.

LEAVING THE VILLAGE
A lemon grove

"I have more questions for you," I say as I pull out my laptop.

"If I remember," Tom says, noncommittally.

"You'll remember."

"Or, I could make something up," he says.

"You could. I already said if something isn't right in here, it's your fault, not mine." I smile.

"Well, I don't like to make things up anyway," he replies.

"I know."

"But, I'm not running for office, so I don't have to tell you what you want to hear," he laughs.

I smile and shake my head and we start talking about when Tom left the village.

Tom left home in 1959 to work. He was thirteen years old and had exhausted all of the education that the local school had to offer. He laughs as he explains that as a graduate of the sixth grade he was one of the most highly educated members of the village. Knowing how to read, write, and perform basic arithmetic made him considerably more learned than his parents.

"Dad went to third grade," Tom tells me. Glykeria's dad finished the same level.

"What about your moms?" I ask them.

"Neither moms," Tom says.

"Women don't go to school over there," Glykeria chimes in. "Why you think I didn't know, Christine?" she yells, before walking into the kitchen and pulling a fresh pan of salted cod and potatoes out of the oven.

"Well, we were just like the Arabs, we didn't want women educated and smart," Tom smirks before getting serious. "Well, those same one as the old timers, I mean. Old time, very seldom you see a girl go to school. After the 50s, when we got a state organized, then they start going to school, at least to the sixth grade."

"They make a law then, they have to go to school. Until then they have no law," Glykeria says, padding into the living room from the kitchen.

"Yeah, for boys did," Tom says, meaning that the boys were expected to go to school before then, even if the girls weren't. "The thing is, we didn't have school, so no one went to school when we had the war. For five, ten years. We couldn't go even if we want to." This didn't directly affect Tom and Glykeria, as they weren't school-age until after the war anyway, but it did impact their older siblings.

With no further schooling available past the sixth grade, and not many opportunities for work, the natural progression was for the men to seek out one or the other outside of the village. "I wanted to go somewhere to do something, it was just something that came naturally. There was nothing to do in the village. So, everybody left," Tom tells me. "After sixth grade, you're grown."

Being grown meant being able to get to work and pull one's own weight.

The men in the family went to work for one to three months, typically leaving the village in order to find a paying gig, while the women stayed at home and tended the children, house, animals, and farm. Bills and debts were paid off in this way. Work often consisted of jobs such as working at a general store, digging stones off someone's field, working on the road with crews, or taking someone's animals to sell at the markets. The closest market about forty miles away, and depending on the weather it could take up to three days to get there. One of the neighbors in the village ran a business this way.

"They'd go to all the families, ask if you had any animals to sell, and they would get them up and take them to the market and sell them. Once the job was completed, the man would make a few hundred drachmas and then head back home to his family.

Tom's first job was working on a lemon tree grove owned by the Kendopolos family. The grove housed a few hundred lemon trees on a property of twenty or thirty acres. The family lived about fifty miles southwest of the village. When Tom left to start work, he had yet to meet the family or visit the farm, so he set off with six or seven other men who were traveling in the same general direction. People in the village avoided traveling alone, if they could help it.

A few of the men had relatives who lived near the Kendopoloses, so they dropped Tom off on their way. On the three-day voyage to the farm, Tom stayed the night at a cousin's house on the way. Tom remembers seeing a well for the very first time at their place. "They had five wells, since they didn't have any other way to get water."

I ask Tom if he was nervous about leaving home. He says he wasn't really nervous, but that it probably wouldn't have mattered if he was. "I mean, I didn't have a choice, anyway," he tells me. He was reassured by the fact that even though his family and the Kendopolos family did not know each other personally, the two families had heard of one another and the Kendoploses had raised one of Papou Lambros's cousins. "We knew who they were. Good people. . . . The Kendopolos family was a huge family. There were so many of them. Some of them, they probably didn't meet each other," Tom says. Stavros and Kelli owned the lemon grove. They had three children aged two to seven.

"I was living there and so I sort of did a little bit of everything." This included taking care of the lemon trees, by trimming them, removing the dead parts and opening the branches to give the sunshine access to the rinds. "Lemons don't produce unless you graft them," Tom explains. "My boss say, 'When you grow citrus trees, they're all the same and they're all wild and then you graft what you want on it. You want an orange or a lemon?' And he showed me how to do it. Once he did, I had no problem with the tree." Tom boasts that about his grafting, "I never lost one!"

The owner was impressed. "Once he started seeing my job—beautiful! He liked that. 'You got a green thumb! Keep doing that!'" the owner told him. Tom became the grove grafter. "He didn't do that anymore." He tries explaining the process to me: "Let the tree grow to a few feet tall and once the graft, the little eye, took it from a real lemon tree with a bud. Put this little triangle with a bud in and wait until it takes. Once it starts growing, chop the rest off." The only thing he didn't do was spray the trees, as there were others who were called in to do this job.

"What did they spray the trees with?"

"Same like they do here for apple trees," Tom says dismissively, right before taking a sip of his coffee.

I nod as if I know what the hell they spray apple trees with, just like I nodded when he explained the grafting process. I might not understand it all, but I listen as best I can and am reminded there is much I do not know. These goat herders remind me that it's good to be humbled now and again.

LEAVING THE VILLAGE
A heaving herder

Tom helped take care of the animals on the property and was in charge of feeding the cows. He'd cut grass for them from alongside a ditch. "Stuff it in huge sacks and bring it back. Just get the shiv and fill up a couple bags for the cow." Tom never liked cows and this experience didn't change his mind.

"I wasn't used to cows. I didn't want no part of that cow. It smelled different. Cow poops so big! Goat poops different, smaller. Doesn't bother me." Add this to the list of why goats are better than cows.

"That's when I stopped drinking milk," Tom says. He grimaces and adds, "It was kinda yellowish. Ugh!"

I wrinkle my nose because that does sound kind of gross, and Glykeria clarifies why it was that color: "First few days after they have the babies, yellowish milk, but then not as yellow." She searches my face to see if I understand what she means.

"Like colostrum?" I ask.

"Yes, Christine," she nods.

Tom shakes his head and makes a gagging noise. "It was always the same. I have hated milk ever since. I tasted it and that was the last time I drank milk. Until here."

Glykeria remembers the one time he drank milk in the States. She was used to cow's milk, so she kept a gallon in the fridge. They also kept a gallon of water in there, to keep it cold.

"Yes, I remember that by mistake he got the milk instead of the water," Glykeria begins, telling me how she heard Tom grab a jug from the fridge. "In '75, I think, in the new house."

"We were in the old house." Tom corrects.

"Yes, that's what I said."

"I thought you said the new house."

"Yes, before we move into the new house," Glykeria replies, before continuing.

"He woke up the middle of the night and grabbed the milk instead of water." After drinking the milk, cow's of course, "All we heard in the middle of the night, 'Hiyyeeeewwww.' Puking all night!" She laughs a tad masochistically and adds, "Everybody making fun of him."

"I used to drink a little bit the old days," Tom discloses. "I'd go to the bars, we'd close the bars. I was a little drunk. I woke up and I wanted a drink. Water. I grabbed the wrong gallon. It's like four, five in the morning. Took a nice swig. Threw up!" he tells me. "When I throw up, everybody knows about it. Wake up the whole neighborhood," he chuckles.

Per usual, Tom finds a way to end this conversation with a rant about why goats are the supreme beings of the animal world. "Not like goat's milk. That I like. Goats is very clean animal, I don't care what they say. Clean, dry. They are different. We loved our goats. Every goat had a baby, we brought it in the house, it lived with us for one or three days until the baby grew up. Those I loved! Even today, I wouldn't mind!"

LEAVING THE VILLAGE
A well-dug well

Since he was basically an expert after seeing his first well on the way over to the lemon grove, one of the first jobs Tom completed while working on the farm was to help dig a well near the grove so the family could irrigate more easily. He was selected for the job because there was one older man, Barba Ted, who was working on the project and, according to Tom, "No one else wanted to do it" with him. The old man started digging with a shovel. Once he got to the point where he couldn't easily shovel the dirt out of the hole, a pulley system with a wheel at the top was put to use. Barba Ted continued digging the dirt from inside the well, while Tom sat perched at the top and used the pulley system to pull up the dirt the old man had dug, dumping it in a pile nearby. When the pile got too big to add to, he used a wheelbarrow to transport the dirt to a new pile, a little further away.

"How deep was the well?" I ask.

"Well went down fourteen meters by seven meters around. It was A LOT of dirt." Tom still seems proud of his work, nodding his head as he describes the finished product: "We went down far enough and it was wide enough." Since the purpose of the well was irrigation and not drinking, there was no need to line the sides of the well with bricks. It took a couple of weeks to complete the laborious project from beginning to end. "It seemed like it took forever," Tom remembers.

When the old man hit gravel and announced that they had gone deep enough, Tom was skeptical, but when they returned to the well the next morning, he was delighted to find it filled with water. The old man had recognized that the gravel he encountered while digging was an extension of the river bed. "I couldn't believe it! Water was nice and fresh, too. Sometimes we drink a bit out of the well, even. Water was clean," Tom says.

LEAVING THE VILLAGE
A cure for tonsillitis

The girls and I go to my in-laws' and Tom is home alone. His wife is at the store. I sit down on the couch and he tries to lure the girls onto his lap.

"*Katsi*," he says. Sit. He pats his lap with his hands and then holds his arms out to scoop them up. "Want to watch cartoons?" he sweetens the deal. They take him up on the offer and he lets them use his Kindle. With the girls on his lap, he tells me more about his first job.

In addition to the lemon grove, the Kendopolos grounds also held a small general store where sugar, flour, candies, soaps, needles, dyes or cups of hot coffee could be purchased. If there were enough people working the fields, he tended the store.

"It seems like running a general store would be a big responsibility for a thirteen-year-old," I say.

"Eh. We didn't have many customers anyway," Tom brushes it off. After a day's work, some people might come in for a coffee or to pick up a few supplies on the way home. Tom remembers a few regular customers that loved how he made the coffee. He remembers one guy in particular: "He was coming in every day. Twice a day. Old friend. I was twelve, thirteen, he was in his fifties. Barba Spiro. That's his name."

"What does 'Barba' mean?" I've heard him use that word so many times before but wasn't sure exactly what it meant.

"It means uncle. Out of respect."

"But, it's not like it really means your uncle, right? Like it could just mean family friend?"

"Sometimes is, sometimes not. Doesn't matter," Tom says. "We call old people '*Papou*,'" he adds. Grandpa. "Out of respect. You know, saw an old man, go up kiss his hands. We used to do that. Not anymore. A lot of things have gone away. Anybody older than you, you call *theia* or *theio*." Aunt, uncle. "You never call anybody by their name. Someone holler at you for disrespecting. But never on like a first-name basis with all the people, no."

I wonder if it bothers him that I call him by his first name, or that I don't always kiss his cheek every time I come or go.

"Like you have here, 'Sir,'" he clarifies further. I nod. That makes sense.

He returns to telling me about Barba Spiro. He shuts his eyes. "I could just look at the guys now, after sixty years. I could still see him," he says. His old friend's face is forever burned in his memory. Barba Spiro would tell the owner, "Stavros, let the kid make the coffee." Stavros wanted to know what it was about Tom's coffee that made it so much better: "'Okay. Whatchyou do? They like your coffee. You put too much sugar in it?'" Tom tosses his head back and cackles. It's impossible not to laugh with him.

"Uh oh," Tom says, after he's done laughing. "Someone has a dirty diaper?" He sounds light-hearted, but I know it's really a plea for help.

"I'll change her." I grab Daphne off of his lap and take her to the back bedroom where we keep diapers and wipes stocked in the closet. Tom does not change diapers. I'm not positive, but I have a hunch that he has never changed a diaper in his life. Even his own kids'.

Barba Spiro was around so much that he got to know Tom well. Tom used to get tonsillitis fairly regularly. Tom's boss was able to get him an antibiotic from a nearby pharmacy when he needed it and his old friend would see him taking the medicine, again and again. "One day he told me, 'Listen, that doesn't work. Go grab a lemon and eat. Every day. Go eat the lemons.'" He told Tom to eat at least one lemon each day.

"So, did you do it?" Tom does what he wants. If he took this guy's advice, I know he must've had some seriously deep respect for him.

"Oh yeah, I listen to him!" Tom followed his advice to a T. "I used to eat lemons better than the oranges! I got so used to it, I didn't want oranges anymore. Naval? Nope! Just the lemon." It didn't take him long to get used to eating them. "First time you get the lemon, you know, your mouth gets ehhhhh," he puckers his lips. "But you eat two, three of them a day and you get used to it."

"So, did it work?"

"Ah! My God, it worked!" Tom cackles, his voice cracking a bit as he tosses his head back. The girls, both back on his lap, look up at him and smile. Penelope pats his chest.

"You never got tonsillitis again?" I ask him, my own lips curling up at the sides in response to his laughter.

"To this day, my tonsils never bothered me again."

"That's hilarious." If only curing every illness was so simple.

"I know! Here, seventy years old, no tonsillitis," he shouts.

"When you left the lemon grove did you keep eating lemons every day?"

"No, but just about everything we cooked in Greece use the lemon. Bean soup? You had half a lemon, whether you need it or not. Fish? Two lemons. *Horta*? Lots of lemon. No matter what you did, you had lemon on it. Once in a while I grab a lemon and eat it, but not as like then, when he told me eat lemons every day. Then, I made a point. I'd walk by the tree and peel the lemon and I ate it."

"You know, I hear there's a thing right now going around about drinking a half a lemon with water every day," I say, referring to an article that's been floating around Facebook.

"They say a lot of things about honey too," Tom adds. "A spoonful of honey and lemon every morning. I don't know, that's the thing." It's hard to differentiate between homeopathic remedies and old wives' tales. The two intertwine. "I guess they didn't have anything else. Whatever they had in the ground."

He chuckles to himself and looks at me out of the corner of his eye, his lips curled up at the corner. "When we got sick, you know what was our medication? A fried egg. Or a hard-boiled egg."

I give him a quizzical look. I'm no doctor, but I'm not sure what an egg has to do with getting over an illness. I haven't seen that article on Facebook, that's for sure.

"We had two chickens. We got one egg a day, or something. Not enough for us. We were seven. So, the treat was to get an egg when they were sick."

"Oh my God." My mouth drops open. It seems so ridiculous.

"I know!" He knows how ridiculous it is. "It's all we had!"

"Did you ever get really sick?" I asked him, getting serious for a second.

"I did. One time." His solemn tone matches mine. "I didn't have the sense enough to know. I was in the first grade. And my mom didn't know what to do. I had so high a fever I was seeing things. I was seeing things flying around like. Oh this, bird, and this and that. I was grabbing them." He pauses for a minute as he thinks how he can describe it to me.

"Hallucinating," he comes up with. "Yes, hallucinating. She called my uncle. Her brother. He gave me a shot of penicillin."

"He just had a shot of penicillin?" I ask, skeptical.

"He was like a cop. A policeman." Tom says. The village constable had a few supplies that most people did not have access to. "Not aspirin, but some other yellow little pills. He had a vial of penicillin. He stuck me with it. . . . Fever wouldn't come down! I remember that. I was reaching up to grab it. And not just little bird. Some rills."

"Rills?" I ask, unfamiliar with the word, even though I'm pretty sure it's an English one.

"The sewing thing. A wooden thing that wire wraps around."

A bobbin? A spool? I figure it's probably one of those and don't question it. I pester him enough, this little detail probably isn't worth it. I'll save my harassment for later.

"We used to play with them. The only time I was that sick as a kid. I had problems with my tonsils, like I said. Tonsillitis! Tonsillitis! So I had to get penicillin. The pink stuff."

"You got that at a doctor?" I ask, thinking of the bubble gum-flavored medicine I remember taking as a child.

"You go to pharmacy and they just give it to you," he said. There was no need to go to the doctor. But he only had access to the pharmacy after moving out of the village. "That was when I left home, when I worked at the grove. It was close by and my boss was getting it for me."

"Before you started eating all the lemons," I say.

"Hahaha! Yes. Before the lemons," he chuckles.

LEAVING THE VILLAGE
A long walk home

In addition to digging wells, tending to the lemon groves and running the general store, Tom periodically babysat the Kendopolos kids. Tom remembers working but doesn't remember seeing a paycheck. He says he thought he was supposed to earn fifteen hundred drachmas a month. During one recounting of this story, he seems a bit agitated about this: "I was working like an indentured servant!" But during another, he implies that it might have been a part of the original arrangement, that his work was compensated largely with room and board. "I slept there, they fed me." It's possible his parents got the money directly.

"Did you miss your family?"

"Missed family a little bit. Once I had my friends, it was okay. It was sort of like summer camp," he replies, before adding, "My dad would come down once in a while." About a year after Tom started at the farm, his brother Andy finished school and started working nearby, for Tom's boss's father. He tended to the pigs and chickens.

"Did you see each other much?"

"Not really, no. We were close, but I was in this little part and he was in his little part and so we couldn't visit that much. We were around, but always working in our own places. Saw him maybe one, two times a week." Sometimes they'd find ways to pop in on each other: "If we were going that way for something, we'd stop by and see each other."

Tom worked at the grove for a year and a half before his first period of employment abruptly ended.

"One day I got into a fight with the guy's wife," he says. "I had a little pocket knife, about three inches long, a small one. It was engraved with a little design. It was beautiful, shiny, it was a very nice one. My old man got me that."

I glance up at him. Maybe for Christmas we could get Tom a pocket knife in addition to his Kindle gift cards. He's clearly drawn to them. Then again, maybe not. Pocket knives seem to have caused a decent amount of unnecessary turmoil in his life. And the old ladies say things always come in threes.

"One day the little boy, he was maybe five or six, he got ahold of it. He probably saw where I was hiding it or something and took it out while I was working. I came back and saw he had started digging in the ground with it and it got really dirty. I used to keep that knife immaculate, really clean, so I got so mad!"

On the first recounting of the story, Tom explains how he "Grabbed that knife away from him, and the kid screamed, he started crying and everything. The mom came out and started yelling and hollering and she was slapping me." On the second recounting of the story, Tom admits that she may have been angry at him for being too tough on her son. "Maybe I slapped him. I was so mad! I was so mad I couldn't see straight." Once the woman started in on him, Tom says he swung back at her. "I hit her once and decided to leave."

His decision was final. "In my mind, that was it." Tom went to the well he had helped dig, pulled up a pail and splashed water on his face, calming himself down. "I pulled up some water from the well and cleaned up a little bit and was on my way out." At this point, his boss had gotten wind of what had taken place. He found Tom by the well. "He gave me a nice swift kick in the butt, so I took off. Right then."

Tom was so infuriated that he left Andy there, tending the pigs, without saying goodbye. He just started walking towards home. "I took off and walked, in one day, from there to my village." Tom's fury carried him the full fifty-ish miles in a single twenty-four hour period. He appears to become energized as he tells the story.

"I was gone!" he shouts loudly. He left the grove around noon and caught up with his cousins, who were walking home from school. He joined them and walked to their house and spent the night there.

"How far was your cousin's house from your house?"

"With the *podi*," the feet, "it's about . . . six-hour walk," Glykeria tells me.

"We didn't have a way to measure that," Tom says. "You leave in the morning, you get there in the afternoon. Well, I could get there in four hours."

"Depends how fast you walking, Christine," Glykeria says.

The next morning he continued his trek home. The exertion took a toll on his body. "I was sick for a week. Dead. Dehydrated, I think. I didn't have much water or any food on the way." He didn't fully regain his strength for about two weeks after returning. Tom's dad, Lambros, went back to the grove to retrieve his things. "I left there my piggy bag. I didn't even take that."

"How did your parents react when they saw you?" I ask.

"Mom was shocked. She was surprised to see me because I was just there for a few days for Easter. She wasn't expecting to see me so soon after that." He adds, "She knew something happened because Theio Andy was still there."

This story, of Tom's return from the lemon grove, comes up again when we're sitting in his living room and rehashing the spinning process. "There was another use for *sfondili*," Tom tells me. He's got a little twinkle in his eye.

"Oh yeah?"

"That was old wives' tale again, okay? I don't know if that helped in any way." He lets me know from the get go that he doesn't necessarily buy into the pseudo-medicinal hoopla. "When you got exhausted, you're twisted, they call it then. We had the old lady put her thumb in your belly button, twist your guts back to make your strength come back, and then they put the *sfondili* in to hold it here."

I raise my eyebrows and purse my lips.

"We believed it though! It worked. I remember that *sfondili*; I had it there for a while. I was exhausted, I was dehydrated," he says. "One thing I was not was untwisted!" he laughs. "Okay, it's hard to describe. People believed it though."

"Was that the one time when you walked home from the lemon grove?" I ask him.

"That's the only time. A day later, I was good again."

"Because you got the *sfondili* twist."

"That's right."

LEAVING THE VILLAGE
A village remedy in a suburban living room

We had guests coming over, so Lambos smoked some brisket in his smoker. He cooks like his mom and there was enough food for thirty, so we invited over ten. Just to make sure there was enough. It's later in the evening now, so the kids have gone to sleep, but most of our guests are still over. I don't know how it comes up, maybe I complain that my back hurt, but my mother-in-law says to me, "You need *vendouzes*." Cupping.

"I've never had that done," I say.

"I do it," Glykeria replies. "Used to do it to Tom all the time."

"What do you need to do it?" I ask.

"Nothing. Cup. Small glass cup," she says. "Little fork, wrap towel around it to make a torch. Some alcohol. That's it!"

"Want to do it now?" I ask.

"Sure!"

We collect the supplies and I lay down on the couch in my sports bra. I'm surrounded by my husband, my parents, my sister-in-law and her husband, and my husband's cousin. Everyone is intrigued and also a little nervous. My mother-in-law is going to be wielding a lit torch pretty close to my bare skin, after all.

She wraps up the tines on a meat fork with a rag, dips it in rubbing alcohol and sets it aflame. I shut my eyes and bury my head in my arms. She heats up the inside of one of the glass tumblers we grabbed from the cupboard and when it's sufficiently heated she places it on my back. I feel my skin pull upwards toward the top of the cup, suctioning it in place.

I'm immensely relieved that I'm not burnt.

She repeats the process, and soon I have five or six cups stuck to my back. She removes the first cup. It takes a bit of effort to remove it. POP! I hear exclamations behind me, about the mark the cup leaves behind.

"Wow! Look at that!"

"A perfect circle!"

POP! POP! She removes the rest of the cups and then starts the process again. It feels good. Like a deep massage. She keeps going until the cups get too hot and actually threaten to burn me.

"Thanks, Mom," I tell her. "That was awesome."

"No problem! Anytime."

The red circles last for a week or so. The memory of how good it feels lasts much longer.

Writing about this reminds me to ask her if she will do it for me again.

LEAVING THE VILLAGE
A murdered relative, a bit of spare change, and a shared bed

On August 6th, the monastery in the area my in-laws grew up in, hosts its annual *panayieri*. I remember Tom telling me that he met up with his cousin at this festival, and that's what spurred his move to Athens.

"What was the name of the church that had that festival?" I ask. I know that the *panayieri* is based on the saint the church is named after, and I am wondering which one celebrated its name day on August 6th.

"Ahhhh, trans, trans . . ." Tom hesitates. "What's it called?"

"Transformation?" he asks himself. "When Jesus Christ transformed from living body to spiritual," he says, describing the event that the church was named after. "Holy Transformation?" he asks himself again. "Ehhh, I'm forgetting the name."

"I thought this was going to be an easy answer, like the name of a saint," I say.

"It was! Christ!" Tom admonishes me.

"Well, yeah . . ." *I guess that counts, huh?*

Glykeria walks over from her kitchen, holding the church calendar she keeps on her fridge. She points to August 6th. "Holy Trans . . . fig . . . ur . . . aton," she sounds the word out, almost correctly.

"Transfiguration!" Tom says, happy to have the name figured out. "I said 'transformation.' Holy Transfiguration of Christ," he says. "My great, great, great papa died in there. They hung him inside the church."

"What?" I was not at all expecting that to come out of his mouth.

"My mom's side. My grandpa's papou. It was late in 1800s."

"Who hung him?" I ask. *How much more don't I know?* I think. There is so much that has happened to this family in the not-so-distant past.

"The Turks," he says with his mouth. *Who else?* he says with his tone.

"Why did they hang him?"

He laughs scornfully because he knows he has to give me another history lesson. "Because he was a priest. It's against everything they believe." He continues, "See, we lived there for four hundred years with them, okay?

And the Greeks and the Turks got along for a while, then somebody revolts, gets his group, fights again. Back again. Back and forth. When the Turks occupied the area, sometimes they'd offer up a consolation prize. 'In order to keep calm and leave me alone,' they'd say, 'I'll give you this piece of land so you can do what you want with it,'" Tom explains. When the Turks were in power and controlled the village land, they'd gift some of the acreage to the religious leaders. It was a smart move—the religious leaders had a lot of political sway. "And still, half the land in the villages around there still belong to the monastery because the Turks gave it to the monks, so they could tell the people not to revolt," he says. "It was 2012 when the Greeks were free from the last Turks."

"Okay, so you decided to go to Athens with your cousin," I prompt, getting us back where we started. His cousin lived there and let Tom know he would have no problem finding a job. It was a large city and employers were eager to hire young kids, since they didn't have to be paid as much as the older workers.

"That's right. We walked across the little river and got on the bus to town."

"Had you been on a bus before that?"

"Me? No! Never saw a bus in my life! Well, we *hear* the cars, the buses or a truck, across the river, waaaaaay up they had a road there, and every day we hear them coming and going and sometimes a bigger truck, we saw it." A huge truck would be a miniscule speck from across the valley. "Oh, we wanted so bad to see!" he laughs. "We wondered 'how does that thing go?!'" he says through his laughter.

Tom's cousin Vasili warned Tom that he'd probably get sick on the bus. Tom was concerned, since he didn't know what to expect. It turned out that Vasili got carsick, but Tom didn't. He was surprised at how the movement of the bus made his cousin puke so much. "He got so sick on that bus, I couldn't believe it."

Tom found a job in the city quite quickly, working as a food vendor at a kiosk. "I spent two days in a shish kabob thing. Those little things, they only had one gyro machine, you had to stay outside. You had to holler, 'Ah, shish kabob! Hot pies!'"

"You only worked there for two days?" This surprises me. Tom's not a quitter.

"Ahhh, I couldn't do it. Couple days, I left it."

"Why'd you leave?"

"I was kinda quiet kid. I didn't like that. I still don't."

"Huh." He doesn't strike me as the shy type.

Vasili worked at a confectionary. One of his customers, an opthamologist who stopped in every morning on his way to work, had mentioned that his dad was looking for workers. As it turned out his dad owned a coffee shop in Athens called Caffeineio Oraios. Vasili connected his cousin with the doctor and Tom was hired. This job stuck.

"I worked there for two, three years. I made good money. I made more money in one night there than in an entire year at the old *caffeineio*." As Tom tells me more about this job, I start to notice a pattern. He says that he got along well with the owner, whose last name was Papa, and with the owner's family. "Except the old lady. She was picky. I don't need to mop the floor three times a day," he gripes. The *caffeineio* sold coffee, ice cream and beer and stayed open until four a.m. This was the second oldest coffee shop in Athens at the time.

"When was it built, do you know?"

"Oh, I don't know. Centuries ago."

There were several shops that all surrounded a large outdoor patio that held dozens of tables. "I thought the whole thing was ours, so I start cleaning tables, chairs. The owner of the bakery next door, nice guy, he said to me, 'Heeyyy, that's mine!'" Tom was embarrassed: "Oh! Oh this tables right here?" He remembers figuring out which tables he was responsible for. The cafe was popular. "Every night it was packed with people. Lemonade. Sodas. Beer." Tom tells me people would sit and sip on a cold drink to cool off. The cafe lived up to its name. "Beautiful," Tom tells me.

"And I was making *so* much money!" He explains the process for figuring out how much he earned: "Every night we had to sit down with my boss. See, how we did then, before I started working in the afternoon, got some tokens. This is coffee token, this is ice cream token, whatever. Every time I went to my boss, or his wife, whoever was tending the bar in other words, I had to give them a token."

He mimes taking a token out of his apron and handing it over to the bartender and says, "Out of my pocket there was a token." He takes a sip of his coffee and continues, "At the end of the night, we started counting. "How many tokens you got?" his boss would ask him. "I was collecting the money," Tom pats the front of his waist, indicating he held all of the cash in his apron.

"'You owe me a hundred fifty drachmas,' or whatever. I count the money I had left, 'Huh!'" His eyes bug out of his head and his mouth opens wide. He was shocked how much money he had left in his apron after paying his boss for the items he had served. "The old man said, 'Why you got so much money? You didn't forget to give me the token or something did you?' I was getting tips. Everybody liked me." He felt rich. "Because me, I was getting a hundred fifty drachmas a month before I got there. And then there, I was getting three hundred drachmas a night." The city later tore the cafe down and there is now a high rise where it used to stand.

"He was making all kinds of money back then, Christine. But he didn't save a penny," Glykeria says, looking at me with her eyebrows raised high.

"Yeah, but how old was he then? Thirteen?"

"Yeah, thirteen," Tom confirms. "Well, you never have money before and all the sudden you have so much." He gives me an example, so I can appreciate how much three hundred drachmas a night was: "For two drachmas, you got a cheese pie or a souvlaki. So that was a lot of money."

"So, what did you spend your money on when you were thirteen?"

"Well, we did things. Every day I watched one or two movies. I went by myself. Everyone else was working during the day, I was working the night. Sometimes I go home and all the beds were occupied, so I had to wait until they left."

"You didn't have your own bed?"

"No!" He says this like it would have been absurd for them to each have their own.

"Drinking . . ." When he says this he makes it sound like a question, but I know it's just that he doesn't want to tell me too much that could be viewed negatively.

"Chasing girls?" Glykeria asks, fishing.

"No, no just easy to spend money if you got it in your pocket," Tom says. "I bought my bed. Mattress."

"You just told me you didn't have a bed." I lift my eyes up to give him an annoyed look as I keep typing.

"Well, I bought one when I moved out. Like a cot. A folding bed. This is a frame. Like a folding frame bed."

Hmmm . . .

"Like a futon?" I try to get some clarity.

"Pretty much. Like a fence."

Not clear yet.

"So, when you folded it up, could you sit on it like a couch? Or did it just fold up so you could move it out of the way?" I ask.

"Just fold it and put it aside," he says.

Okay, sorta clear.

"But once I had it in the room, it's there for everybody. Open."

"So you just all shared a bed?"

"Oh yeah, we'd sleep together. Just wherever you found room, you just lay down."

"They all knew each other, Christine," Glykeria points out.

"Friends, cousins," Tom confirms. "Just lay down and go to sleep. I mean, it sounds weird now, but it wasn't. We didn't have a problem just sleeping with someone in the same bed."

"What else did you buy, besides your bed?" I get us back on track.

"I bought my soccer shoes and my socks. Carry them around. Maybe we weren't smart enough to get a bag," he laughs. "Socks and shoes around the neck." He puts his hands up close to his ears and bring them down to his shoulders, closing his fists around invisible socks and invisible cleats with the shoelaces tied together. "I don't know, everyone was doing the same thing. We never had a bag!" His voice starts to get louder. "Now, the kids, everywhere you go they've got the backpacks!" I nod. He gets even louder: "I'm not talking about schools. I know they got books and all that stuff. I'm talking in Athens now even the politicians, they got a backpack. All dressed up and have a red backpack on their back!"

"That's weird," I concede. We're getting off track.

"Yes, it is weird!" he shouts. His voice booms. He appears to be passionately anti-backpack.

"Calm down, Tom," Glykeria whispers.

"You were talking about how you spent your money," I remind him.

"I had my stereos, my discs. A lot of stuff. And anywhere we went, I was the only one buying. I was always treating them. I was the only one who had money." He takes a sip of coffee out of his Styrofoam cup. "Always broke. Always broke," he says about his friends. "But I didn't mind." He looks at Glykeria and starts listing people he often paid for: "Your brother, my cousin. Well, my cousin did have money, just too stingy. Too tight. But I didn't mind."

Tom spent a lot of his free time working out. He went to a complex near the beach three or four times a week. "I was into lifting weights, the rings, parallel bars. Gymnastics. All at a complex with soccer fields, basketball courts, gymnastics equipment, all set up by the beach, free! You had to check the weights out if you wanted those, but the rest was all free. Usually five or six of us went together to play soccer with another group," he explains. "We practiced with some first division teams when they came to Athens. That was the only practice fields they had," he adds. "I was pretty well built up, you know, good shape. I was into arm wrestling."

"Really?"

"Oh yeah! Only one guy beat me in arm wrestling," he claims.

I smile as I type, imagining my father-in-law as a Hellenic Popeye. A highland version instead of the maritime one, eating a piece of spinach pie instead of spinach out of a can.

"Sometimes worked out with this guy, used to come into the store. He sold imported liquor, he had some money, he was a distributor," Tom says. "You couldn't buy imported liquor from everywhere," he points out. "He was a good friend. I was sixteen, seventeen, he said, 'I gotta get you in the Olympic boxing team.' He was involved as a promoter in 1964 and wanted to sponsor me." Tom was not interested. "I wanted no part of it," he tells me.

"Why not?" It seems like something he would enjoy. I remember him telling me once that he used to get into bar fights, so maybe this could have been a way to channel some of that energy. Get out some of his aggression.

"I had a nice clean face. I didn't want to mess it up!" Tom snorts.

"Oh my goodness." I laugh out loud. I would never expect him to be vain. "But, didn't you used to beat people up?" I call him out.

"Eh, nothing serious. Just teenagers getting into a squabble. You end up friends after anyways," Tom says dismissively. "No guns, no knives, nothing. Just a slap here, slap there. Who cares?" he says, before adding, "Although, I had black eyes and cut lips most of the time anyway, from late night . . . you know . . ."

"What?! No, Tom, I have no idea what you mean about the late night whatever." I envision something on par with *Fight Club*.

Tom tries to explain: "It happens, no matter what you do. I wasn't the one trying to get into a fight, I didn't care, but if we gotta have a fight, I wasn't going to back down." I look at him, with his large hands and wide knuckles. His broad cheekbones and his roman nose. Even though what I see now is him holding his grandchildren with those hands, cuddling their smooth faces against his weathered one, I can tell he used to be a scrapper.

He's pretty mellow now, but the stubborn temper in the core of his being threatens to penetrate through his calm exterior. Tom cements this impression I have of him when he tells me he acted like the bouncer of their group. "If someone had a problem with someone else at the bar, they'd say, 'Oh, let the *vlaxo* take care of it!'" The shepherd. "'He can take care of him, no problem.' Late night someone wants to be a tough guy, so we'd beat him up!" Apparently he only worried about keeping his face pretty when he wasn't out late at the bar.

LEAVING THE VILLAGE
A new bakery, a bath house, and a poisoning

When Caffeneio Oraios closed, Tom acquired a position working as a delivery man for a bakery. "Can't remember the name of the place, but it is still there." He delivered bread on a bike, a little three-wheeled trike, with a basket on the front that he loaded with fresh bread. Athens is a city full of hills, so Tom got in shape quickly doing this job. "It's hell going up with that thing!" he says, lifting his hand up to illustrate the inclines. "Whew!"

He worked there for about two months, before Papa hunted him down and asked him to work for him again, at another *caffeineio* that he had just recently opened up. "My old boss couldn't sit still. Like Dimos," he says, referring to his brother-in-law, who is the hardest worker any of us know. Dimos is the kind of guy who will chop down a dozen pine trees in his backyard and then plant new ones in the same spot, just to have something to do.

"So he went half a block down the road where Oraios was, and he rented that one. He said, 'Come on back, we opened a new one!'"

"So it was the same guy who you used to work for?" I make sure I have the story straight.

"Same guy. Same old lady, arguing all the time. Never got along with her."

"What was the new place called?"

"Same name. Cafe Oraios," he tells me.

The new cafe was a smaller place than the original. "Three tables in there. And then the sidewalk, a couple tables. Always put a couple tables in the sidewalk. Little dump, no windows, nothing. One light on the ceiling."
It doesn't sound like this venue quite lived up to the name, like the old one did.

Tom worked at the new *caffeineio* for about another year. He explains his role there: "Someone calls from another store or whatever, shoemaker or whatever, coffees, pop, water, couried. To-go items. Back and forth." Beautiful delivery instead of beautiful scenery, I suppose.

He remembers an exchange with another vendor: "Next door, really fancy bakery. Older lady, nice customer, good tipped, always polite. One day, I came out and my jacket was kind of dirty, had to take them to the cleaners every so often. We had two jackets. One got dirty, had to get other one," he explains. "She looks at me. 'Hmmm . . . nice. Nice and clean,'" she said sarcastically. "I turn around, go back in, put on a clean jacket. But, the pocket was ripped. So she looked at me and said, 'Oh. Clean AND sewn up,'" he laughs. "I was so embarrassed. Ah, we were just a cheap place. Cheap coffee. That's what we sold."

Tom continues: "We had a pinball machine in there. That's all we had for entertainment. We had two, three guys, who spent all their time. This guy became so good, he'd put in the first drachma, and he kept winning—free game, free game, free game. Finally, Mr. Papas said, 'Okay, he's not playing anymore.' He'd get a ton of free games, let his brothers play, and when the number of games got too low, he'd play again and get them back up," he shakes his head remembering this. "He sold fresh produce, so whenever no customers, he'd want to play," he adds. "Everyone delivered everything. Even a little kiosk on the corner, you call him up and he'll send you a pack of cigarettes. Groceries. Richer people, they never went to the grocery store, they'd call and deliver." He takes a sip of coffee, his rant about the rich over.

After Andy finished school, he moved to Athens and rented a room with Tom and their friend Odessea. The old house that they lived in was located on one of the highest hills in the city. There was a faucet outside, but during the day, when water usage was at its peak, the water pressure was too low to use. "We had the water, the municipal water, but during the day, we were so high up, once everybody opened up downtown there was not enough," Tom says.

At night, when the stores and restaurants were closed, the water levels would rise enough to supply the faucet that was outside their apartment. They would fill up a special bucket that had a spigot at the bottom and bring it with them to an enclosed area in their complex that was designated for showering and toileting. The room was rustic, at best, and was shared by everyone who lived in the apartments. Tom and his roommates would fill up buckets at two or three in the morning. "You had to catch it at that time, to use it for the next day." The boys had to be sure to fill up the water in the can to have it for shaving, showering or washing up. A simple solution to the lack of bathroom in the apartment was going to the public bath house. "You paid two drachmas, would get a bar of soap and one of those grass rough things . . ." He can't think of the word.

"A loofah?"

"Loofah. Clean yourself up. We did that a couple times a week, once we started smelling bad. It was the cheapest way."

LEAVING THE VILLAGE
An autograph

After several years working for Papa in his *caffeneios,* Tom got a job at a restaurant in the Plaka, near the Acropolis. "This place was a five-star restaurant; it had great food." The clientele at the restaurant was elite. "I used to get great tips from Prince Constantine before he became King. I also saw Kirk Douglas. He signed quite a few autographs. I had one autograph my whole life. I gave him my tablet, that I used to take orders on, and he used up the entire tablet with his signature. I still have the autograph he gave me somewhere."

"I definitely want to see that," I say as I sip on a glass of wine in my mother-in-law's kitchen. If she ever wants a glass of wine, she always asks me to drink with her. She knows I'll accept. She doesn't want to drink alone.

"There was a photographer from the local paper there," Tom continues, "and I asked him to take a picture of me with Kirk Douglas and his wife." According to Tom, he was standing a step or two above them and the photographer, so he wouldn't appear so short in comparison, and the photographer ended up cutting off the top of Tom's head in the picture. "I thought if I went up one step we'd be even," Tom says, holding his hands up to indicate that their heads would be the same height.

"What kind of photographer cuts off the top of someone's head?"

"He working for a big newspaper, too!"

"He really didn't care about you in the picture." I point out the reality of the situation.

"No, no, no." Tom acknowledges this is probably true.

"Yea, I want to see that too," I tell him.

"*Pou einai?*" Glykeria asks Tom. Where is it?

"I have no clue, *mori*, I never look for those things," he says. "Up until recently I had it in my wallet. The autograph. Until I came here, a few years ago," he says. "Kinda worn out."

"Until you came HERE?" I ask, pointing to the floor. *"Here" as in the U.S. forty years ago or "here" as in this house I'm standing in that you've lived in for four?*

"Here, yeah," he says, copying my motion and pointing to the dark wood floor.

"You carried it around in your pocket all that time?" *For decades?*

"Yeah. Since 1969. Since I got the original card. I mean my social security number card. It's in my wallet."

His social security card and Kirk Douglas's photograph. His two prized American possessions.

"I took it out two, three times maybe," he says, referring to the social security card. "Once I memorized it, never take it out," he says before adding, "I hope *that's* still there." He laughs, takes a sip of his coffee and turns back to his book.

"Now she got me think that," he says a minute later, putting his book down.

"She got you thinking about what?" I ask him – not realizing that 'she' was me.

"My pictures." He stands up and walks out of the room.

"*Pege nah vre ti photographia*," Glykeria says. He went to find the pictures. "I knew where they was before, but when we move here, I don't know where he puts it," she says.

Glykeria and I sip on our wine and from the kitchen we can hear him rummaging through boxes.

"I gotta go get a new one before he dies." Tom enters the kitchen, laughing and holding a small piece of paper in his hands.

"No way! You found it?!" He's been talking about this autograph for years but I hadn't ever seen it, so I figured I never would.

"Get some tape! Get some tape!" my mother-in-law shouts, as she runs to get the scotch tape herself.

"Worn totally out," Tom says, inspecting it. It was folded in half, and then half again, and when he opens it up the paper rips across the seams and there is a hole in the center. "Worn totally out," he says again as he scans it. "9-11-1964," he says.

"I got it! I got it! Let me tape!" Glykeria says. I move the wine glasses out of the way so they don't get tipped and stain the paper.

"That's okay, *mori*. That's okay. No big deal. But it's worn out. I better get Kirk Douglas now. I think he's still alive yet," he snickers.

Glykeria grabs the autograph, turns the paper over and lays a strip of tape along the back seam.

"Wow," I say. "That's awesome." I'm still amazed that he has this after all those years. "Wait, 9-11 . . . on your birthday?" I look at Glykeria incredulously. September 11th is her birthday.

"No, months are backwards," he says. *Ah. November 9th.*

"Well, let's take a photo of it," I insist. My husband snaps a photo of the front and back of the paper that once lived in my father-in-law's pad of guest checks.

"Take a picture with it, Tom!" I hand him the autograph. He's got a huge smile, something rare when a camera is being shoved in his face, and he holds up the paper.

"No, no!" Glykeria yells out.

What the hell? She's been just as excited as I am about his autograph until this moment.

"You got a hole in your shirt!" A cigarette burn, it looks like to me, on the side of his stomach.

"I'll cover the hole," Tom appeases her. "I'll cover the hole with the autograph. The only one I ever got!" He puts the paper with the hole in it over the hole in his shirt and his smile gets even wider.

LEAVING THE VILLAGE
A few cut corners

"Try it." Glykeria shoves one of her white CorningWare platters in my face. It's loaded with sliced *loukanika*.

"I just ate. I'm so full," I tell her. I just had lunch with my friends, otherwise I'd be shoveling those babies right in.

"Try it, Christine."

I don't have a choice.

"Okay," I relent.

"A little bit more cumin, I think," Glykeria says as she pops one in her own mouth.

"A little bit more salt," Tom says.

"A little bit salt," Glykeria agrees.

"That's okay," Tom says. "I mean, I ate it anyway."

I nod. Still delicious.

I take another bite. "Tell me more about the restaurant you worked at in the Plaka." The Plaka is the tourist area beneath the Parthenon.

The waiters at the restaurant wore black pants and white wool sweaters. The clothes were purchased at a store that became a favorite of Tom's, made of fine-quality, store-bought wool, a luxury Tom was not accustomed to.

"We would get to the restaurant at five p.m. and set out the 'reserved' signs on all of the tables." If they didn't recognize the people who walked in and asked to be seated, they said the tables were all reserved. Apparently this made the restaurant look more appealing.

The restaurant owners valued the five-star rating, but they had to cut a few corners to obtain it. Tom shares one sketchy detail: "In order to be a five-star restaurant, to get the highest rating, you had to have a three-person band. We only had two people. So, if an inspector came in, one of us would grab a green jacket and sit on the stage with the band." He gives another example: "We also were supposed to get a day off, and weren't allowed to work every day of the week. So, if an inspector asked our name, we'd give someone else's name and just run away."

During the summer months, the walls of the restaurant were taken down, creating an open-air environment. To increase profits during the summer, the staff extended the dining room floor by putting tables out in front of the restaurant, making rows all the way into the street, blocking the intersection. It must have really paid off for the owners and staff. "We would get tickets and just pay the fine. No one got mad, people just drove around the tables."

To further the sketchiness, Tom reveals this tidbit: "When we closed, we would shoot craps there. One day we got caught and the older people got arrested for illegal gambling. The kids got off; they thought we didn't know anything about it." Tom was able to look beyond the minor infractions he saw around him. Never in his life had he felt so rich. "That's where I made money. Theio Andy was making four hundred drachmas a month. I made two thousand plus drachmas a night. I stayed there until I went into the army in 1962."

Tom made more money than anyone in his family was used to. "One time my dad asked if he could borrow some money, so I just gave him what was in my pocket. One day's pay. With that one day's pay, my dad was able to pay my brother-in-law to tear down the old two-story house I grew up in and built another one with the same stones. Another time my dad needed money, he came to town to get his teeth fixed."

Tom tried to get Andy to work with him at the Plaka. "My brother worked at the grocery store. I tried to get him to go work in a restaurant—we used to make so much money. I couldn't get him out of there. Four hundred drachmas a month, he stuck there. We made three thousand a night. I used make more money in one night than he made in one month."

"Why wouldn't Andy get a job in the restaurant?" It seems like a no-brainer to me.

"He was a shy guy, too. He didn't want the restaurant business. He didn't want too much . . . I don't know. He just never got into it, I guess."

Even though Tom was forced to work as hard as a grown man, he was still just a boy and he made sure to find time for fun in Athens. "I would have had more money if I would have saved anything, but after work we would go to the *bouzoukia* every night." Bars with live music. "Rent was only a hundred drachmas a month. And even though I made two, three thousand plus drachmas each night, Johnny Walker Red was about fifteen hundred drachmas, so I spent it all. It was fun though. Careless years. You didn't care when you left home, you didn't care when you come back. It could be a week. Other than that, you were gone. Tonight spend the night with this friend, tomorrow spend the night with that friend, go get drunk with that friend. Wherever you got drunk, you stayed. Slept in your clothes," he says. "Well, usually slept in your shorts," he corrects himself.

"Shorts or *vraki*?" Glykeria teases him.

"Same. Always. Not jockeys. Briefs."

"We call them *vraki*, Christine, okay?"

I have no idea how we just started talking about my father-in-law's underpants. I didn't anticipate learning that he always has, and always will, wear briefs instead of boxers, but there we have it. You don't know what you'll learn when you ask your in-laws to tell you their life stories.

LEAVING THE VILLAGE
An army outpost, an army meal, and an infestation

My in-laws have come over after working all day, cleaning their rental properties. They each have a gas station coffee in their hand, even though it is early evening. They are exhausted. My mother-in-law sits down at our counter and rests for about thirty seconds before my husband says, "Mom, come see if our oregano is ready."

She gets up and walks over to the dining room table, which has been covered in oregano for the past couple of weeks. "Tom, I'm going to ask you about the army," I shout before going to help her.

I return after we have determined that the oregano has dried sufficiently to be removed from the stems, crushed up, and placed into the glass jar to be used for cooking. "Okay. Tell me about the army," I demand. I've been interviewing them for so long, we're past pleasantries in many ways.

"Army was not a big deal in Greece, because nothing going on. Just one year of your life.

"One year only?"

"One year for me."

"What made you so special? Normally it's a two-year requirement, right?" I ask. Every male in Greece is required to serve in the army.

"Yeah, the rest was twenty-four to thirty months, depending on the branch and your specialty," he says. He sips his coffee from the Styrofoam cup. "I was the oldest guy. When you have a lot of kids in the family, the oldest son goes one year only. Three or more," Tom says, quantifying "a lot" of kids. "I was the oldest one. Male child. Girls don't count. Yeah, I served one year and ten days."

"Ten days. He did something not right, so they punish him," Glykeria rats him out.

"Ten days discipline," Tom nods.

"But during peacetime, eh, nothing!" He waves his hand. For him, the army was a piece of cake. "You have your guard duty here and there. Small stuff. I didn't mind it a bit; it was fun for me."

"How old were you when you were in the army?"

"Almost twenty years old when I went in." He takes another sip of his coffee. "So you go there, the post, the base. I went in the day before anyway. Nothing better to do, so just went in, a couple of us, the day before we were supposed to. We get our hair cut. 'Zzz Zzzzzz!' And you check in your boots, uniform, you know, what they give you there," Tom tells me.

The first seven weeks, he had basic training in Thebes.

"You have to marching, the guns, train you how to take them apart, put them together, clean them. But mostly exercises. Running, jumping jacks. Or peeling potatoes. We had to peel potatoes couple times a week too. I mean, PILES of potatoes, not just one or two. And then your guard duty. Once a night, depending on your shift."

After basic training, Tom worked as a cook. He moved around quite a bit. He was sent to Gytheio, Thessaloniki, and a hidden outpost "waaaaaay up in the mountains. We had ammo depot inside that mountain. You couldn't even see it. We had a big door in front of it. You see three houses, unless you knew, you couldn't tell it was there. I was there three months maybe."

This post was Tom's favorite location. It was tiny; he was cooking for seventeen people during the week and thirty-five on the weekend.

"That was the best time," he says. "That was like being at camp every day. That's what it is. A nice house with bunkbeds inside. You had your living room, your card tables." Compared to his house growing up, the outpost might have seemed luxurious.

"Every day they bringing me the food what we had for the day. Depending on what the base had, they send me my share, in other words. We had to go get the water every day or every other day. We didn't have any water, we haul it from the Jeep."

I'm starting to wonder if he was handpicked to cook at this location. Someone from the city might have had a rough go of it. "Nothing in the kitchen, I had to use wood. So it was just like a campfire," he says. I imagine he had an advantage in this aspect, since he cooked over a fireplace in the village as well. "Sometimes they sent you food that you needed the oven. I didn't have oven! No matter what it was, it got cooked on the fire," he laughs.

Daphne walks over to the pantry, opens the door, and demands crackers that she can see but not reach. Glykeria walks over and grabs the box, scanning the expiration date before opening it and pouring a generous amount into a bowl for her.

"Expiration dates." Tom clucks his tongue. "We never have that. In the army, 1967, we had these crackers. Never expired. Twenty-years-old packs. Thirty years old. We had them for emergency, you know. You don't have fresh bread during the war or something. That's what you eat. You had to soak that thing in bean soup half a day to make it soft enough to eat them."

"That sounds like there should have been an expiration date."

"They were like bones. That hard." Tom shakes his head and chuckles as he heads into the kitchen to fill up his coffee cup.

"You get him started and now he's not going to stop today, Christine." I can't get enough of the stories that my mother-in-law has probably heard a million times.

"We had a frozen side of beef," Tom continues. "Twenty years! That beef was older than I was! And it was fine, tasted fine! Now beef is over a week and it's expired."

I grimace.

"My brother came to visit and he saw me chopping a side of beef with the ax. I had the beef on the floor. We didn't have no cutting boards or anything like that. Just right on the floor where we walked."

"Tom, that's disgusting!" And I thought the story was gross before that last bit.

He laughs.

"He came up for a soccer game, and since he was there in Thessaloni he came to the bus and figured, 'I'll go see Tom too.'" He takes a sip of his coffee before adding, "The floor was perfectly clean. We only walked on it."

The water they hauled into camp with the Jeep was kept in a large tank. "One night, the wintertime, it start getting cold out there. Nobody thought about it, our water tank outside. It froze up!" He laughs at the error, since the only consequence was in the morning. "No chai! Usually chai and feta for breakfast!" Tom learned his lesson: "Oh, next time we need to get the water in during the day. Fill up a couple pots and keep them inside." He grins. "Ah, we spent most of the time playing cards. Or crapshoot. Man, it was fun!"

After a few months, Tom got moved back to Thessaloniki, where he spent a majority of his time. He was responsible for feeding his platoon. "Total base had three, four thousand, but in my platoon, in other words, I had around two hundred." The number varied by the day, ranging from one hundred seventy to two hundred twenty. "I didn't have a certain amount, because a lot of people traveling or they assigned someplace else for the day."

Each day an exact head count was done. Tom would get his ingredients needed to cook for the day based on this count. "Every day we had to know how many people there. They gave you EXACTLY the amount you wanted for everything. Need one hundred grams of rice per person. Or sixty-eight grams of meat. Or sugar. And that's all you got. You had to get it exactly there," Tom says. "Because the guy in the store is responsible for everybody," he explains.

"But the thing is, at the end I was a little uh, little trouble with that. Because rice, I was never getting the whole amount. I didn't want it. I didn't eat it," Tom tells me. Apparently he thought the army gave out way more rice than the recipes he cooked needed. "You make soup, you only need less than half the amount. So I was over the amount of rice like five or six hundred kilos." He was questioned about why he was so under ration for rice. "They called me up before I got discharged: 'Why so much rice there?' You gotta explain to them. 'Well, if I got soup twice a week, only need that much rice.'" There was a reason behind their questioning. "Lot of people—the sergeant, the lieutenant, lot of people—load it on the truck, load it on the market, black market, and sell it," he nods.

He was under on rice, but he was over on bread. "I was short four hundred loaves of bread," he remembers.

Even when given the most specific of recipes, when they're *ordered* to follow them, my Greek in-laws refuse.

"Well, that seems like it makes sense, if you made soup that much. Need something to sop up the broth," I concede. *Especially when you withhold all the rice.*

Tom remembers that as head cook he was responsible for every square inch of the kitchen. "I was in charge of the chain on the stupid skylight.

Ten meters high in the roof and I was in charge of the chain. What happen to the chain? You sign for everything there!" He's starting to yell. It's hard to decipher, as always, but this sounds like an angry yell.

"Shhhh, calm down," Glykeria says to her husband. "Oh my God, Christine," she says to me.

"Playing soccer outside and they broke the window on the roof. The sky. The big window. Whatchya call them? The skylight. 'What happened?' 'I don't know what happened.' But still, the kitchen is yours and you're responsible. Everything around is your responsibility. I got away though, I didn't have to pay anything. I had to stay after ten days."

"Because you go out, get drunk." It seems like Glykeria has been waiting to tell me this.

"I go out," Tom confirms. "From four to eight, they don't ask questions. But if you want to stay a couple hours later, you have to get a pass. But I never got a pass," he says stubbornly. "I want to go out, I go out," he says.

This doesn't surprise me. Tom is the most stubborn man I know, other than my husband, but he explains his refusal to get weekend passes wasn't only because he was so headstrong: But, I didn't have to report. Every day they take oral report. If you there or not. I didn't have to be there though. I was excused because of my job. In the morning too, I didn't have to go to the assembly there. But one night, this guy, he was a lifer there, he was a master sergeant but he was a mean son of a gun. Then he says, 'Where's the cook?' 'Oh the cook doesn't have to be here,' says the sergeant on duty. 'He doesn't have to be here, must be in the kitchen.' 'Okay, go get him.' He sent somebody. I was not there, so when I came in, he reported me. 'You weren't here.' 'But I don't have to be there!'" Tom explains what he felt to be an unfair situation. "That's the army," he says, rolling his eyes.

So out of one side of his mouth he tells me he didn't have to report to roll call like the rest of his platoon, but out of the other side he admits, "One day we didn't come in 'til one in the morning. So, that's the time I got caught. We had a few drinks too."

"That's what I said. They got drunk so he had to go back." Glykeria seems to enjoy pointing out his misconduct.

"We went back into the colonel's office, the base commander. He chewed me out. He sits me down the steps and gave me a nice buzz." Tom chuckles as he explains how, after being in the army for a few months, his hair had grown out. It was easy to tell that Tom had received punishment and was knocked back down to newbie status. "When they give you punishment like that they take your pay away. I was making thirty-five dollars a month. Enough for shoe polish and envelopes. They take it away. So, I didn't have enough money for cigarettes."

The colonel gave Tom twenty days penalty. "Restricted," Tom says. "So you lose your pay and you couldn't go out from the base. Small stuff like that." Luckily for him, he was friendly with the lieutenant. "But the lieutenant though, who keeps records, he comes in the next day and he was a nice guy, we became friends, he said, "You know what? I'll mark down for five days instead." He cut Tom a fifteen-day break.

Tom didn't learn any lessons from the discipline.

"And the next time, I did the same thing. I had sixty-five days total." He remembers the exact number of additional days he racked up as punishment. "But I end up staying over ten days because of that guy. He did me a good favor," Tom says. "Some nice people, some not very nice." The lieutenant was clearly on Tom's nice list.

"And you one of those, you not very nice," Glykeria says to him, boldly.

"I was the nicest guy in the army," Tom counters.

"You didn't follow rules though," Glykeria states.

"Yeah, you go out with five, six guys and I have to leave because I don't have the pass?" He waves his hand, dismissing the need for the pass. "I went out Friday night, and coming back Sunday. Every weekend I was going out," Tom says.

It wasn't just the weekend pass regulation that Tom ignored. It was also the dress code. Remember how he prefers briefs to boxers? "I took them to the army with me. I couldn't wear those sack cloth or whatever," he cackles.

A sack cloth?!

Apparently part of the army uniform included government-issued boxer shorts, which Tom, I now know, has quite the aversion to. "One size fits all. Hah!" he roars. "Well, every day I was in charge of collecting the laundry.

I had to take them. Once a week I had to collect that stuff," he says, having regained some composure. "When it came back, you didn't always get yours. Same size usually, that's it. But no one was inspecting the kitchen, so I wore civilian stuff." This explains how he was able to wear his precious briefs, even then.

"There was this one guy," he starts in on a new story, "and he wasn't like us, village boys. They were out camping. They had to go to the border, in other words. They came back two months after." I'm not sure where this is going.

"I looked at the guy. He was scratching and itching, scratching and itching. 'Man, look at this little thing,'" Tom mimes pulling a tiny bug out of his armpit. "He was showing me the lice. I told him, 'That's lice.' He said, 'No, that's from sleeping bag from when we were sleeping.' See, he didn't know what lice were. Maybe he never seen, never heard, I don't know. Ahhhhhhh!" He tips his head back and his eyes are watering again. "He had lice all over!" he says, shaking his head.

Tom was very familiar with what lice looked like. "We had them as kids in school. We always caught lice. Every year. As soon as school start." He finishes his story about the lice guy, but suddenly his voice gets very quiet. He whispers, "We took everything off and boil them in the same pots we was cooking the next day."

"TOM!!!" This might be the loudest he's ever heard me yell.

"Well, we only had two pots." He makes it sound like a question. *What else were we supposed to do?* He shrugs.

"That's disgusting," I say, my gag reflex kicking in a bit. "Hghh!" This is much worse than the beef.

"They didn't care," Tom says. "But *psires!*" Lice. His voice goes up a couple of octaves: "Lot of *psires*!" he howls.

It takes us a while to get back on track after this discussion. Tom is cracking up and I am disgusted. Once we do, I find out that Glykeria's brother Giorgos was serving at the same post, at the same time as Tom. "How did they decide who had to serve in the army when?" I ask.

"Original," Tom says. He means to say it depended on your place of origin. Eligible men were issued duty assignments as a group, based on location. "People from Patras, people from Athens, every three months they had a different section of the country."

"Huh. I didn't know that. Do they do that so you're already tight-knit?" I wonder. Tom isn't sure what the reasoning was behind the logistics.

"When I got discharged, I didn't even go back to my job," Tom says, referring to his restaurant job in the Plaka. "I knew I wouldn't be there long."

"Did you head to the States right after you were in the army?"

"Got out August, left in January," he says. It took him a few months to get his paperwork in order.

"When did you know you would be going to the States at some point?" I couldn't remember when he first knew he would be moving to America.

"In '65. When Father Gregory invited over. But he couldn't invite everybody. He invite his sister. Class A relative." His uncle Greg brought over his sister, Yiayia Athena, who then brought over five of her children.

"So you had to wait until after you served in the army then?"

"Boys had to wait until they got discharged," he confirms. "And, in the back of my mind, Vietnam," he adds. "Once you served in a NATO country, your service counts. The United States recognizes my service. I knew I'd rather serve in Greece." He knew that if he had already served in Greece it would be recognized by the US and he wouldn't have to fight in Vietnam.

Tom remembers he was working every day and wasn't able to see his mom and sister off when they left to head to the States. "I wasn't allowed vacation time because I was serving just that one year," he explains. The army during peacetime was a weekday job. "Weekends, yeah. If you wanted to stay out, get the pass," he says.

"But you never got the pass anyway."

"Nope," he chuckles.

LEAVING THE VILLAGE
A family friend

It turns out that Tom knew several members of Glykeria's family before he met her. He was best buddies with her brother, Giorgos. The two men are the same age and first became acquainted in elementary school, even though they attended different buildings. The specifics of how they became friends during school excursions brings up a whole other story. I'll try to keep it brief.

One of Glykeria's cousins, Adelphius, lived with her and her family for a substantial chunk of time, somewhere in the neighborhood of seven years. I assume that his family was so poor that even the impoverished Economou family was rich by comparison, and that is why he was taken in. His brothers, Cleades and Hero, each spent time living with her family as well, but those two rotated years, so only two of the siblings were staying with them at any given time. Meanwhile, a fourth sibling, Achilles, was living with Tom's family. The four boys were also Tom's cousins. Even though their parents did not want to split up their children, the family had no other option, being so poverty-stricken that, as Tom puts it, "Not even a mouse could live comfortably in that house."

Every so often, the neighboring schools merged together to attend a field trip as a group, and on these occasions the siblings would be briefly reunited as a whole unit. Tom vividly remembers them hugging and crying with emotion; they were so happy to see each other again, after weeks or months apart. It was these siblings who first brought Tom and Giorgos together on these field trips, George alongside Adelphius or Hero, and Tom beside Achilles. If you're a little confused, let me help you out here: Tom and Glykeria are third cousins, or something like that. They're the type of cousins that when they explain it to you, you still can't figure out exactly how they're related. You'd need a flow chart to keep the connections straight. Instead of a family tree, they joke that they have a family wreath.

Giorgos and Tom knew each other only superficially from these elementary school jaunts, but when they both lived in Athens, between the years of 1961 and 1969, they became quite close. The men would hang out often in the city, visiting each other's apartments, going out for a coffee or a beer, or meeting up for a game of backgammon. They saw each other almost daily; country boys navigating the metropolitan area as a team. A group of their fellow mountain men coalesced within the bustle of the city, enjoying speaking the village dialect that was not found anywhere else in Greece and keeping up the old traditions. One of the friends in their group spent a lot of time and energy trying to preserve the village history, collecting paraphernalia that reflected the culture of their *xorio*.

Being such close chums, Tom got to know Dimitri Economou, Glykeria and Giorgos's father, when Dimitri visited his son in Athens. This is partly why Glykeria's dad felt comfortable sending his daughter to America with a man she hardly knew; he had already gotten to know Tom and thought highly of him. In addition to knowing Glykeria's brother and father, he also knew her cousin, George quite well ... since George was also one of his cousins.

"How well did you know Dimitri - Glykeria's dad?" I ask.

"All my life, just about."

"Did you? I didn't think you met him until you moved to Athens."

"Well, I knew who he was. He was kinda . . . not family, but . . . You go to the coffee shop, that's where he is," Tom tries to explain.

"Small village," Glykeria adds.

"When he was going to leave Athens to go visit his grandma, he used to travel the bus to go to the village with my dad," Tom says. "I knew who he was, and then George."

"So, knowing her dad and her brother really sealed the deal for them to agree for her to marry you, huh?"

"Oh yeah. Every day I go see him," he says about Glykeria's brother. "I go see him in the morning. I didn't work during the day; we didn't open until nine at night. I'd go see this George or the other George. Other friends too, from work. Let's go swimming today or go play soccer," he says.

"Knowing them made him more comfortable with you, but it probably also made you feel better about marrying her," I say.

"Oh yes. I depended on those people. Oh yeah, the family, you know, they gotta be okay. You know what I mean? Oh yeah," he says again. "That's what I relied on."

He would sometimes stop by the store where Giorgos worked for most of his adult life, selling and repairing Hoover vacuum cleaners. From these periodic visits, Tom got to know Giorgos's now-father-in-law, Xristo, as well.

"He was selling chestnuts outside the door. He had a little grill and depending on the season, in the fall roasting chestnuts, he'd sell a bag of chestnuts, that was his job, and during the summertime, when the corn was up, he was selling corn on the cob. A lot of money he was making like that."

Tom knew that Giorgos "had a little thing" with Xristo's daughter, Katina, "but of course I couldn't say that to the dad!" he snickers. "See, you had to keep it a secret. I don't think Xristo knew about George and Katina." They ended up getting married a year before Tom and Glykeria did, but Tom explains how it worked when couples were dating: "Seeing each other, but away from everybody else. You didn't want anyone to know about it. They probably bmmsffmmdout," he mumbles.

"What?" He doesn't usually mumble to himself like that.

"They probably beat you up if they find out," he states, more clearly. "Anyway. Little different than it is now." Ah. He hates to talk about things that he doesn't really want me to know about. Like him fighting all the time at bars. I asked him once what he wanted his grandchildren to know about him and he said, "There's a lot I DON'T want them to know!" He only wants his grandchildren to remember his good parts.

LEAVING THE VILLAGE
A job in the city

"My sister moved to Greece, 1969," Glykeria starts telling me.

"Greece?" Tom points out her misspeak.

"Ahhhh, I mean *sto* Athens." To Athens, she meant. She shakes her head. "My sister got married. February 28 or 29, 1971 her anniversary was. So I left the village and came to Athens for the wedding, and then I stayed in Athens. I didn't go back to the village."

"That always happens," Tom says. "Somebody, they take you along," he explains, illustrating how, one by one, everyone made their way out of the *xorio*.

"My brother didn't want me to come," Glykeria says. "He was afraid. He was living a bunch of boys. 'I want you to stay there?' he said to me."

"So, whose idea was it for you to stay then?" I ask. I had always assumed it was her brother's idea.

"My uncle. My dad's sister's husband. He say to my brother. He said, 'What she going to do in the village?'"

Giorgos conceded the point and Glykeria moved in with him. For the first time, Glykeria lived away from home and worked a wage-paying job.

Her sister Ismini was working at a local factory and got her a job at the same place. "Worked in a factory making notebooks, lined paper notebooks, plastic cover outside with a pocket. I was pressing the covers." It sounds like she enjoyed the work. "We had competition, who would make more," she says.

Glykeria hopped on a bus that stopped close to her house, and then transferred to a second bus that took her to work. Her commute took forty-five minutes. She didn't mind the travel time because she had a friend who got off a few stops after her and the two would chat on the bus on the way home. Every other week, she alternated working first and second shift.

"A month or two later, my sister, one of her friends, she said someone looking for girls to work. Close to her house." Glykeria accepted the job closer to home. It was only about a block away from where she was living so she was able to walk. It was another factory job, but instead of notebooks they made boxes. "Making all kinds of boxes. Shoe boxes. For books. For everything. All different boxes. Brown, white, different colors to wrap packages, pharmacy boxes," Glykeria tells me.

"What's a pharmacy box?" I ask.

"Everyone's making fun of me," she says, evading my question.

"Why?" *What's to make fun of about making boxes?*

"I don't want to say."

"You have to tell me now," I insist.

"They used to make boxes for . . ." she hesitates and whispers, "the man protectors."

Man protectors?

Then it hits me. "You were making condom boxes?" I try not to laugh because clearly she is uncomfortable. But I don't try that hard. My mother-in-law is so innocent, and the thought of her moving to the big city and getting a job making any product that is sex-related makes me giggle.

Yes. She can't even say it, she just nods it.

Other than being embarrassed about the packaging she made, she really enjoyed that job. "You had to cut them, got the extra papers and folding the box and put them in order." I can see her enjoying a job like that. She's a hard worker, she likes to move, and she feels good about getting things done. "Ten, fifteen people worked there. Like a family there. We used to collect money and all go out to get lunch together. A different person would go out to get lunch for everyone every day." Two brothers owned the company and one of the wives worked at the factory. She loved Glykeria so much that she passed along a lot of dresses and other clothes to her. Glykeria worked at the box factory for about two years.

I sit at her kitchen table. I'm typing and typing, cleaning up some of the text from the interview on her time at the box factory, and she brings me a cup of coffee. I nibble on a bowl of Cheetos that she gave to the girls but they forgot about. A while later, I'm still typing and she brings each of my daughters a small bowl of fruit. She brings one to me and says, "And here's one for mama." She cleans the bowls up when we are done. She washes my coffee cup when I put it in the sink. Later on, she pulls out the leftover pita. The one that I ate half the pan of yesterday. I eat more. "Good," she says. "Eat it all." I stop myself from eating it all, but just barely.

"Did you drive when you lived in Athens?" I ask. I assume the answer is no, since after being in the States for decades she is still only comfortable driving a handful of familiar routes and she's never gotten the nerve to drive on the highway (it's the merging that worries her), but I am not one hundred percent sure.

"Didn't drive," she confirms.

Tom lets me know this wasn't all that unusual: "No one had cars, not like here." It was easy to get around without a car; they could easily walk or take public transportation where they needed to go. This was a good thing, since it would have been expensive if they needed one. "The rich had cars," Tom tells me. "Ninety percent of Greeks didn't drive. The rich had chauffeurs." Glykeria eventually got her license in 1983, after living in the U.S. for nine years.

"Did you do anything besides work? Anything fun?" I ask her.

"Whatever I wanted to do, my brother wouldn't let me do it," she tells me. "I couldn't go anywhere without my sister or my brother. And then my brother got married and I used to go to the movies, go everywhere with her." She and her sister-in-law Katina are close. "We used to go together four, five of us, friends go together have ouzo, snacks. My sister-in-law had the kids and we'd go to the park." Whenever she went somewhere, she was chaperoned. "But not by myself, nowhere." Getting together with cousins, friends, and family was her main source of entertainment. She didn't even go to the Acropolis by herself.

"Wouldn't even let you ride the bus by yourself," Tom pipes up. "So strict. Overprotective."

"Didn't want you to go anywhere by yourself," Glykeria reiterates. "They have to go with you. But then my sister got pregnant and stayed home with the kids and then I would get on the bus by myself." Usually by herself. "But my brother, sometimes he popping up on the bus. You know they have the holders and you're packed in the hallways, hanging on?" she asks me as she mimes holding onto one of the handles that hangs from the bus ceilings.

"Mmm hmmm," I nod. My mouth is too full of *pita* for me to say more than that.

"One day, he comes up from behind and puts his hand over mine on the handle. Scares me! I turn around, and it was him. He keeps eye on me, you know, checking on me."

"Oh yeah. They want to keep them in line, you know," Tom adds.

"Not boys, boys didn't care too much, but the girls, you know, for reasons, they're afraid the girls go out to the boys, they're going to be pregnant and that's going to be embarrassing. That's it. No one wants you with babies and stuff. That's why I was afraid of it."

I guess this explains why, even now, she rarely goes out on her own, and if she does it's to shop or go to church. Other than that, her family members pretty much dictate her social calendar. Birthday parties, barbeques, babysitting. Every now and again, Tom will take her to the casino. That's about it.

"What did you and Katina do when you went out?" I ask her.

"Just go to the movies with her sometime. Didn't have a lot of money to go out anyway," she tells me.

Glykeria had gone home to visit a few times, but she had no intentions of returning there to live. She planned on living in Athens forever. "I loved it because in the village there was nothing, and in Athens that was where the jobs were." She liked to work in the city and make money, get paid.

"When you imagined your life when you were younger, did you imagine you would eventually live in Athens?"

"I thought that would not happen, so I was surprised. I never going to leave the village," she tells me.

"Really?" I'm surprised. She's such a go-getter.

"No. I never thought I'm going to leave the village because they never let us go anywhere and it was a big surprise for me," she tells me.

If anyone or anything could make *her* feel this way, I can't imagine how it could impact others in her situation. She is so much stronger than most.

LEAVING THE VILLAGE
A search for a spouse

"So, did you ever have a crush on anyone else, besides Tom?" I ask Glykeria.

She leans towards me. "No. But I didn't have a crush on TOM either!" she cackles.

"Touché," I reply. "Okay, but were there any other prospects?"

Glykeria had a couple of potential suitors before Tom showed up. She vaguely remembers one guy meeting her at her house, with her father, but apparently negotiations fell through before she got to know him well. In Athens, one of her sister-in-law's cousins brought someone to meet her, but nothing came of that either. Most matchmaking was done without the input of the individuals getting married, particularly the women. She also met a handsome taxi driver who lived in Athens. He was the cousin of her friend Alexandra. She met him at her friend's house and the two talked a bit. He wrote home to discuss the potential marriage arrangement with his family and was waiting for a reply.

Alexandra warned him that Glykeria was planning to meet Tom in the near future, though they didn't know exactly when. While the taxi driver was figuring things out on his end, "Tom shows up and we got married." Things move quickly with arranged marriages. Glykeria remembers running into him while heading back to Athens, after her wedding in the village. "We came back to Athens, to the bus station, and went to take the taxi home and it happens to be him! We were in the back seat and Tom's arms is around me and he sees our rings." The two did not acknowledge that they knew one another. "He just looking at me from the mirror. He was looking at me and looking at me. It was funny," Glykeria says. "I recognized him too, but Tom didn't know anything," she adds.

"You didn't say anything to him, did you?"

"No, I didn't say anything there."

Those are the only suitors I hear of until one day Glykeria tells me,

"I don't know if anybody knows about this. I told Tom." She glances at her husband. I nod. Spouses don't count. "Maybe my brother knows but he never mention. Back in the village, before I left in Athens, my dad receive a letter. It was posted to me, it had my name on it, but I never see the letter. My dad open it. "Was 1970 when he sent that letter. I still don't know exactly what happened. It said, 'I like you,' but I couldn't figure out who the letter was from. My mom ask me when I went to the dump truck—when I went to pick some cottons to get paid—my mom ask me, 'Did you meet somebody down there? Did you do anything you shouldn't?' I told her, 'No, I don't know nobody.' So after that, they keep an eye on me. To this day I don't know, who was it?"

"Could you read it?"

"Mmm hmm! He was writing down, 'I like you and I want you but I can't meet up with you.' The way he was writing down seems like he thought I was more rich than him. How poor must he have been?! To this day I still don't know who sent it. So, after that, my dad kept an eye on me. Just popping up with not expected somewhere. He thought I was doing something secret, you know."

Tom had the one prospect: Soula. "I was dating before I came to the States. She was living in Athens. We dated for a couple months before I came to America, and she would have liked to have come over."
Tom and Soula had kept in touch, writing back and forth to one another after he moved to the States.

"How often did the two of you write back and forth?"

"Geehhhhhh," Tom lets out an exasperated sigh and waves his forearm towards me. He does this a lot when I pepper him with my questions. But despite any dismissive arm flaps he throws my way, he always answers. "A few letters, I guess. A couple times a month." The two continued to correspond during the five years Tom was living in America.

Tom first met Soula on the train from Athens up to his village, which passed through her hometown. Tom can't remember why he was heading home on the day he met her. "Maybe elections?" he asks himself out loud. He gripes about how Greece had some "stupid law" which required people to vote at the location of their birth, instead of where they were currently living. Much more interesting than why he was heading up to the village, though, is what he used to carry around with him—the item that piqued Soula's interest, and started the two talking.

Tom tells me he used to carry around his "portable" record player, about the size of a hat box, and a huge stack of 33s. "Had that thing all the time," he says. "Wherever there was a plug."

"So, what kind of music did you listen to?" I ask. In my mind, I imagine him playing rebetika records: Greek folk music, chock full of tangy chords strummed on the bouzouki and ecclesiastical chanting that came from the diaphragms of men whose mouths were trimmed with dark, thick mustaches.

"Pos se lene?" He turns to his wife and asks her what the name of the music was that he liked. "Not pop, but like *bouzoukia* type of stuff," he tells me. Greek night club music. "Instead of clarinets and violins. Country music, in other words. Not too much there." No one listened to folk music in Athens. "Every night we had the bouzouki-type things," he tells me. "We tried to go to every artist or singer or whatever. They give us one or we buy a record for a dollar," he says, indicating that a lot of the records he listened to were local artists. "That's where my money went too, by the way. All my money," he says.

"Johnny Walker Red, right?"

He nods. "The thing is, you knew, go back tonight and make it again. So you didn't care too much. Next morning have ten drachmas for cigarettes or something. I'll get it tonight. No problem." Every night he'd blow the money he made working at the restaurant, knowing he'd have more in his pocket the following evening.

"I listened to everything, pretty much. Classical . . ." he says.

"Really? Like what?"

"Mozart. Beethoven. Chopin."

On the train, Soula broke the ice by flipping through his stack of records, saying she really admired his taste in music. The two talked during the entire five-hour train ride, getting to know each other fairly well. Tom even met her mother, who was with Soula on the trip. Before parting, the pair ended up exchanging numbers. Once they were both back in Athens, they talked on the phone regularly and would get together every once in a while, usually on Tom's days off, since she worked days and he worked nights.

"She was an architect. She went to the biggest architecture school in Greece.

The guy who built I-75 started the college in Greece, or something like that." He tells me he thought she might not be the most fitting wife for him, because she was so well-educated.

Glykeria can't help herself, she interjects, "See what happens when you go for education, lady? Haha!"

During one of our interview sessions at a later date, Tom admits he was intimidated because she was so much "above me." As he says this, he gestures with his hand above his head, meaning she was far more educated than he was. Tom only finished the sixth grade back in his village, though he did continue his education in the U.S. as an adult.

Despite these misgivings, Tom met up with Soula and her family at the beginning of his trip back home, thinking she might be the one he would marry. But he ultimately decided that they didn't get along as well as he remembered.

"She was a hippie-type girl and I wasn't like that." Tom makes it a point to tell me that he was not a hippie every time any discussion of the 1960s or '70s comes up. Every single time. He continuously defends the fact that he wore bell bottoms, saying it was impossible to purchase any other style of trousers at the time.

He goes on to list reasons why Soula wouldn't have made a suitable bride: "She was modern-type girl, from the city. She liked to go out a lot; she was very modern. I figured she wouldn't last very long here in America." Tom had settled in Saginaw, Michigan. "Saginaw wasn't Athens. People hated Saginaw then. People still hate Saginaw. So, we broke up." Amicably, so he tells me. He adds later, "She kept calling my cousin after the fact, asking why."

It turns out that there were several possible wives for Tom. There was another prospect, named Christina. She was from the same tiny village in central Greece as Tom and Glykeria, and was one of Glykeria's very best friends. One of Tom's cousins called Christina and invited her to come to Athens to meet Tom, for the most important of blind dates. She did end up heading to Athens, but by the time she arrived Tom was already on his way up the mountaintop to marry Glykeria. Christina phoned Glykeria at one point and told her, "I'm in Athens, I'm here to meet Tom," and Glykeria replied, "Too late, he's with me." Clearly neither one of the girls held a grudge, as they are still good friends and talk occasionally to this day.

Tom recalls another prospect: "When I went home to the village, my Uncle Stephanos gave me the name of another girl from our same village. I went to school with her. Her name was Roula."

I squint at him. "Roula?"

Roula is the name Glykeria has gone by ever since she came to the United States. It's the nickname Tom gave his wife when they married. Glykeria is known as Roula to her coworkers, her neighbors, and all of her friends. I start to wonder if he met so many girls during this time that he got their names confused and it just stuck.

Glykeria and Roula were also friends, though they were not as close as Glykeria and Christina. Glykeria didn't know that Roula had been another potential prospect until after she and Tom were already married, but she does remember her friend asking her numerous questions regarding her wedding plans and her pending trip to America. Apparently, several of Tom's uncles argued about which of the two girls would make a better wife for him. Tom placed the most value on the opinion of his mother's brothers, John and Gregory, who were rooting for Glykeria.

BONUS! YIAYIA'S BEAN SOUP RECIPE
Fasolada

You will need:

Pinto Beans: 1 large jar. Yiayia uses Randall's.

Carrots: Just a couple; too many and the soup will be too sweet. Diced.

Celery: A few stalks, diced.

Onions: Chopped.

Tomato Paste: About ½ of a small can, dissolved in water.

Crushed Tomatoes: A 16-oz can.

You will do:

1. Sauté the carrot, onion, and celery in the bottom of a large pot.

2. Add the beans and tomatoes (including liquid for both).

3. Simmer for an hour or so.

Serve with Yiayia's white bread and feta.

TOM AND GLYKERIA'S WEDDING

Finally, we've reached the wedding story. The original interview that began in the car and has been rehashed dozens of times since. This is where it all began. Everyone loves a good love story. Even one that began before there was love.

Tom took his first steps onto American soil during the winter of 1969. His mother, Athena, and sisters Effie and Romi had emigrated to the States a couple of years earlier. Effie secured him his first job in the United States, working with her, Romi, and Yiayia Athena. They worked at Mr. Hotdog: a family restaurant of the Coney Island variety, with a secret sauce recipe, one that everyone in his family still raves about and every so often tries to replicate from memory in their own kitchen. Tom experienced a bit of culture shock.

"I had my mom here, my two sisters here. It was their life, there was nothing for me here. I went to the bars or the disco, it wasn't for me. Totally different," he says, describing how life changed for him once he moved to the States. "Sometimes we just stay home and have wine or a drink. But nothing. Totally different lifestyle. I kind of settled down, in other words. I don't know if that's the word," he struggles to explain. "I changed completely the next day. That's it," he tells me.

He was a new person in the new environment. "We didn't have the TV watching Greece," he says, referring to all of the Greek channels he subscribes to today. "All we had was a few records, if we bought them - if we went to Detroit and found a 45 . . ." he trails off.

"Everything American," Glykeria clarifies. He wasn't in the old country anymore.

"Besides the church," Tom points out. This was the exception, the one place where he felt connected to his old life. "We got to church every Sunday. Uncle Gregory came by every Sunday and picked me up," he says. His tone changes a bit and he adds, "Whether I wanted to go or not."

After five years of working and saving as much of his paychecks as he could, he decided to head back to Greece for a month-long trip to visit family. Tom was twenty-seven years old and decided he was ready to settle down. "Well, you're twenty-seven, if you plan on doing something you might as well do it," he explains. "Why wait until you're forty? I was going there, I didn't have any . . ." he pauses. "It's not like you can afford to go every six months or a year. I was there. I figure, better get married now and get it over with," he says.

"He make up his decision go there instead of spending money again," Glykeria chimes in.

"I had enough of that life, so you decide to settle down. That's all."

Per family tradition, Tom was looking for an arranged marriage. Sometimes he gets a little defensive about it, as if I'm judging him. "Yeah, it was like an arranged marriage. It was usual. It's not like I was the first one doing that."

"But he wasn't going back for me, Christine!" Glykeria shouts out.

"I wasn't going back to Greece for Glykeria," Tom confirms. "I was going back to visit and maybe to marry another girl. Soula," he says, glancing my way to make sure I remember hearing about her.

"That's right. I remember that. So, how did you and Glykeria end up getting together?"

"Well, her dad sent a letter to Father Gregory and just mentioned the idea of trying to find a husband for his daughter. Wanted to know if he knew anybody." Tom's uncle, the priest, was the first member of his family to emigrate to America, having done so in the 1940s. He started out in Massachusetts, and had moved to Saginaw, Michigan when an opening as a priest presented itself at St. Demetrios Greek Orthodox Church in 1951. When Father Gregory dropped Tom off at the airport to head back to Greece, he passed along a photo of Glykeria and said, "As long as you are going over there, you should go have a look and check this girl out. We know the family. She comes from a good family." Tom shrugs. "And this and that. I stuck the picture in my pocket. Nothing to it."

With all of the other prospects I know existed for both of them at the time, I have to ask, "So, what was it that ultimately made the two of you end up together?"

Tom laughs for a minute and then replies, "They made me an offer and I couldn't refuse."

"What's that?" I ask.

"Sausages."

Glykeria nods.

I should have known it would be her cooking.

Both remember that they met on January 31, 1974, but as they tell me the story they bicker back and forth from the back seat of my car about what day of the week it was. Tom states assertively, "I went over there on a Wednesday night. January 31, 1974."

In a classic marital move, Glykeria interrupts, shaking her head, saying, "No, it was a Tuesday."

Tom maintains his position. "I'm positive it was a Wednesday! Because Achilles had to work and he came up after that night."

I grab my phone and looked it up online while they bicker in the back seat. January 31 was a Thursday that year.

"What? How you get Thursday from?" Tom asks me, accusingly.

The internet, Tom. The internet. It remembers.

Tom's blink lasts significantly longer than usual and his speech pauses momentarily while his eyes are shut. After a moment he finishes his sentence: "and we decided to go to the village and get married." I think he's taking a breath, but after a moment I realize he just stopped talking. I'm smacked in the face with his brevity. Maybe he's pissed about the whole day of the week thing, or maybe he thinks he's getting out of telling me all of the juicy details.

Come on, Tom.

Luckily for me, they are trapped in the back seat of my car so I am able to continue badgering them to tell more of the story that I want the particulars of so badly. I kept prodding.

Glykeria had been living with her brother Giorgos in Athens for the past three years, employed at a packaging plant, making boxes. She was in the middle of her shift when their cousin George called Giorgos and said, "We're coming to your house." He was bringing Tom over to meet Glykeria.

Right then.

Even though Tom had talked with Giorgos about meeting his sister, no date or time had been established. Getting Tom to make plans ahead of time is impossible now, and apparently he was the same way back then.

Her sister-in-law Katina walked up to the factory, rang the bell and told the employee who answered that she needed to talk to Glykeria immediately. They let Katina in, and she told Glykeria, "You have to come home, someone is coming to meet you. You have to come home now." Glykeria was embarrassed by her sister-in-law's sudden appearance and the spectacle it caused. She was uncomfortable with the questions she received from her coworkers. She wasn't sure how to answer when they asked "Where are you going?" and "What do you have to do?"

She evaded their questions. "I don't know, something came up," she stammered. She didn't share with them that she was meeting her potential husband. "I don't remember what we say, but didn't say the truth." Her face reddens; that she is still self-conscious about this experience is evident, over thirty years after the fact. "Everyone was making fun of me," she says. Perhaps it was the prospect of admitting to her peers that she was getting set up in an arranged marriage, or perhaps it was simply being told what to do and having to leave work without giving her employer any notice. Despite how uncomfortable the situation made her, she obliged and punched out.

As Glykeria explains how she felt about the situation, Tom adds matter-of-factly, "You didn't have a choice. No one asked you, they just told you what to do." He turns to me and says, "That's how things worked back then. For us."

"That's right." Glykeria confirms this with a nod.

Glykeria left work and went home to get ready.

"What did you wear?" I ask, curious.

She places her hand high on her thigh and says, "Mini mini mini skirt."

I raise my eyebrows. "Really?"

"It was all I had!" She shrugs.

I think I know her well enough to know that that is a bunch of bullshit, but I let her continue anyway. "And a yellow shirt with polka dot stripes on the chest and a multicolored plaid jacket with a wide collar. I love that jacket, Christine. I wore that for years. Even here." I recall seeing pictures of her in this jacket while flipping through family pictures that had been pulled out of the closet.

"I wouldn't remember that," Tom says. "After a bottle of ouzo, it all looked the same." I remind him that that is why I asked *her* what she wore, and not him. I look at her and roll my eyes.

Glykeria tells me about their first encounter: "I served him coffee, then ouzo, then *loukanika*," homemade sausages, an appetizer to go with the ouzo.

"Very salty," Tom jokes, his laughter almost silent until the guffaw at the end.

She explains the humor behind the joke: "We didn't have refrigerators so the sausages *had* to be salty, okay?" Meat was relatively rare, but every Christmas Glykeria's family butchered one of their pigs, often making sausages that could last for two or three months after the holiday. Her mother would grind the pork, add leeks, salt, pepper, parsley, garlic and oregano, and use a wooden dowel to push the spiced meat mixture through a funnel into casings made out of the swine's own intestines. The sausages were strung up across the kitchen to dry. Even though Glykeria says she found Tom attractive, she wasn't interested at all in moving to America. She had pictured continuing her life living in Athens.

Her cousin George came to the kitchen, catching her alone for a moment and asked, "What do you think?"

Glykeria answered honestly: "George, I don't want to go to America."

"Shut up and go make some coffee," was his reply.

"And that was it," Glykeria says as she looks at me pointedly.

Tom ribs her about them being too salty, but he says the *loukanika* were delicious. Mouthwatering savory links. They must have been at least partially factored into his decision. After finishing them, Tom turned to Giorios and said, "Okay" which apparently was all that needed to be said to indicate that the wedding was on. "Had some sausages. A little ouzo. That was it. They got me drunk, actually. So I couldn't say no." He grins.

Even though Glykeria was worried about going to a country where she didn't know the language or anyone who lived there, she didn't protest again. George had been to America a few times and knew that there were many opportunities for Glykeria that she would never have if she stayed in Greece. Tom adds that George knew that "if she didn't come to America with me, she could end up staying in the village chasing goats around." Glykeria says that maybe she would have ended up living in Athens, married to the handsome taxi driver. They shrug their shoulders. There's no way to know.

A blood test was required before couples were allowed to marry.

Glykeria's blood work was already on file, but Tom's was not. Tom says, "That night I went to my doctor's office. My brother called him and up and said, 'We're coming up.'" The three of them went to the physician and, without Tom actually getting any blood drawn or tested, the required paperwork was signed. Neither Tom nor Glykeria know how much Giorgos paid for this expedient service.

From the doctor, the trio headed to Glykeria's sister Ismini's house. Katina had filled Ismini in a bit earlier in the day, but Glykeria hadn't yet had the chance to talk to her sister.

"She had no clue at this point," Glykeria says, about the details of her sudden betrothal. When the two met face-to-face, Ismini shouted, "Oh my God, I didn't expect this! Nobody told me anything!" She may have been referring to the engagement or she may have been referring to the surprise visit. "She didn't have her hair done or anything," Glykeria says. She may not have primped, but Ismini was still a competent hostess. When the group arrived, she was cooking chickpeas. "Tom sat down, ate the whole pot. He said, 'I come here and eat the best food.'" It runs in the family. Glykeria spent the remainder of the evening with Katina, Ismini and Ismini's twin boys, who were one at the time. Achilles came over to visit, and he and Tom ended up going out to grab a drink at a local bar where one of their mutual friends worked.

"Next day we went for dresses and shopping," Glykeria tells me. The day after they met, Tom and Glykeria went shopping in Athens with Giorgos and Katina for their wedding essentials. Once in the city, they rented a wedding dress (this was a common practice at the time; only the uber-rich bought dresses). While Glykeria tried on dresses, Tom gave his opinion, saying no to the ones he didn't like. He chose the dress she wore.

"What did your wedding dress look like?" I ask.

"Short sleeves with long white gloves. It went down," she says, making a sweeping motion with her arms, from her chest to her hips. "It was not fancy, Christine, it was simple like the rest of it."

Simple as the whole wedding may have been to her, I remind her that I want to know details surrounding the simplicity, and ask if she has a picture that shows her as a bride. When we're at her house one day, she digs through a cardboard box full of unsorted photos in the bottom of her linen closet. She brings me a couple of blurry snapshots from her wedding day. Even through the blur, I obtained so much more information visually than I had received verbally.

She wore an A-line dress, its deep scoop neck lined with an inch and a half of stiff white ribbon that contained within it three or four rows of stitching, each row spaced about a centimeter apart. Over the white taffeta rested a layer of finely woven lace with scattered, diamond-shaped, beaded embellishments, adding just a bit of shine. The dress hit her ankle bone and had no train. She wore opaque white stocking and white pumps, with straps that crossed over the tops of her small feet, and low, square heels. On the crown of her head she wore a headpiece of scalloped ribbon and lace. Her outfit looks so much more dignified and ornate than I originally pictured it, as the simple village attire she described.

Once they had settled on the dress and accessories, Tom purchased two identical rings: broad bands of gold, simple in style, lacking any engravings, etchings or other ornamentation on the outside. Glykeria runs to her bedroom and fetches the rings. They are usually nestled inside her jewelry box instead of on their fingers.

She allows me to inspect them. Inside each ring is an inscription; they both have the other's first and last name (her maiden name, I notice) and their wedding date, with the block letter text covering a little less than half of the internal loop. In addition to the rings, Tom bought a necklace for Glykeria, which she still has.

"Is rusty now," she says. (The necklace had become tarnished, so Lambros's sister Athena took it to her jeweler to have it cleaned up. It came back shiny and breathtakingly beautiful. The large gold pendant is a few inches in diameter, the Greek key encircles a gold cutout of the Acropolis.)

Glykeria wanted to buy Tom something in return, so she ended up buying him an umbrella. I walk outside with Tom while he takes a smoke break in the garage. He holds his Winston with his right hand and grabs a beat-up black umbrella off of a hook hanging on the wall of the garage with his left. He still has the gift, over thirty-five years later. He's visibly excited to show off this worn, charcoal umbrella. He says, "This used to be the cutest thing! It used to collapse into itself and you could put it into a little pouch." It no longer collapses into itself, the mechanisms on the inside is as broken-down as the tattered nylon of the exterior. He repeats, "It was the cutest thing!"

I'm not sure if I've ever heard my father-in-law use the term "cute." He's gruff. A man's man that lives off of cigarettes and black coffee. He has few material needs. He does what he wants, when he wants to. He's the type that never goes to the doctor, even when he's doubled over in pain. I enjoy the novelty of hearing his reaction to the wedding gift much more than I enjoy seeing the gift itself. We head back inside and continue to rehash the details, picking up the story from where we left off, at the umbrella purchase.

It was a long day of shopping and traveling, and by the time they reached the bus station, it was about four-thirty in the morning. The betrothed, still accompanied by Giorgos and Katina, spent the night in the depot and waited to catch the next bus back to the village. Glykeria shows me a photo of her waiting at the station, in the dark of night. She's wearing a lavender pea coat, her hair already set for the ceremony the next day, her dark tresses pulled up into a simple, elegant bun on the back of her head. The weather was fine so the bus trip "didn't take much time," only three hours or so, which was quite quick compared to how long it might have taken if conditions were poor.

The bus took the group as far as the river, where the route ended. Their destination, Glykeria's village, was still two miles away. Tom and Glykeria dispute the details of this part of the story.

At first, Glykeria tells me that her father came to the river to help them, bringing with him two mules for them to ride atop of, to make crossing the rough waters more manageable. She tells me he took the women first, then went back to get the men.

Tom shakes his head and insists that her brother Giorgos carried each of them, one at a time, across the width of the river on his shoulders.

Glykeria then changes her story a bit, insisting that her father helped them across, but that he only brought one mule with him, which she rode on, and she declares adamantly that her father stripped down to his underwear and carried Tom across the river on his back.

Tom shakes his head again, and allows her the fact that he did, once, ride across the river on his half-naked father-in-law's back. He adds that he almost fell into the rapids that time, but denies that this was the method of crossing on the eve of their wedding day.

On every retelling of this story, both manage to consistently concur that the celebration was important enough to warrant the butchering of one of their valuable lambs. Or goats. The exact species of ungulate changes from one telling of the story to the next, but regardless of which hooved mammal was eaten, they're at least in alignment on this part.

The day before the wedding, they went to church for the rehearsal. Tom wore his burgundy corduroy bell bottoms. "Had a thirty-inch waist, thirty-two-inch bells!" Tom says, using his hands to show me how wide the flares on his pants were. "My older sister Eftehia said to me, 'Give me those pants, I'll make two *fustas* out of them!'" Skirts. Tom announces several times that these were the only kind of pants you could purchase at that time.

"I wasn't a hippie or anything," he says for the millionth time. His four-inch, black, platform boots boosted him up to the height of six foot two, and all of the Greeks he towered over gave him the nickname of Tall Guy.

"Saturday we went to church," Glykeria tells me. "Went to church Saturday morning," she repeats.

"What you talking? I didn't go to church," Tom disputes.

"No, no, no, we went up and left from there," Glykeria states firmly, sure that Tom was with her.

He points to himself and silently shakes his head back and forth. *No.*

"Little details . . . makes no difference to anybody else anyway," he says.

Sometimes though, it's those little details that I find fascinating.

The *koumbaro*, the best man, came up from Athens. The pair had chosen Achilles. Achilles bought the wedding necessities for the ceremony, as tradition imposed. It's a significant honor and a fairly large financial investment to be the *koumbaro* in an Orthodox marriage ceremony. The *koumbaro* is expected to be a reputable member and role model of the Orthodox religion, as he often ends up as the godparent of the couple's first-born child. The *koumbaro* purchases the *stefana* (wedding crowns), *lambades* (candles), the *boubounieres* (favors) and, in this case, material that is wrapped around the shoulders of the bride and groom during the wedding ceremony, binding them together with the material just as they are about to be bound together in God's eyes. Glykeria remembers that the material was brown, with a floral pattern. After the wedding, she used the material to sew herself a dress.

Tom's *theio* Ianni shook up their plans a bit. "That day he said, 'Who's your *koumbaro*?' 'My cousin.' 'Oh no no no. I'll get you a *koumbaro.*'" Tom replays the conversation.

"Why wasn't it okay for you to have Achilles as your *koumbaro*?"

"Because the kid was living in his house all through school. Too close of relatives," Glykeria answers.

"Like your brother be your best man or something," Tom adds. "Had to get somebody else from outside."

"You're not allowed to have your brother as a *koumbaro*?" I ask. I don't see what's wrong with having your brother as the best man.

"It's not like a rule, it's what my uncle wanted and who's going to argue with that guy? You don't argue with that guy . . ." Tom trails off. I'd love to meet the one guy on Earth Tom wouldn't argue with.

"So he calls one of my neighbors. 'Hey, come on down. We need you there. Come on down. You don't need anything.'" Tom remembers him saying.

"Who was the neighbor?"

"Leonidas. Old neighbor," Tom says. "And uh, that was just a little . . . I didn't have any choice, I liked Achilles!" he blurts.

"We brought him up from Athens for that!" Glykeria adds.

"Was he pissed?" I asked.

"Yeah, yeah, you know how it is," Tom says. "Didn't make any difference," he concedes. "It's a family friend too. I knew that guy from a little kid. Neighbor. My dad's best buddy and that's why he wanted him anyway," Tom tells me.

Four days after their initial meeting over ouzo and sausages, their wedding day arrived. On Sunday, February 3, 1974, the pair got married at the church, called *Panagia,* in the village. The church's name refers to the Virgin Mary. Katina helped Glykeria put on her gown and boosted her onto the gray mule she rode to the church. The mule wore an ornate lace blanket across the width of its back, which she sat upon. Tom left his uncle's house donning a black suit. A colorful striped wool blanket was draped across the back of the mule he rode on. The pair met at the church.

The Orthodox church is apostolic, meaning that sacraments and services have remained unchanged, as much as possible, since the beginning of Orthodoxy itself. Church services and holy ceremonies do not vary depending on the priest or the parish, like other denominations often do. Their wedding ceremony was performed in traditional Greek Orthodox fashion. I ask Glykeria if there was anything that stood out from her wedding that she thinks is worth noting, and she feeds me this little morsel: "If you want the men to listen to the wife, you step on his toes when the priest says to start going around the altar."

Repeating actions three times is commonly seen in Orthodox rites and symbolizes the Holy Trinity. During the wedding service, the bride, groom, and *koumbaro* are led by the priest around the altar three times. It is considered their first walk together as a married couple. I am curious to know if she was successful in her attempt to step on her husband's toes.

"So, did you do it?"

"I tried, but I couldn't do it! Tom had a big shoe on and I couldn't get my little toe, my little foot on," she says.

Based on what I know of their relationship, Tom completes projects around the house, takes charge of the finances, and does what he wants, when he wants, without much regard to his wife's preferences, while Glykeria, stereotypically female, does all of the cooking, cleaning, and knitting, and defers to her husband for practically any decision that involves leaving the home, with the exception of the occasional shopping trip. Not being able to step on his toes at their wedding seems like it was a pretty damned accurate foreshadowing.

Tom explains that it was customary for newlyweds to ride their mules from the church to the bride's house, and on this return trip the couple traded animals; Tom rode the mule that Glykeria rode to the church and Glykeria rode the one that carried Tom to the church.

"Yeah, the way back, just because of tradition, the groom's horse, the bride has to ride that back." He recalls the gray mule: "They gave me a little little short one. It was SO short! My legs, I thought they were dragging. Hahahaha, oh man!" Tom dies laughing when he tells this part of the story. Every. Time. A deep belly laugh. About halfway back he said, "Forget it. This is stupid. I walked most of the time."

"No, you didn't walk at all!" Glykeria disputes.

"Yes, I did!" he argues. His eyes are watering because he has been laughing so hard. "Ah, it was fun," he smiles.

They spent the night at Glykeria's, celebrating with a spit-roasted lamb dinner and a few dozen friends, family and neighbors. The couple note that while the celebration was a good one, some of their close family members missed out on the festivities. Two of Tom's sisters, Eftihia and Chyrsanthe, missed the wedding ceremony because they had difficulty getting to the mountainside church due to inclement weather, but they arrived shortly after.

On the way to the wedding, his "sisters hear the old ladies all yapping about these crazy bell bottoms." He laughs as he pictures his sisters overhearing gossip about their brother. Even though they themselves ribbed him about the bell bottoms being as big as skirts, they took great offense at hearing someone else badmouth their brother's garb. Siblings can be the most cruel, because they know how to hit where it hurts, yet they can also be the most protective, ready to fight to the death for their sibling's honor, even if the actions of the aggressor are virtually the same as their own. Maybe especially when this is so.

The girls apparently ended up yelling back and forth, arguing with the old ladies. Chyrsanthe was so mad she couldn't even speak by the time she reached the village, her voice too hoarse from hollering. Eftihia wasn't nearly as concerned about the situation, so she didn't yell that much and thus arrived, after the ceremony had taken place, with vocal chords intact. The bell-bottomed suit that caused the argument was one of Tom's favorites. "I wore that suit for a long time," Tom tells me. "I had it over here. I was so skinny though. Thirty-two-inch waist. Ahhhh, it was fun."

Glykeria's sister Ismini couldn't attend the wedding because traveling up the mountain with her one-and-a-half-year-old twins, Christos and Dimitri, would have been too difficult. She had not been able to make it to the wedding of their brother Giorgios either, since at the time of his wedding she had recently had her twins and, per religious custom, wasn't supposed to leave the house. Greek Orthodox religion imposes several forty-day timelines.

Examples include the forty-day churching for a newborn, where the mother and child leave the home and enter the church for the first time after childbirth, and the forty-day memorial, where family members gather to honor the recently deceased. With these timelines come recommended restrictions. For example, newlyweds don't attend funerals within the forty days after the marriage and mothers aren't supposed to leave their houses with their babies until after the forty-day blessing has occurred. Ismini felt so badly about missing her sister's wedding that, years later, she made it a point to fly to the United States to attend all three of Glykeria and Tom's children's weddings.

In addition to missing some key guests, there was also no music or dancing at the wedding; Glykeria had a relative who passed away within forty days of the wedding date, so the family was considered to be in mourning. Ordinarily a wedding wouldn't be scheduled during this time, but there was a rush to marry as Tom had already booked his return flight to the United States for February 10. Even missing these things, both remember the day as one of merriment.

The day after the wedding, Glykeria and Tom were supposed to catch a bus from the village to the closest town and from there transfer to a bus that would return them to Athens. The travel conditions were horrible, since asphalt roads were nonexistent. "There weren't any roads, and this is going from the top of the mountain to the bottom. It was raining, so the bus we were supposed to take wouldn't take us because there were no roads; the roads were washed out," Tom explains. The pair stayed one more night in the village, and the next day the two started walking down the mountain towards the next closest bus station, about forty miles away.

It would be nice to think that Tom and Glykeria huddled close together under the umbrella she bought him, the gift a perfect symbol of how she was able to take care of her husband during stormy times, and the two of them stayed dry and cozy. In reality, it was so windy walking down the side of the mountain that the umbrella kept turning inside out, a useless, wavering nylon "u" above their heads, collecting droplets. To top it off—as if walking down the side of a mountain without roads or guard rails, carrying suitcases, on a rainy February day wasn't bad enough—Tom had the additional burden of carrying about twenty pounds of hay seed that needed to be delivered to his brother-in-law Harithimo's house. "We have a little suitcase and a bag of seed. Hay seed. To take it down since we were going down, drop it off to my brother-in-law. About ten, twenty pounds; it wasn't that big," Tom explains.

"It got wet though," Glykeria says, her voice deepening.

"Well, if we did what I planned in the first place wouldn't have all that in between problem. But we started going there and somebody calls, 'Oh, come back here, the bus is coming,'" Tom says. They ended up second-guessing their original route and turned back to catch the bus at a different point. "We went the other way, which made it worse. Rain got worse! It never stopped! It rained like twenty-four hours straight," Tom elaborates on the conditions. "I had brand new boots," he says.

"The four-inch platforms?" I smile at him, letting him know I have not forgotten about those.

He nods. "It was so wet that the heel of my right boot fell off! We were soaking wet from head to toe."

"So now you're hobbling down the mountain, in the rain, carrying a twenty-pound sack of seeds?" I confirm. I shake my head.

"That's right, Christine!" Glykeria says.

I think about how the morning after my wedding I slept in, woke up late and rolled over lazily on a plush mattress in a honeymoon suite, before hopping in the shower and heading to the continental breakfast. Not quite the exciting start to the marriage that they had.

"Finally the bus showed up in afternoon," Tom says. It ended up coming a few miles before they thought it would. They hopped in. "Just us, one other couple."

"She was pregnant, she was going to have a baby," Glykeria remembers. "We thought she was going to have the baby on the bus."

"The bus was leaking all over the place!" Tom howls. "It was worse than being outside!" he shouts. "Bus was rocking from the wind. Bus was leaking all over, didn't matter where you were sitting," he says.

"Bus was full of water," Glykeria adds. "I was so scared."

"I had a garbage bag over our heads so we wouldn't get wet," Tom tells me.

"More wet, you mean?" I snort.

"We were soaking wet."

Glykeria continues the story: "We got the taxi and went to Tom's sister's house. Went to his sister's house and his sister wasn't back from the wedding yet." Eftihia had come up for the wedding, but she hadn't yet made it back home. She took her time on the return trip to avoid slogging through the soggy territory, so only her husband and her kids were there to greet and house them for the evening. "We slept and the next morning there was a snake IN THE BED. I'm not going to forget that," Glykeria shudders. I amaze myself by refraining from any juvenile honeymoon jokes about her spotting a "snake" in her bed for the first time.

The two continued to travel, stopping briefly to visit Tom's uncle. A day after that, they finally arrived in Athens. From the train station, the two took a taxi to Glykeria's brother, Giorgos's house.

You remember this taxi ride, right? Glykeria and the handsome driver locking eyes through the rear-view mirror? Tom oblivious to the fact that his wife and the driver could have easily been married, had Tom not swept in when he did? Yeah, that was this taxi ride.

Tom stayed with Glykeria in Athens for a couple of days and then left on his return flight to America. Back in the United States, he filled out the necessary paperwork, so that his bride could join him. It took a few months for the process to be completed, and she followed him here in June. When Glykeria came over, he started calling her Roula. This was a new nickname for her—up until then she had gone by Glykeria, or Ria.

While at their house, confirming details and asking them clarifying questions about the wedding for the umpteenth time, Tom picks up his sixteen-month-old granddaughter, Penelope, and says to her, "When you grow up, I'm going to send you to the *xorio* and set you up with a nice *gambro*, a nice husband. A *vlaxo*." Tom must think that the arrangement worked out quite well for him, if he wishes, even jokingly, the same for this granddaughter he adores. Glykeria understands that this is Tom's subtle way of paying her the biggest of compliments, a rare gesture on his part. She smiles.

EPILOGUE

"What do you think is the most important thing about getting these stories written down?" I ask them.

"The memories they gonna have. That's all. The memories. Memories of my life. Where we did," Glykeria says.

"That's all. So they know what life I had." Tom nods.

"When we were there, we hate it. Oh my God, we hated it. We cried every day, 'Oh I'm tired of it.'" Glykeria says.

"Complaining," Tom confirms.

"You did? I didn't know you complained. You never complain. I thought you were super-people."

Glykeria is sitting at the kitchen table, her elbows resting on the edge. She puts her face in her hands and sits like that for several minutes. Her emotional response startles me. "To remember all those things . . ." she trails off. "It's hard to think about that stuff, even now. But I would do it over again. I was poor, hungry, but I'd still do it over," she tells me.

I thank them for letting me interrogate them about their lives over the past several years. For letting me dredge up and poke around all of their memories—the good and the bad.

"Ahhhh, c'mon." Tom waves my thanks away with his hand.

"Thanks for what, Christine? We don't do nothing," Glykeria says, backing him up.

I shake my head. They don't know how to give anything less than all of themselves.

ACKNOWLEDGEMENTS

GRATITUDE. So much I can barely articulate it, for the following individuals: Glykeria and Tom Skoutelas, for letting me into their lives. My husband Lambros Skoutelas, for not giving me flack for how much time I spent staring at my computer screen. My editor, Chelsea Johnson, who worked so efficiently and who was kind enough not to yell at me every time I added new text to a section she had already edited. My assistant editors, Dan Riney and Laura Ross, for helping me get started and for cheering me on along the way. I would also like to express my appreciation for everyone who patiently listened to me ramble on about this project while I worked on it, and who kindly smiled and nodded their head.

ABOUT THE AUTHOR

Christine Skoutelas is a special education teacher by day and a half-assed blogger, freelance writer and mixed media artist by night. She loves spending time with her family, practicing yoga, and drinking red wine. She hates mornings and mean people. Christine is addicted to caffeine, nachos, and finding new hobbies. Christine posts her writing and her art under the name, A Morning Grouch. You can find her on the web at amorninggrouch.com and on Instagram.

RECIPE INDEX

Avga kai feta (eggs and feta), 165

Baklava (honey and walnut pastry), 56

Dolmades (grape leaves), 125

Fasolada (bean soup), 278

Gigantes (baked giant lima beans), 35

Horta (cooked greens), 122

Koulourakia (twisted butter cookie), 155

Kouloukithopita (greek pumpkin pie), 46

Loukoumades (fried dough balls), 217

Makaronopita (greek mac and cheese), 226

Melinzanes (eggplants and onions), 160

Psomi (bread), 170

Rizogalo (rice pudding), 177

Salata (greek salad), 95

Spanakopita (spinach pie), 6

Tiropitakia (cheese triangles), 16

Tzaziki (greek yogurt sauce), 113

Yemista (stuffed peppers), 66

www.ingramcontent.com/pod-product-compliance
Lightning Source LLC
Chambersburg PA
CBHW071558080526
44588CB00010B/950